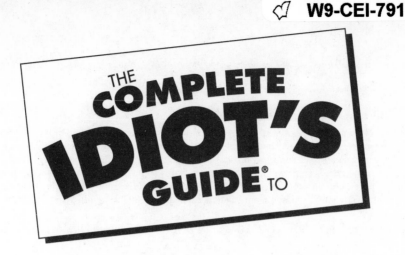

THE COMPLETE IDIOT'S GUIDE® TO

Prayer

Second Edition

by Mark Galli and James S. Bell Jr.

ALPHA

A member of Penguin Group (USA) Inc.

To the memory of my mother, who first taught me to pray. —MG
To my wife, Margaret, the greatest prayer warrior I know. —JB

International Standard Book Number: 1-59257-245-6
Library of Congress Catalog Card Number: 2004101846

06   05   04   8   7   6   5   4   3   2   1

Interpretation of the printing code: The rightmost number of the first series of numbers is the year of the book's printing; the rightmost number of the second series of numbers is the number of the book's printing. For example, a printing code of 04-1 shows that the first printing occurred in 2004.

Printed in the United States of America

Note: This publication contains the opinions and ideas of its authors. It is intended to provide helpful and informative material on the subject matter covered. It is sold with the understanding that the authors and publisher are not engaged in rendering professional services in the book. If the reader requires personal assistance or advice, a competent professional should be consulted.

The authors and publisher specifically disclaim any responsibility for any liability, loss, or risk, personal or otherwise, which is incurred as a consequence, directly or indirectly, of the use and application of any of the contents of this book.

Most Alpha books are available at special quantity discounts for bulk purchases for sales promotions, premiums, fund-raising, or educational use. Special books, or book excerpts, can also be created to fit specific needs.

For details, write: Special Markets, Alpha Books, 375 Hudson Street, New York, NY 10014.

Publisher: *Marie Butler-Knight*
Product Manager: *Phil Kitchel*
Senior Managing Editor: *Jennifer Chisholm*
Senior Acquisitions Editor: *Renee Wilmeth*
Development Editor: *Lynn Northrup*
Production Editor: *Janette Lynn*
Copy Editor: *Drew Patty*
Illustrator: *Richard King*
Cover/Book Designer: *Trina Wurst*
Indexer: *Tonya Heard*
Layout/Proofreading: *Ayanna Lacey, John Etchison*

Contents at a Glance

Contents

Foreword

Everybody prays. Prayers can be chanted or moaned or sung or whispered, shouted or simply offered in complete silence. Prayers are offered in beautiful churches, in lonely hospital rooms, in football stadiums, in the halls of the U.S. Congress, on busy freeways, and, as I know from personal experience, in speeding airplanes racing across the sky. Even atheists pray in foxholes, so the saying goes. Even nonreligious people, the kind who would never be caught dead in a church, or perhaps, better, would only be caught in a church dead, even these people pray. When they stub their toe, or mash their finger with a hammer, and cry out "God d—!", what is that but a prayer? In the ultimate sense only God can damn, or bless. Intuitively, we all know this and reflect it in the common curses and minor blasphemies of everyday life.

All persons pray, but not all prayers are created equal. This book is a kind of primer on Christian prayer. It will introduce you to the most famous of all prayers, the Lord's Prayer, which Jesus taught his disciples to pray, and which Christians of all traditions have been praying for two thousand years. This book also discusses the fear of praying. It acknowledges that one can get bored with prayer, and tired of prayer. These problems are faced by everyone who prays. We should remember that even the great saints and heroes of the faith struggled with prayer, just as all of us do.

The Complete Idiot's Guide to Prayer, Second Edition, is a book for beginners, for those who want to enroll in the kindergarten of prayer. But there is a funny thing about the life of prayer: We never get too old, or grow too mature, or become too spiritual but that we still need to come back to the basic formulas of prayer we first learned perhaps as little children. I recently heard a great religious leader tell about an experience he had not long ago. He had been rushed to the hospital with stabbing pains in his chest. The doctors recommended immediate open-heart surgery and soon he found himself being prepared for this ordeal. Lying on the operating table as the anesthesia was beginning to take effect, he said the thing that kept running through his mind were the Bible verses and simple prayers he first learned as a little boy. The little bedtime prayer his mother taught him years ago kept coming back to him now: "Now I lay me down to sleep, I pray the Lord my soul to keep; if I should die before I wake, I pray the Lord my soul to take." In that moment prior to surgery, he did not know exactly what his earthly future would be, whether in fact he might not die before he awoke. But in that moment, he said he felt closer to the Lord than he had for many years.

So this book is for everyone. For no one is really an expert in prayer. We are all in kindergarten, beginning anew learning how to pray, for what to pray, to whom to pray. Welcome to the great adventure of prayer, to the pilgrimage of the heart.

Dean Timothy George, Ph.D.
Beeson Divinity School
Samford University, Birmingham, AL

Introduction

You've opened this book because you're at a loss about prayer. You don't know how to get started, or you don't know how to continue. Whatever the reason, you're confused about prayer. Welcome to the club.

We've each been at this prayer stuff for years, and we're still learning. We've known people who've spent their whole adult lives in prayer—as monks—and they are the first to admit that they always feel like newcomers to prayer.

That shouldn't intimidate you as much as encourage you. The great classical guitarist Segovia said that the guitar is the easiest instrument to learn but the hardest to master. That's true of prayer, but we'd put it this way: Prayer may be the hardest human activity to master, but it is the easiest to learn.

And that's the point of this book: to help you learn to pray, or to reacquaint you with the basics of Christian prayer.

Getting Specific

Note the adjective: Christian. As much as we'd like to write a book on prayer as it is experienced in all the world religions, we can't. We're Christians, raised in the Christian tradition. We've worked for Christian publishing houses. We attend Christian churches. We know Christian. We don't know Jewish, Buddhist, Hindu, Islam, and others.

But we're not convinced that this is a problem. First, nearly every person who picks up this book will have been born and nurtured in the West, particularly in North America. This is a part of the world steeped in Christian culture. According to repeated Gallup polls, three out of four Americans describe themselves as Christian. Other polls regularly indicate that two out of three pray every day at home—most likely in the Christian tradition. Christianity pervades our communities, our literature, and our everyday expressions ("at their wit's end," "apple of my eye," and "scapegoat" all come from the Bible). Whether we like it or not, and whether we believe or not, Christianity is in our cultural veins.

And that means that if you're exploring prayer, Christian prayer is the logical place to start. Kathleen Norris, a well-known writer on spirituality, tells this story in her *Amazing Grace: A Vocabulary of Faith:* "A young man I know was stunned when he went to Thailand and tried to join a Buddhist monastery. 'Go back home and become a Christian monk first,' they told him. 'Learn your own tradition.'"

Perhaps you're interested in comparing and contrasting prayer with different traditions, or maybe exploring Eastern traditions. You are wise, then, to understand the tradition of your own culture first.

The Complete Idiot's Guide to Prayer, Second Edition, explores prayer as it has been and as it continues to be practiced in the broadly Christian tradition: Catholic, Orthodox, and Protestant. New chapters have been added on fasting and prayer technology, as well as new appendixes that list recommended books, Internet sites, and prayer retreat centers. In addition, more stories of answers to prayer are scattered throughout, and Prayer Hotlines give practical tips for prayer.

And this book will explore only prayer to God. Praying to saints is a long-standing tradition in some Christian circles, but we don't believe it belongs in the category of the "basics" of Christian prayer. We won't be getting into that here.

The Power of Strange Words

A book on Christian prayer is going to have to stick with biblical vocabulary. This doesn't mean that the book will sound pious. The fact is, for Christians, the Bible is *the* prayer book. Not only are there a ton of prayers in the Bible (see the Book of Psalms alone), but a lot of the language used in prayers handed down through the ages comes straight out of the Bible.

Even though the Bible sounds strange to modern ears at times, there's something powerful about biblical language. This is the reason the Bible has hung around for thousands of years—it really does speak to human beings in all times and cultures.

We'll be quoting a lot of prayers for the Bible, as well as the teachings on prayer in the Bible (especially those taught by Jesus, the master of prayer). We believe that you cannot learn about Christian prayer without learning what the Bible teaches about prayer—and in the language it uses to teach prayer.

The other vocabulary item to bring up at this point is the pronoun to be used for God. The Bible, and especially Jesus, talks about God as "Father." As such, the constraints of language tend to force writers into referring to God as "he."

Let's make one thing clear, though: God is not male. Nor is God female, the great goddess. God is beyond male and female.

On the other hand, Christian theology teaches that God is not an *it,* an impersonal force. God is not just the "Creator," but a "loving heavenly Father." God is personal—more personal than we can imagine. Thus, we choose to use a pronoun like "he" to refer to God. This has been a part of the Christian tradition from the beginning; "she" (or alternating "he" and "she") causes confusion to most readers—and using "he" just makes writing a heck of a lot easier (especially after quoting a saying of Jesus, who has just called God "Father"). But when we use "he" or "him," we mean to suggest only that God is a personal being.

A Long Tradition

Christian prayer is not something that has just developed, nor something that must be recreated in every age for each new generation. It's a long tradition, one that has been practiced for nearly 2,000 years. Along the way, many men and women who have grappled with prayer have had insights that have helped others understand prayer a bit more. You cannot understand Christian prayer without listening to these people, so you'll find that we quote a lot from this Christian tradition. Many of the names will be obscure at first, but hang in there: By the end of the book, some of the names will start to become familiar.

Cure for Restless Hearts

Augustine, one of the greatest theologians in the Christian church, said this in a prayer to God: "You awaken us to delight in your praise; for you have made us for yourself, and our hearts are restless until they rest in you."

Prayer is for everyone created by God—even novices when it comes to prayer and religion. We cannot know ourselves fully, we cannot settle (as much as it is possible to settle) the large issues of life, we cannot have the strength and courage to make a difference in the world until we find our rest in God. And the way we do that, more than any other way, is through prayer.

Wherever you are on your spiritual journey, we invite you to explore Christian prayer to see if it doesn't move you closer to your journey's goal.

Extras

Along the way, we've included boxes that quote from the Bible or other sources, define terminology, make things clearer, or take interesting little side trips. Here's how the boxes are labeled, and what you'll find in each:

> **From the Good Book**
>
> These quotes come from the Bible, the prayer book of Christianity, and address the nature of prayer.

> **Snapshots of Answered Prayers**
>
> Here are examples of biblical characters who prayed for and received answers from God.

> **Prayer Pearls**
>
> These quotes about prayer come from saints, monks, mystics, and great pray-ers from the past.

 Prayer Hotline

Here we've provided answers to questions and helpful information to encourage prayer.

Acknowledgments

To keep confusion to a minimum, Jim took responsibility for almost all the supplemental boxes, quotes, prayers, and appendixes; Mark wrote the running text and the Prayer Hotlines. Thus, all the references to "I" and "me" in the running text and prayer hotlines refer to Mark, and the personal examples all come from his life.

Thanks to Renee Wilmeth and Lynn Northup, whose editorial skills, patience, and gentle prodding made this a better book.

We would also like to thank our families for their continued love and support through another writing project for each of us.

Trademarks

All terms mentioned in this book that are known to be or are suspected of being trademarks or service marks have been appropriately capitalized. Alpha Books and Penguin Group (USA) Inc. cannot attest to the accuracy of this information. Use of a term in this book should not be regarded as affecting the validity of any trademark or service mark.

Part 1

Let Us Pray

Prayer (in Jewish/Christian tradition, anyway) has been around for a long time—at least 4,000 years. Yet for all that experience, prayer is still something that's pretty hard to get a handle on. It is ultimately a mystery. God is a mystery, certainly—that we can communicate with God is even more a wonder. But through the centuries, many people have experienced that mystery and have found it—well, wonderful.

This has been an astonishing experience for generation after generation because of what prayer is and what it does. Before we can look at the mechanics of prayer, we need to understand exactly what we're talking about when we use the word *prayer*.

What Prayer Isn't (and Is)

In This Chapter

♦ Clearing up confusion about prayer

♦ What prayer is: a conversation with God

♦ The purpose of prayer

♦ Creating a relationship with God

One reason many of us are intimidated by prayer is that a lot of people such as ministers (like I was), writers (like I am), and theologians (like I wish I was sometimes) have taken something that's basically pretty simple and have managed to make it pretty complicated.

Yes, prayer is a mystery, but let's not make it more complicated than it really is. To begin with, let's clear up some misconceptions about prayer.

Clearing Up Some Confusion

I've run across some pretty interesting definitions of prayer over the years—okay, not so much "pretty interesting" as "pretty confusing."

Prayer as Work?

The poet Gerard Manley Hopkins said, "To lift up the hands in prayer is to give God glory, but a man with a dungfork in his hand and a woman with a slop pail give him glory, too." Indeed, people in most any activity can give glory to God in their chosen activity. But some people have gone a step further and said, "Building a chair or bundling hay or fixing a flat tire—anything we do to God's glory is a prayer." Nope. Fixing a flat tire is, well, auto mechanics. Building a chair is carpentry. Certainly, you can do these things well—so well that they make the world a better place and so well they give you honor and God glory. These activities can be *like* prayer (focused, devoted, selfless), but they are not *prayer*.

> ### Prayer Pearls
>
> Prayer is the rope that pulls God and man together. But it doesn't pull God down to us: It pulls us up to him.
>
> —Billy Graham, evangelist

Hyperspiritualizing

How about this one: "Prayer is a supernatural activity." This is an example of a definition that makes prayer sound more spiritual than it really is. Certainly, in prayers we're getting in touch with a Being who lies beyond nature. But prayer itself is a common, ordinary, everyday sort of activity, like talking. Natural people in natural settings use natural words when they pray all the time.

Self-Help

Then there's this: "Prayer is a way of lifting ourselves." As if we had the power to lift ourselves into the presence of God. As if we need to lift ourselves in order to talk with God. Again, the problem lies in overspiritualizing things. If anything, God lowers himself to us in prayer—more on that later.

Cosmic Shrink

I hate this one in particular: "Prayer is God's psychotherapy for his children." This isn't so much what prayer *is* as much as what prayer *does*. In other words, according to this misguided understanding, prayer helps all those weaklings who need a crutch to get through life—you know, the type of people who need therapy. So these people go to God. Not only are his rates cheap, but it turns out that he's also an awfully good listener. Let's get something straight at the beginning of this book: Prayer is for the strong, the weak, the smart, the stupid, the wise, the foolish, people in their better moments, people in their worst moments. It's for *everybody*.

Wishin' and Hopin'

One preacher said, "A prayer in its simplest definition is merely a wish turned Godward." I almost like this one. It's human, at least. We know what a wish is, and we can figure out what it means to turn Godward. But put this definition in the wrong hands, and it perpetuates the childish stereotype that prayer is about asking and getting things from God.

Shhhh!

Given my previous reaction, you may think I love this definition: "A man prayed, and at first he thought that prayer was talking. But he became more and more quiet until, in the end, he realized that prayer is listening." Nice sentiment, but it's not really true. Listening should be a part of prayer—in fact, much more a part than we usually make it. But prayer is more than shutting your mouth or your mind when in the presence of God.

Getting Formal

The formal definitions of prayer that you find in dictionaries and encyclopedias aren't much help, either. The *Encarta Encyclopedia*, for example, says this: "In its broadest sense, prayer is any ritual form designed to bring one into closer relation to whatever one believes to be the ultimate." Unfortunately, people have some pretty creative ideas about what is "the ultimate." For some it's fine art, for others it's *Captain America* comics, for others it's sex (okay, close). For Kevin Costner in the movie *Field of Dreams*, baseball was the ultimate. When he built a baseball field in the middle of his cornfield, it was *like* an act of worship. Steady meditation on the *Mona Lisa* is *like* prayer. The ecstasy of sex is akin to the ecstasy some have experienced in prayer. But none of these activities are *prayer*.

> **Snapshots of Answered Prayers**
>
> God rescues Jacob from the clutches of his brother Esau, after Jacob's "dirty tricks" in previous years. See his prayer in Genesis 32:9-1.

Talking to God

Clement of Alexandria, a third-century Christian philosopher from Egypt, said it best and most simply: "Prayer is conversation with God." Pretty simple, huh? Let's make sure it's clear, though.

If prayer is conversation, it means first that we *talk* to God. Prayer is not just wishing and hoping. It is not meditating on ultimate things. It is not doing things for God. It is not lifting ourselves into a foggy spiritual state. Prayer is talking to God and expressing our thoughts, feelings, hopes, dreams, and fears to God. Most of the time, this means using *words*. Some mystical types say that mere human words cannot adequately convey the feelings and thoughts they wish to express to God. Certainly, words have severe limitations; any writer will admit that. And, of course, there are nonverbal ways to pray: guided imagery, music, painting, and so on. But let's not give up on words too quickly. Think about it: Words are one of the main ways God has communicated with us—in the Old and New Testaments (lots of words there!). Furthermore, the words of Jesus, as much as his death and resurrection, have inspired people through the ages. And when the Bible sums up who Jesus is, it says this: "In the beginning was the Word. And the Word was with God, and the Word was God." (John 1:1) Biblical scholars say "the Word" here means much more than "words." But it means *at least* that much—that is, Jesus is God's way of communicating to us.

<table>
<tr><td>

Prayer Pearls

At the profoundest depths in life, men talk not *about* God but *with* him.

—Elton Trueblood, Quaker philosopher

</td></tr>
</table>

The word is so important to God that he's willing to use it as a name. I may give my children presents; I may coach their soccer teams; I may give them kisses in the morning and hugs at night. But if I never speak with them—and especially if I never say to them, "I love you"—there is a large void in our relationship. In the same way, there are many ways to nurture my relationship with God, but the key way is by speaking with him.

Schizophrenia or Prayer?

On the other hand, if prayer is conversation with God, it means that God also speaks to us. "Sure he does," you say. Maybe it's a one-way conversation, you think, but not two-way. A Moses or an Isaiah—or people locked up in state hospitals—may hear God speak, but most of us don't care to keep that sort of company. But as comedian Lily Tomlin put it, "Why is it when we talk to God, we're said to be praying—but when God talks to us, we're schizophrenics?" The problem here lies in the stereotype: a deep, booming voice falling out of the sky, sternly setting out instructions of one sort or another. Another stock image is the dreamy, mystical encounter: no voices, just a bright light that surrounds and beams down on the person, who freezes in wonder, staring into the light, countenance shining with beatific delight, silently taking in the secret message. One of the things prayer teaches is that God speaks to us in more ways than we can count, in "voices" we can hardly imagine. It also teaches us how to hear God. And speak to us he does; we miss out on one of the great wonders of prayer if we neglect this part of prayer.

Forgetest Thou Queen Elizabeth I

If prayer is conversing with God, it helps us toss out a lot of unhelpful stereotypes right at the start. For one, the idea that God understands only people who talk like Shakespeare and litter their prayers with "thee" and "thou" and "shouldst" and "wouldst." There's a time and a place for such prayers, just as there is a time and a place to watch a Shakespeare play. But it's not something you should do at home (at least without a grammarian present!), nor is it a very effective way to converse with God.

This also means that prayer is not a formal speech. If asked to pray—before a meal, for instance—most people will balk. They become nervous, hesitant, awkward. "Uh, well, I don't know. You know, I'm, not really very good at praying. Why don't you ask someone else?" That's because they think good English is demanded and that a formal outline is to be followed, after which they'll be judged for their performance. In other words, they think they're being asked to make a speech—something like, "O Lord God, creator of heaven and earth, giver of all blessings: We would give you hearty thanks for the bountiful meal set before us, and for the hands that have so lovingly prepared it. In the name of him who loved us and died for us. Amen." There are occasions when formal prayers are called for: at weddings and funerals, at graduation ceremonies, when installing someone into office, at worship. But in everyday life, prayer is not a speech *at* God as much as a means of speaking *with* God. Therefore, it doesn't have to elicit any more fear than talking to another person. When it comes to mealtime graces, for example, it should be no more difficult to say "thank you" to God for the food than it is to say "thank you" to the host for cooking: "Lord, thank you for this food and for those who prepared it. Amen."

> ### Prayer Pearls
>
> Sometimes when your child talks, your friends cannot understand what he says; but the mother understands very well. So if our prayer comes from the heart, God understands our language.
>
> —D. L. Moody, nineteenth-century evangelist

A Close Relationship

When it comes to praying to God, you see, it's not much different than speaking with your spouse, a friend, or anyone else you're trying to have a close relationship with. In her classic book *Prayer: Conversing with God*, Rosalind Rinker put it this way:

"Prayer is the expression of the human heart in conversation with God. The more natural the prayer, the more real he becomes. It has all been simplified for me to this extent: Prayer is a dialogue between two persons who love each other." Prayer is not a religious speech to a divine audience, or the groveling petition of a servant to an arbitrary master, or vague spiritual thoughts directed to no one in particular. It is one key means of drawing ourselves closer to God and opening ourselves up so that God might draw closer to us. Of course, in terms of Christian theology, God is always close—closer than we are to ourselves—and he knows us better than we know ourselves.

One of the Psalms puts it this way:

> O Lord, you have examined my heart and know everything about me.
>
> You know when I sit down or stand up.
>
> You know my every thought when far away ….
>
> You know what I'm going to say even before I say it, Lord ….
>
> Such knowledge is too wonderful for me, too great for me to know. I can never escape your spirit!
>
> I can never get away from your presence!
>
> If I go up to heaven, you are there;
>
> if I go down to the place of the dead, you are there.
>
> If I ride the wings of the morning,
>
> if I dwell in the farthest oceans,
>
> even there your hand will guide me,
>
> and your strength will support me.
>
> —Psalm 139

> **Prayer Pearls**
>
> Christ as a light, illumine and guide me. Christ as a shield, overshadow and cover me. Christ be under me. Christ be over me. Christ be beside me, on left hand and right. Christ be before me, behind me, about me. Christ, this day, be within and without me.
>
> —St. Patrick

And how do we better understand this hand that silently guides us? How do we take in this strength that quietly supports us? You guessed it: prayer.

Problems Are No Problem

Some people, however, can't imagine that God has anything to say to them. Some wrestle with low self-esteem or are haunted by guilt, and they can't imagine that a holy and omnipotent God who rules the universe has time for them or has any interest in their "petty" little problems—let alone have a relationship with them. Others fight against the idea of prayer as conversation because they're afraid it may be true. If they acknowledge it and try to listen to God, some fear that they'll be told to sell their possessions and take up a missionary life in Africa. Others fear that by speaking with "the way, the truth, and the life," they will be forced to explore troubled regions of their inner self—areas they'd just as soon let be.

I have a friend who for a time found himself deeply troubled by the thought that maybe God was calling him to "speak in tongues"—that is, use a prayer language that sounds like nonsense but which some have experienced as a type of profound mystical prayer (more on this in later chapters). For a while, he found his heart thumping wildly whenever he went into prayer because he thought he might end up doing something crazy! He eventually learned that speaking in tongues is not about going into an ecstatic, uncontrolled state, and that this wasn't his gift. But for a time, prayer was a pretty scary thing for him.

Others say they've tried prayer and that it didn't do any good. Or, they don't have the patience for it. Or, that they pray by doing good works. Some say it sounds too simple to be true. And on it goes. There are lots of reasons—many of them good ones—to distrust all this talk about conversation with God. Indeed, in many respects, it *is* preposterous to believe that God exists and that God wants to be in intimate relationships with people like you and me. But we are not the first age to have doubts about prayer—after all, it is a mystery, something that can never be fully explained or fully understood. It is something that believers have marveled at for centuries. One of the Psalms put it like this:

> When I look at the night sky and see the work of your fingers—
>
> the moon and the stars you have set in place—
>
> what are mortals, that you should think of us?
>
> mere humans, that you should care for us?
>
> —Psalm 8

Then again, any relationship is a mystery. After 40 years of marriage, a husband and wife still look at each other some days and wonder, "Who in the heck are you?" and "Why do you still love me?" Yet without fully understanding, the relationship goes on and is enjoyed immensely.

From the Good Book

The Lord bless you and keep you; the Lord make his face shine upon you and be gracious to you; the Lord turn his face toward you and give you peace.

—Numbers 6:24–26

In the course of this book, we'll look at these and other problems that prayer presents, and we'll examine the ways Christians have handled them. As you'll see, though, problems are no reason to stop praying. Nor is the fact that prayer is ultimately a mystery. The most mysterious and complex things of life can be expressed in the simplest ways. When I say to my wife, "I love you," there's a lot going on there—a lot of history, a lot of pain, a lot of ecstasy, a lot of wonder. But this remains a pretty darn good summing up. Prayer has history, pain, ecstasy, wonder, and a host of other dimensions—but, in the end, it is conversation with God.

The Least You Need to Know

- Prayer is a conversation with God.

- Prayer is less like making a speech and more like talking to a friend.

- Conversation with God through prayer is a means of getting closer to him.

- Just because you have doubts about prayer doesn't mean that you can't pray and get something out of it.

Chapter 2

What Prayer Promises

In This Chapter

- ◆ How prayer helps us experience God

- ◆ How prayer changes us

- ◆ How prayer changes others and circumstances

- ◆ Whether God is changed by prayer

It seems that a lot of religious types like to tell others that they *should* pray, as if prayer is a duty. I know that I, for one, can become lazy and forgetful, and sometimes I need a kick in the pants to get me back on my knees.

But prayer is less a duty than a gift. And what we usually need is not a scolding, but a reminder of the promise of prayer and the many gifts that God can lavish upon us through prayer.

The Best Gift of All

First things first. With prayer come a lot of gifts: faith, hope, courage, wisdom, and so on (more on that in a bit). But the key gift of prayer is God himself. If prayer is a conversation, it's about a relationship with God—and a relationship with God is less about things he can give us and more about getting to know God.

This is at the bull's-eye of the Christian faith. Some people think Christianity is a set of morals or a certain way to worship or a philosophy of life. That's partly true, but primarily it's about experiencing God.

Let's do a quick primer on a key biblical theme: Because of sin, people are alienated from God and cannot experience him truly or fully. Jesus, the Son of God, died and rose to new life to forgive people and make it possible for them to experience God again, in this life and forever.

That's basically it. And though we can experience God in a variety of ways, such as sitting in the woods or contemplating the stars, prayer—conversing with God—is one of the most direct ways God has given us.

People experience God in prayer in a number of ways. Let's look at four and illustrate them with prayers that are found in Psalms, the prayer book of the Bible.

> **Prayer Pearls**
>
> Our prayers go all around the world, without anything definite being asked for. We do not expect anything. Many people would be greatly surprised if God did answer their prayers.
>
> —D. L. Moody, nineteenth-century evangelist

Gratitude

One of my college roommates was a religious skeptic—and a stubborn one, at that. We spent more than a few nights, sometimes going deep into the morning hours, debating theology and philosophy.

One 3 A.M. as we concluded another long philosophical debate about the existence of God, he said, "The only time I'm tempted to believe in God is when I'm in love."

That's because, I believe, he was looking for someone to thank. Though we can be manifestly selfish a great deal of the time, there are moments when we're overwhelmed with the goodness of life. Maybe you have just taken in the sweeping vistas of the Grand Canyon, or studied a rose up close for 10 minutes. Maybe you've enjoyed a delightful meal with friends, or have just made love with your spouse. Perhaps you've just escaped some crisis, or maybe a child or a spouse has come through an operation. Whatever the cause, you're flooded with joy and a sense of deep appreciation, and you have this urge to say, "Thank you."

It's not enough just to "be thankful." This is the sort of drivel textbooks feed children these days when they discuss Thanksgiving. One of my kid's history books said the Pilgrims celebrated the first Thanksgiving because they "were thankful." Uh, not quite. They wanted to say "Thank you," and, being devout Christians, they wanted to say it to someone in particular—and it wasn't the Indians (though they were invited to say thanks as well). When the human heart is thankful, it wants to say "Thank you."

The interesting thing when we express our gratitude to God is this: We don't run out of gratitude—instead, we're filled with even more gratitude and joy. That's why the Psalms are littered with prayers of thanksgiving. One example, from Psalm 138, will do for now:

> I will give thanks, O Lord, with all my heart;
>
> I will sing your praises before the gods.
>
> I bow before your holy Temple as I worship,
>
> I will give thanks to your name
>
> for your unfailing love and faithfulness.

Even some of the Psalms that begin with desperate pleas ("Lord, help!") end with a note of thanksgiving ("Nevertheless, Lord, I will praise you!"). More on the Psalms later.

Prayer Pearls
Prayer is when heaven and earth kiss each other.
—An anonymous Jewish mystic

Transcendence

This large word expresses a large idea: To experience transcendence is to experience something that goes beyond (transcends) what we can see, feel, hear, smell, or touch.

Several beer commercials on TV have recently focused on people at the beach or at a barbecue, playing, laughing, generally having a good time, with a beer in hand. Then someone says, "It doesn't get any better than this." Sometimes life—just life—is pretty darn nice (even without beer).

But then there are other times when life boxes us in. It seems small, petty, and pointless. And that's when we say, "Is that all there is?"

Well, no, it isn't. There is something, *someone*, who transcends this world, one whose Spirit is *in* the world but not *of* it, one who can enlarge the soul, expand the mind, and help us experience something beyond this world—the Uncreated, the Infinite, the Immortal. One of the great mysteries of prayer is that we can experience this someone who cannot be adequately described, thought of, or imagined.

It would be a pretty dumb thing to say that we can experience the inaccessible, if it weren't for the fact that people have done so for thousands of years. The Psalmist refers to this experience when he writes:

Every time I come to God in prayer, my approach must be with praise and thanksgiving. It is a rude imposition to come to God asking for anything without saying thanks for past blessings.

—Lehman Strauss, author and teacher

Come, let us sing to the Lord!

Let us give a joyous shout to the rock of our salvation ….

For the Lord is a great God,

the great king above all gods.

He owns the depths of the earth,

and even the mightiest mountains are his.

The sea belongs to him, for he made it.

His hands formed the dry land, too.

Come, let us worship and bow down.

Let us kneel before the Lord, our maker.

He's struggling to sing about the great God he has experienced, greater than his mind can fathom. One of my favorite hymns, which is titled by its first line, expresses it this way:

Immortal, invisible, God only wise,

In light inaccessible hid from our eyes,

Most blessed, most glorious, the ancient of days,

Almighty, victorious, thy great name we praise.

Forgiveness

Modern psychology has taught us that we sometimes feel guilty about things we have no business feeling guilty about. Some have run with that insight and have concluded that a healthy human being shouldn't experience guilt at all. Wrong! Emotionally healthy people *should* feel guilt when they've done something wrong.

This is especially true when we turn to God in prayer. God is good, holy, and infinitely perfect in love. We, however, are not good, nor are we holy or very perfect in love. Healthy people feel bad about that. As one prayer, used in many liturgies, puts it, "We confess that we have sinned against you, in thought, word, and deed, by what we have done and by what we have left undone." That about sums it up—and that's guilt.

Some people, though, feel so guilty they can't find the courage to face God. So they stop praying. I was a youth pastor for a number of years, and in one church, one young man had a habit of drinking on Saturday night. Then he'd skip church the next day, he said, because he felt guilty coming to church.

I understand the feeling, but he didn't understand that one of the best places to go when you're guilty is to prayer. In prayer, we can experience the forgiveness of God as we can nowhere else. More on this in later chapters, but for now, let me quote sections of perhaps the most joyful experience of forgiveness ever recorded: Psalm 103.

> Praise the Lord, I tell myself,
>
> and never forget the good things he does for me.
>
> He forgives all my sins
>
> and heals all my diseases ….
>
> The Lord is merciful and gracious,
>
> he is slow to get angry and full of unfailing love ….
>
> He has not punished us for all our sins,
>
> nor does he deal with us as we deserve ….
>
> He has removed our rebellious acts
>
> as far away from us as the east is from the west.

Love

This brings us to the essence of experiencing God: experiencing his love. This arises from a gradually increasing awareness that God loves not just the world, not just humankind, not just people—God also loves *me*, an individual with a personality and memories like no other, a person with unique faults, special talents, particular sins, and even moments of unusual kindness.

The awareness of God's love grows as we meditate on the teachings of Jesus (a form of prayer we'll talk about later) in passages such as Matthew 18:12–14. Though Jesus is speaking here specifically about children, biblical scholars recognize that the point applies to every human person: "If a shepherd has 100 sheep and one wanders away and is lost, what will he do? Won't he leave the 99 others and go out into the hills to search for the lost one? And if he finds it, he will surely rejoice over it more than over the 99 that didn't wander away! In the same way, is it not my heavenly Father's will that even one of these little ones should perish?"

Or take another saying: "Not even a sparrow, worth only half a penny, can fall to the ground without your Father knowing it. And the very hairs on your head are all numbered. So don't be afraid; you are more valuable to him than a whole flock of sparrows." (Matthew 10:29–30)

Don't think you can squeeze out of this: God cares about you even if he can't number the hairs on your head because you don't have any. (Believe me, I know this more and more every day.)

Anyway, you get the idea. No wonder the Psalms are full of praise to God for his goodness and love to us:

> Shout with joy to the Lord, O earth,
>
> Worship the Lord with gladness.
>
> Come before him, singing with joy …!
>
> For the Lord is good.
>
> His unfailing love continues forever,
>
> and his faithfulness continues to each generation.
>
> —Psalm 100

Snapshots of Answered Prayers

Abram asks God for an heir and his wife Sarah, a 90-year-old woman, subsequently gives birth to Isaac. Find it in Genesis 15:2,3.

It Changes Us

We are changed by the people we come to know—usually for the better. I'm a different—and mostly better—person after having lived with my wife for these 25 years. I don't lose my temper as often; I'm a much better listener; I'm more sensitive to other's needs; I even eat my vegetables now.

I don't know that experiencing God will help you like vegetables, but knowing God does have a way of changing a person at the very core—and in a number of ways.

You Understand Yourself Better

Socrates knew what he was talking about when he said, "Know yourself." All improvement in the character of our lives begins with self-knowledge. What Socrates didn't see was that you can know yourself better by knowing God.

This only makes sense. If you know the creator of something, you'll know a lot more about the things he or she has created. If you understand, for instance, that a fiction writer lost her father when she was a child, you'll understand better why in so many of her novels a father figure plays an important role.

Likewise, if you understand the being who created you, you'll better understand yourself. As the author of Genesis put it, "God created people in his own image; God patterned them after himself." (Genesis 1:27)

Theologians debate (as usual) exactly what this means, though they all agree that it has nothing to do with looks. But there is something central to our nature that is very much like God's nature. The better we understand the original, then the better we'll understand the image.

Wisdom

According to the Bible, a wise person is someone with "street smarts." It's not someone who spouts off important-sounding phrases about the meaning of life, but someone who knows what to do and what to say in all sorts of situations.

What exactly do you say to your boss when he asks you to do something you think is immoral? How do you figure out which college to go to? How do you handle your neighbor who leaves his garbage cans on your lawn?

This is the stuff of life, and we need wisdom to handle such situations. Prayer can help us grow in wisdom.

This doesn't mean that God will tell us exactly how to handle each situation that puzzles us. It *does* mean that, in prayer, we'll gain insights into ourselves and the situation we face. And those insights will help us gain "life smarts."

Courage and Hope

We'll cover these topics together because they go together in real life: We're more likely to have courage if we have hope. And life has a way of assaulting us so that we need regular doses of both.

Sometimes it's the big things that knock the wind out of us: A friend is battling colon cancer; a neighbor woman finds herself alone after 19 years of marriage because her husband left her; you discover your teenager is taking drugs; you've been fired.

Then again, sometimes it's lesser things that overwhelm us: a co-worker who is a constant irritant, a bad back that throbs, a dead-end job.

Optimistic self-talk, willpower, and gritting one's teeth will only get you so far. (Well, actually, they usually don't get me very far at all.) We quickly run out of resources to deal with these things and, almost instinctually, turn to God for courage to see us through and to work things for the good.

Building Character

To handle life's challenges and enjoy life's blessings, we need to be better people. You're never going to be able to help others unless you learn love and self-control. You're not going to be able to handle stress unless you get some peace into your heart. You're not going to be able to fully enjoy marriage or friendship unless you learn faithfulness. And on it goes.

 From the Good Book

I prayed to the Lord and said, "O sovereign Lord, do not destroy your people, your own inheritance that you redeemed by your great power and brought out of Egypt with a mighty hand. Remember your servants Abraham, Isaac, and Jacob. Overlook the stubbornness of this people, their wickedness and their sin."

—Moses, Deuteronomy 9:26, 27

Many places in the Bible summarize the most essential traits human beings need to possess and the way they can grow in them. One of my favorites is found in a letter the apostle (an *apostle* is "one who is sent out," such as the apostles who were sent by Jesus to spread his message) Paul wrote to the Galatians. He not only lists the traits, but he says that these come from an intimate acquaintance with God's spirit: "When the Holy Spirit controls our lives, he will produce his kind of fruit in us: love, joy, peace, patience, kindness, goodness, faithfulness, gentleness, and self-control." (Galatians 5:22–23)

You can't get any better than this.

It Changes Other Things

It has been said, "Prayer changes things? No! Prayer changes people, and people change things." Don't believe it—at least, not all of it.

Yeah, most of the time it's me who needs changing. If a co-worker is driving me crazy because he pops into my office and wastes my time with his drivel about his pet iguana, I've got to change a few things. I may need to learn more patience. I may need to become more assertive and tell him to get back to work. I may need to learn to like iguanas.

When I pray, "Lord, help good old Pete not to come into my office so much," God may make it plain to me that *I'm* the one who needs to do something. In fact, most of the time, that's exactly what God will do. But that's not the case all the time. Sometimes God really will change Pete. He may help Pete understand that he's being a bore, maybe by planting a thought in his head or by having someone else yell at him.

Other people say that prayer doesn't change circumstances, but only people. Don't believe that, either. Sure, it doesn't happen every day, but once in a while God changes circumstances regardless of people. This is called a miracle.

When I pastored a small church, we would invite people during worship to announce prayer requests before we prayed. Most weeks, people requested prayers for someone's flu or operation. Once in a while, we'd hear really bad news, like the week one woman mentioned that her brother had inoperable cancer.

As I did every week, I prayed that God would heal all those who were sick, recognizing in my own mind that most of the time God heals people through doctors and medicine. I didn't have a whole lot of faith or hope about this woman's brother.

About a month later, before the Sunday service was about to begin, this woman told me before the service that her brother had gone in for a check-up and that the cancer had disappeared. I said, "How wonderful!" but inside I was shocked—and disappointed that I, a minister of the gospel, was shocked when God acted like God and that the prayer worked.

Prayer Hotline _____

Many people have stories to tell. God does, in fact, heal people miraculously—and it's not an everyday thing, as some will lead you to believe. But neither should you throw in your lot with the skeptics. A reasonable person has to look at all the stories of healing and say, well, it may not happen all the time, but once in a while God does indeed change circumstances.

Does Prayer Change God's Mind?

Here's one more saying to think about: "Prayer does not change God, but changes him who prays." That's a philosopher speaking, one whom I happen to like: Søren Kierkegaard. I think he's *mostly* right.

Here's the deal according to Kierkegaard and others: God knows everything that's going to happen ahead of time. God has a perfect will. No puny human being is going to get the infinitely wise and perfect God to change his mind and do something stupid. Nor is God going to change the future he has mapped out because some poor Harry in Bismarck, South Dakota, needs some help.

But here's the deal according to Jesus (a "philosopher" with a tad bigger following than old Søren): "You parents—if your children ask for a loaf of bread, do you give them a stone instead? Or if they ask for a fish, do you give them a snake? Of course not! If you sinful people know how to give good gifts to your children, how much more will your heavenly Father give good gifts to those who ask him." (Matthew 7:9–11)

Jesus assumes that prayer doesn't just change only us—it also makes a difference in what God does.

If you know any classic Christian theology, you know that what I've just said borders on dumb. God is supposed to be "immutable"—that is, unchanging. That's because, as I said, he's got a perfect will that doesn't need changing. We change because we're not perfect; when a better idea comes our way, we say, "Good idea. Never thought of that." Then we abandon the old way. God, on the other hand, never says, "Good idea. I never thought of that." He already has thought of it, believe me.

But then we have this Jesus fellow—who seems to know God better than anyone—saying that if we ask God for things, it makes a difference in what he does.

Major mystery time! Here's one way to think about this ultimately unsolvable problem: God will not change his mind about some things, no matter how hard we pray. If we ask God, "Help me to rob this bank," or "I'd like you to give me the strength to kill my boss," he's not going to do it. He's never going to change his mind about things like that.

There are other things God is going to do whether we pray or not. No need to pray, "Lord, I pray that the sun will rise tomorrow morning," or "Lord, I really hope gravity continues working all day."

But apparently there are things that God doesn't have a definite plan about, and these things he leaves open-ended. He'll do them if we pray for them; he won't do them if we don't pray. It's not so much a matter of changing his eternal, wise plan—it's actually *part* of his eternal, wise plan that we get to decide some stuff.

Here's how Presbyterian theologian Donald Bloesch put it: "God's ultimate will is unchanging, but the way in which he chooses to realize this will is dependent on the prayers of his children. He wants us as covenant partners, not as automons or slaves."

That's how it works with my kids and me. Some things I'll never permit, no matter what ("Dad, can we each have TVs in our rooms?"). Some things I'll do whether they ask for it or not—I'm going to pay the mortgage every month. But with some things, I'm open. For instance, I want my kids to try to play an instrument for a few years, but I really don't care which ones they play. I might direct them toward piano because I like it best—and if they don't say anything, they'll end up playing piano. But if one of them says, "Dad, I'd like to play the flute," that's fine. Otherwise, they're going to get piano lessons.

So, no, prayer doesn't change God or his perfect will. But part of his perfect will is that we learn how to use our own wills wisely. That's one of the things prayer is for. In some cases, it helps us determine God's perfect will and align our wills with his. The well-known archbishop of Canterbury, William Temple, put it this way: "God is perfect love and perfect wisdom. We do not pray in order to change his will, but to bring our wills into harmony with his."

In other cases, prayer gives us the wisdom and courage to shape our lives within God's larger will. One of the lifelong learning curves of prayer is to learn to distinguish when we should just accept God's will and when we should keep pleading for him to do what we think seems to be best. As one famous prayer, called the Serenity Prayer (said to be authored by theologian Reinhold Niebuhr), puts it, "Lord, grant me the serenity to change the things I can, to accept the things I cannot, and the wisdom to know the difference."

> **Prayer Pearls**
>
> Day by day, dear Lord,
> Of thee three things I pray:
> To see thee more clearly,
> Love thee more dearly,
> Follow thee more nearly,
> Day by day.
> —Richard of Chichester

The Least You Need to Know

- Prayer helps us to experience God; it is the main way we can sustain a conversation with him.

- Prayer changes us because a sustained relationship with a holy and loving God cannot help but change us.

- Prayer sometimes changes circumstances.

- Prayer helps us understand God's will for our lives.

What Prayer Requires

In This Chapter

- How much faith is necessary to pray?
- The importance of honesty in prayer
- Why humility is key
- Why patience is necessary

Some people make it sound as if you must have superhuman faith and the perseverance of a medieval saint to pray. Here's how E. M. Bounds, a writer famous for his books on prayer, put it:

> Prayer is a rare gift, not a popular, ready gift. Prayer is not the fruit of natural talents; it is the product of faith, of holiness, of deeply spiritual character …. Perfection in simplicity, in humility, in faith— these form its chief ingredients. Novices in these graces are not adept in prayer. It cannot be seized upon by untrained hands …. Master workmen are required, for mere journeymen cannot execute the work of prayer.

Well, not quite. Prayer *is* designed for journeymen, for amateurs, for the inept, for complete idiots. Sure, in the right hands (or knees), prayer can reach dizzying heights of spirituality, and seasoned veterans may get a lot more out of prayer than rookies. But don't be fooled by anyone who says that prayer is only for the talented or that the school of prayer has steep prerequisites. Prayer has prerequisites, all right, but they are the type that even complete novices can fulfill. Let's look at four of these: faith, honesty, humility, and patience.

Faith

You certainly need faith to pray: You must believe in God, you must believe that God hears prayers, and you must believe that somehow prayer makes a difference. But you don't need a whole bunch of faith. In fact, some teachers of prayer have challenged the skeptical with this: "Pray every day for 30 days straight, *acting as if* God exists." That's pretty minimal faith, but it is surprising to hear of the number of skeptics who, for the first time in their lives, become aware of God's presence as a result of this little one-month experiment. Jesus spoke often about having faith the size of a mustard seed—which, by the way, is pretty darn small: A few thousand would fit in the palm of your hand. Nonetheless, Jesus said even this much faith could work wonders. He once told his disciples, "I assure you, even if you had faith as small as a mustard seed, you could say to this mountain, 'Move from here to there,' and it would move." (Matthew 17:20)

 From the Good Book

> "If you will save Israel by my hand as you have promised— look, I will place a wool fleece on the threshing floor. If there is dew only on the fleece and all the ground is dry, then I will know that you will save Israel by my hand, as you said." And that is what happened. Gideon rose early the next day; he squeezed the fleece and wrung out the dew—a bowlful of water.
>
> —Judges 6:36–38

Now get this: If mustard-seed faith is mature and powerful enough faith to move mountains, then the amount of faith required to begin the life of prayer is microscopic—maybe the size of an amoeba. Maybe smaller.

No matter how small, this faith has to be focused in the right direction. We're not talking about faith in yourself: You don't have to be self-confident, assured, or floating on a cloud of high self-esteem. We're also not talking about faith in prayer. Prayer is merely the means to a greater end, coming to know God. And we're not talking about faith in faith. That's one of the craziest things people say: "It doesn't matter what you believe, as long as you believe." I don't think so. I don't really have a lot of confidence in someone who really believes the earth is flat. And I don't think it's possible just to have faith. There is always an object to faith—always. You either have faith in your own abilities to solve the problem, or you have faith that someone else will solve the problem, or you have faith in fate, that some impersonal force will work things out.

So, the faith that is necessary for prayer is faith *in God*, faith that he exists, and faith that he hears and responds to prayer.

When it comes to faith, Jesus says some remarkable (although some would say ridiculous) things, like this: "Listen to me! You can pray for anything, and if you believe, you will have it." (Mark 11:24) This and other sayings like it have led to a lot of misunderstandings. Some people think that faith must be some sort of self-talk or self-hypnotism that helps us feel more confident when we approach God—like football players gathering on the sidelines before a game, arms wrapped around each other, chanting "Go, go, go, go …" or "Let's do it!" or whatever. They bounce up and down, work themselves into a mild frenzy of enthusiasm, and then head for the field full of faith in their ability to annihilate the opponent.

That is not what Jesus was talking about. Some people have turned this statement into a magic formula for consumerism. They take it literally, and they encourage people to pray for a $500,000 home, or a new Lexus, or a vacation in Hawaii. Given that Jesus was pretty down on materialism, this is probably not his take on it. Still others think this saying means that if we don't receive answers to our prayers, it's our own fault: We didn't have enough faith.

Let's think about that one. Jesus himself, the man of perfect faith, prayed that he would be spared from having to die on the cross. God didn't answer his prayer, but I don't think it has much to do with Jesus' faith or lack thereof. (More on unanswered prayers in Chapters 16 and 17.)

So what type of faith is Jesus talking about here? In this instance, it is special faith indeed, a special gift from God. Let me give an illustration. When I was in youth ministry at a church in Fresno, California, we decided that we wanted to raise some money to help alleviate hunger. We were debating about how much we should set as a goal, and we were throwing around the numbers we usually shot for—$200, $300, in that range. Then we decided to pray about it and see whether we could sense what God might have us do. We spent some time in prayer—and a lot of it listening in prayer. When we ended the prayer, I asked what numbers came into people's minds. For more than one of us, it was $2,000.

Well, this was an unimaginable amount to us, but we felt confident that this was the figure planted in our minds by the Holy Spirit. We began making plans on how we were going to raise that kind of money. Well, one thing led to another, and we organized a marathon week-long softball game; we got pledges from the church and community, donations from local businesses, and players who played in 12-hour shifts, morning and night. At the end of the week, we stood proudly on the field as we had our picture taken after our triumph. Then we counted the pledges. We'd made our goal plus some.

Certainly this sort of thing can be "explained" on a number of levels, but all those who participated had a deep sense that we had been given a special gift of faith—what was for us a *large* amount of faith—to pray for and work for a large goal. It was a special moment for all of us, certainly for me.

It's not often in my life that I get a sense that if I pray for something, it will come to pass, even if it seems absurd at the time. Sometimes it turns out to be wishful thinking, not something given by God. Other times, it has proven to be a divine gift. There is no formula for knowing when something comes from God. But part of faith is trying to listen, acting on what you sense is true, and trusting God for the results. It's not so much a puzzle to be solved, but an adventure to be lived out. But let's be clear that, most of the time, adventure requires the simple faith: God exists and he hears prayer.

Honesty

You can't fool God, although a lot of us try. Some people imagine that they must bring their very best selves to God. Let's say that Joe is resentful of his brother, Tom, who has just made a killing in the stock market the same day Joe has lost a lot of money. Joe, trying to be a good Christian, prays, "Lord, I'm thankful that my brother made a lot of money in the stock market. Please bless him and help him use his money wisely."

This is a noble prayer, but it's a lie. What Joe is really feeling is that his brother is a jerk, that he always gets lucky, and that it's not fair that Tom, who already had a lot of money, should hit it big in the stock market when he, Joe, could really use the extra income.

But let's say Joe is reasonably honest. He might pray, "Lord, I admit I'm jealous of Tom. Help me to rid myself of this jealousy, and bless Tom and his family."

That's better, but still not exactly what Joe is feeling. Probably the most honest prayer would be, "Lord, I hate Tom right now. And to be frank, I'm not too happy with you. Why should he get another break? And why didn't you give me a break? I'm the one who needs it. This is pretty unfair."

Now we're praying, because prayer is an honest expression of our hopes, dreams, fears, and wants to God. It isn't as if God doesn't know what we're really feeling, as if we can hide our true feelings from him. So why not just lay everything on the table?

This type of honesty is found throughout the history of prayer, and the Bible is full of expressions of it. One of my favorites is in the obscure little Old Testament Book of Habakkuk, which begins like this:

> "How long, O Lord, must I call for help? But you do not listen! 'Violence!' I cry, but you do not come to save. Must I forever see this sin and misery all around me?" (Habakkuk 1:2–3)

Habakkuk is not a happy camper: His nation is increasingly corrupt and violent, and he has been praying about it for years. But things are only getting worse. It's only natural that he'd get ticked off. And it's only honest that he tell God what he's feeling instead of praying some pious prayer.

> **Prayer Pearls**
>
> Your desires are probably not in complete harmony with God's will. Pray instead that God will lead you to want the right things. Ask for what is good and for what is best for your soul. There is no way you could want these things for yourself more than God desires you to have them.
>
> —Evagrius Ponticus, Egyptian monk

Jeremiah is another whiner to God. At one point he says to God, "Lord, you know I am suffering for your sake. Punish my persecutors! Don't let them kill me! Be merciful to me and give them what they deserve!" (Jeremiah 15:15) Not very nice, and at some point Jeremiah had to move to higher moral ground. But the refreshing thing about him and all the biblical prayers (especially in Psalms) is their utter honesty before God. Age after age has discovered that when it comes to prayer, honesty is the best policy.

Humility

Humility has gotten bad press in our day. To many, it means to grovel before others or never to say anything good about yourself. To some, it's the same as low self-esteem.

Not quite. To be humble is not to have a high or low view of yourself, but to have an *accurate* view. In terms of prayer, it means to have an accurate view of yourself in relation to God. That is, you must essentially say: God is great, good, holy, just, wise, eternal, all powerful—and I am not.

This may strike some as obvious, but it isn't so obvious in day-to-day life. I'm upset with my wife, let's say, for forgetting to be home at 6:00 P.M. to watch the kids while I go to an appointment. It's closing in on 6:30 P.M., and she's still not home. I'm furious by now, and I have a mouthful of venom to spew at her when she walks in the door—she's always inconsiderate; this is going to ruin my meeting; how could she be so self-centered, and so on and so forth.

The entire time, though, I haven't prayed. I've acted as if I'm good, holy, just, and wise—not only toward my wife, but also toward God because I haven't thought him worth consulting in this matter. *I* know what's going on, and *I* know what needs to be said when she walks through the door.

Of course, when it turns out that, uh, I never *told* my wife that I needed her home at 6:00 P.M., I feel pretty humbled. Feeling stupid is not the main issue, though: It's living my life as if I didn't need the patience and wisdom that come from God.

So humility in prayer means simply recognizing where our strength comes from and then seeking God for it. You can see why this is a prerequisite of prayer: If you're not humble enough to admit that you have any needs—not even a need for God—then you're probably not going to pray.

Humility has another dimension as well. To enter into a life of prayer means to be willing to enter into an experiment of sorts, but the experiment is unlike any other. By their nature, scientific experiments put us in control. We mix the chemicals, we perform tests, and then we analyze the results. To enter into prayer, however, is to put ourselves into another's control. It is to allow ourselves to be shaped, tested, and analyzed by another.

In this regard, the most important prayer we can pray is the one Jesus prayed the last night of his life. He was sure he was heading toward his execution. He had prayed until he sweat blood to avoid death. But in the end, he simply said, "Yet I want your will, not mine." (Mark 14:36) As theologian Donald Bloesch put it, "There is a time to argue and complain to God, but there is also a time to submit."

The one thing we can be pretty sure of is that God is not going to ask us literally to give up our lives when we begin the life of prayer. But he is asking us to take the first step in a lifetime of giving control of our lives over to him.

For me, it's like going on a roller coaster. Whenever I sit in one, I realize I'm putting my life in the hands of a lot of other people: the designer of the roller coaster, the maintenance crew, the operators. For me, that's a scary proposition. But it's also a heck of a lot of fun, with a number of jerks and drops along the way. Prayer is not much different a lot of the time. It doesn't require a huge amount of humility to begin—just enough to buy a ticket and stand in line at first. But that's enough to get you started on this adventure.

In his classic book *Prayer*, Ole Hallesby summed it up this way: "Prayer and helplessness are inseparable. Only he who is helpless can truly pray. Your helplessness is your best prayer."

Patience

Scott Peck begins his best-selling book *The Road Less Traveled* with this: "Life is hard." I could have begun this book with a similar sentence: "Prayer is hard." Don't let anyone tell you different.

Okay, I admit that I just got done telling you it is different: I've said it was "fun" and an "adventure" and a bunch of other stuff to get you to consider taking prayer more seriously. I'm not saying those things are not true. I'm just about to explain to you the fine print.

Prayer is hard work a lot of times. Sometimes it's so boring that you'll fall asleep. Sometimes it feels like God isn't there. Sometimes no prayer you pray will be answered. Sometimes you will feel that God has abandoned you. You will doubt prayer and God and everything else. You'll be sure you've been hoodwinked into prayer. You'll scorn people who pray, calling them fools. You'll never want to say another prayer the rest of your life.

And then you'll find that you really can't live without prayer. And however angry, bored, or doubting, you'll turn to God and say, "Okay, let's give this another try."

> **Prayer Pearls**
>
> Do not let it be imagined that one must remain silent about one's feelings of rebellion in order to enter into dialogue with God. Quite the opposite is the truth: It is precisely when one expresses them that a dialogue of truth begins.
>
> —Paul Tournier, Christian psychologist

In other words, if you're going to enter into a life of prayer, you'll have to have patience. If Rome wasn't built in a day, a meaningful prayer life isn't built in a week or a month—or a lifetime. Let's just say that like any other serious endeavor, you will always feel you could know more, be doing more, or be experiencing more. It's like marriage. I've been married for 25 years now, and I love my wife more than ever. I believe I'm a better husband than ever and that our relationship is better than ever.

Are my wife and I satisfied with our relationship, though? No. Do we want it to be better? Yes. Do we feel like taking the trouble to make it better? Not all the time. Is it an adventure, fun, hard work, dreary, joyful, frustrating, or satisfying? Yes.

Such is a life of prayer with God, as long as patience is part of the picture.

With a Little Help from the Friend

A difference between prayer and all other pursuits is this: The very thing we need to embark on a life of prayer and then continue in it comes through the activity itself.

When you take up golf, let's say, you know you're going to need a lot of patience to play it well. But golf itself does not grant you patience—it only *tries* your patience. Patience must come from somewhere else.

But if you need more patience in prayer, you can simply use that very means to gain the patience you need. Faith, honesty, humility, and patience are not only prerequisites of prayer, they also are qualities that can be sought and received in prayer. And Jesus promises gifts such as these: "You can pray for anything, and if you believe, you will have it." (Mark 11:24)

A story from the Gospels (Mark 9:14–29) shows this dynamic in action. Jesus was speaking with a man whose son had epilepsy. The man had brought his son to Jesus, only to have the boy fall to the ground "in violent convulsions, writhing and foaming at the mouth." Jesus asked the father, "How long has this been happening?"

The man replied, "Since he was very small. The evil spirit [thought to be the cause of epilepsy in that day] often makes him fall into the fire or into water, trying to kill him. Have mercy on us and help us. Do something if you can."

> **Prayer Pearls**
>
> To be a Christian without prayer is no more possible than to be alive without breathing.
>
> —Martin Luther, German theologian

That was a weak prayer, if you ask me. Jesus seems to agree: "What do you mean, 'If I can'?" he replied. "Anything is possible if a person believes." The father then blurted out, "I do believe. Help my unbelief!" And Jesus then healed the boy.

Here was a man who had the minimum prerequisite of faith: He believed there was at least a small chance that Jesus could do something to help his boy. He had faith, but he needed more.

That is also the case with the other prerequisites of prayer, and we need a prayer to help us through a lifetime of prayer:

> Lord, I come in faith; help my unbelief.
>
> Lord, I come in truth; forgive my dishonesty.
>
> Lord, I come in humility; rid me of pride.
>
> Lord, I come with patience, but not enough. Amen.

The Least You Need to Know

- The four prerequisites of prayer are faith, honesty, humility, and patience.
- We need only minuscule portions of each to begin praying.

◆ We will need more of these qualities as we continue in prayer, and we will be given more as we ask for more.

◆ Prayer can be hard work, but it is well worth the patience and perseverance required sometimes.

Part 2

The Heart of Prayer

Before we can talk more specifically about how to pray in the Christian tradition, we have to look more specifically at what prayer means in that tradition. More specifically: Who exactly is this God we're praying to? And how exactly am I supposed to approach this God?

Answering these questions will get us into the very heart of prayer. They'll help us better understand what we're doing and help us to pray more effectively. And one prayer, the "Lord's Prayer," more than any other, answers these questions. So we'll begin there.

Chapter 4

Getting Insider Information

In This Chapter

- Getting beyond trendy resources
- The greatest written resource on prayer
- The greatest teacher of prayer
- The most important prayer of all

I've already said a number of things about prayer, and a careful reader (namely you) has probably asked, "Says who?" You've probably looked at the back of this book and read the introduction and noticed that I've got some credentials suggesting I may know something. But why trust me?

Well, you shouldn't. Frankly, there are a lot of crackpots out there spewing all manner of half-truths about prayer—and, as far as you know, I could be one of them. So, if you shouldn't trust me, who should you trust? Where do you go to get good, reliable, insider information on prayer?

Prayer Book Hall of Fame

The temptation, of course, is to scan the religious best-sellers list, log on to Amazon.com, and order something contemporary. The problem is that you'll have no idea whether the guidance is sound or merely trendy.

It takes a while for any good book to establish itself as a classic, and you probably don't want to waste your time on stuff that is still proving itself when there are literally hundreds of prayer books that have already stood the test of time.

One place to look for this insider information about prayer is in the greatest devotional books of all time—books like Thomas à Kempis's *The Imitation of Christ*, Francis de Sales's *Introduction to the Devout Life*, or Harry Emerson Fosdick's *Prayer*—among hundreds of others (see Appendix C for a longer list). Such books are still in print after decades, and sometimes centuries, precisely because they still have something profound and relevant to say.

To be sure, some of these are not easy to read. Some still rely on older translations; some are wordy by modern standards of prose; some are a bit mystical in parts. But the effort required to digest them pays off with huge spiritual dividends.

> **" " From the Good Book** _____
>
> Then Hannah prayed and said: "My heart rejoices in the Lord; in the Lord my horn is lifted high. My mouth boasts over my enemies, for I delight in your deliverance. "There is no one holy like the Lord; there is no one besides you; there is no rock like our God. Do not keep talking so proudly or let your mouth speak such arrogance, for the Lord is a God who knows, and by him deeds are weighed."
> —Hannah, in 1 Samuel 2:1–3

The Prayer Book for Christians

One thing you'll find in reading the classics in prayer is that they all ground themselves in another book—still *the* prayer book of all time. It's not an accident that the Bible has been around for more than 1,500 years and is still the best-selling book in America—and this in a society that is supposedly not all that interested in religion.

So what's so great about this book?

For one thing, it's got a lot going on in it, including some pretty fascinating stories and characters: Moses dukes it out with Egyptian pharaohs. King David steals another man's wife and then murders the husband. Babylonian armies lay siege to Jerusalem and exile the population. Jesus, the Son of God, confronts the authorities—and loses. Paul instigates riots in Ephesus.

The Bible is also a book of sublime religious poetry. Lots of passages could be quoted here, but the most famous, Psalm 23, will do for now:

The Lord is my shepherd, I shall not want.

He makes me to lie down in green pastures.

He leads me beside the still waters.

He restores my soul;

He leads me in paths of righteousness for his name's sake.

Yea, though I walk through the valley of the shadow of death,

I will fear no evil.

For you are with me,

Your rod and your staff, they comfort me. You prepare a table before me in the presence of my enemies;

You anoint my head with oil;

My cup runs over.

Surely goodness and mercy will follow me

All the days of my life;

And I will dwell in the house of the Lord

Forever.

(New King James Version)

The Bible also contains some stories that speak to issues every culture in every age is concerned about: the creation of the world (Genesis); the meaning of unjust suffering (Job); and the goal of history (Revelation), to name a few.

On top of that, the Bible is a practical book that gives the world some of its most profound ethics. That includes not only the Ten Commandments, but also Jesus' highest commands: "Love God with all your heart, all your soul, all your mind," and "Love your neighbor as yourself." (Matthew 22:37–39)

The Bible, however, has one more dimension: For Christians, it is *the* authority in matters of faith and practice. That's why we call it the word of God. We believe that through this collection of books, God teaches us about himself and how we should live.

> ### Prayer Pearls
>
> Prayer is the key of the morning and the bolt of the evening.
> —Matthew Henry, Bible commentator

He also teaches us how we should pray. The Bible is not just a book of theology and ethics, it's also a prayer book. It teaches *about* prayer and also teaches *how to* pray. This only makes sense, because one big theme in the Bible is how people can know God. As we've noticed, prayer is about getting to know God.

The Bible doesn't have a part dedicated to discussing just prayer. Okay, maybe the Psalms—a collection of prayers/songs—could be considered that (more on that in Chapter 18). But other than that, it's a snippet here, a paragraph there on prayer.

So when you open this big book, how do you decide where to start?

The Center of the Bible

Well, go to the center of the Bible. By that I don't mean the physical center, which is somewhere in Psalms. Look at the central figure of the Bible: Jesus Christ.

Jesus is central because he is the one to whom the Old Testament points. Lots of Old Testament passages speak about the great longing for justice and peace and look to the day when a messiah, or savior, would arise out of the Jewish people. Here's one: "Out of the stump of David's family [that is, King David, the greatest Jewish king] will grow a shoot … and the Spirit of the Lord will rest on him—the Spirit of wisdom and understanding, the Spirit of counsel and might, the Spirit of knowledge and the fear of the Lord …. He will defend the poor and exploited. He will rule against the wicked and destroy them with the breath of his mouth. He will be clothed with fairness and truth." (Isaiah 11:1–4)

> **Snapshots of Answered Prayers**
>
> Nehemiah prays that King Artaxerxes would hear his plea to return to Jerusalem to assist in its rebuilding after the Babylonian captivity. See what happens in the second chapter of the Book of Nehemiah.

For Christians, the messiah foretold by this and other Old Testament passages is Jesus Christ.

Jesus is central also because the New Testament says that he will bring history to a magnificent conclusion. At the end of time, Jesus will say, "It is finished! I am the Alpha and the Omega—the Beginning and the End. To all who are thirsty I will give the springs of the water of life without charge! All who are victorious will inherit all these blessings, and I will be their God, and they will be my children." (Revelation 21:6–7)

Furthermore, the New Testament teaches that in Jesus' life, death, and resurrection—especially his presence with us today—he answers our deepest questions: What is the purpose of life? Can I be forgiven? Am I loved? Is there hope?

You can't get much more central than that.

So if you're looking for a way to make sense of the many books of the Bible and its 31,000 verses, you could do worse than by focusing on Jesus Christ.

Not surprisingly, of the many things Jesus did and taught, prayer was at the core. The fact that Jesus prayed often and at length is regularly noted in references such as this: "The next morning, Jesus awoke long before daybreak and went out alone into the wilderness to pray." (Mark 1:35)

This obsession with prayer began to rub off on the disciples, who became curious about prayer one day.

The Prayer to Start All Prayer

"Once when Jesus had been out praying," writes Luke, "one of his disciples came to him as he finished and said, 'Lord, teach us to pray.'"

Jesus replied by saying they should pray like this:

> Father, may your name be honored.
>
> May your kingdom come soon.
>
> Give us our food day by day.
>
> And forgive us our sins—just as we forgive those who have sinned against us.
>
> And don't let us yield to temptation.
>
> —Luke 11:1–4

Sound familiar? This is what is commonly called the "Lord's Prayer," that is, the prayer that the Lord, Jesus, taught his disciples. Some people call it the "Our Father," after the first two words. This version, from the Gospel of Luke (11:20–4), is only one biblical version. The Gospel of Matthew (6:9–13) is the basis of the version said by most people today:

> Our Father, who art in heaven, hallowed be thy name.
>
> Thy kingdom come, thy will be done
>
> on earth as it is in heaven.
>
> Give us this day our daily bread,
>
> And forgive us our trespasses

as we forgive those who trespass against us.

And lead us not into temptation,

but deliver us from evil.

For thine is the kingdom,

and the power, and the glory,

forever and ever. Amen.

Note one thing: Many churches pray that line about forgiveness like this:

Forgive us our debts as we forgive our debtors.

We'll look at the meaning of each of those words—*trespasses* and *debts*—in Chapter 6. For now, just be aware that when you're in church and the minister says, "Let's pray the prayer that Jesus taught us," you'll know what he's talking about.

Different versions aside, this little prayer is the most important thing Jesus said about prayer. It is a model prayer, one that we can pray. It also teaches nearly everything Jesus wanted to teach about prayer.

Let's look at the take of both Protestants and Catholics: *The Catechism of the Catholic Church* quotes the early Latin church theologian, Augustine (often referred to as Augustine of Hippo): "Run through all the words of holy prayers [in scripture], and I do not think you will find anything in them that is not contained and included in the Lord's Prayer."

 From the Good Book

As for God, his way is perfect; the word of the Lord is flawless. He is a shield for all who take refuge in him. For who is God besides the Lord? And who is the rock except our God?

—David, 2 Samuel 22:31, 32

The famous nineteenth-century Protestant preacher, Henry Ward Beecher, put it this way: "I used to think the Lord's Prayer was a short prayer; but as I live longer and see more of life, I begin to believe there is no such thing as getting through it. If a man, in praying that prayer, were to be stopped by every word until he had thoroughly prayed it, it would take him a lifetime."

Not bad for just a few lines. I'm not going to take a lifetime to explain it, though—just two chapters. Still, I think you'll soon see why this can aptly be called the mother of all prayers.

The Least You Need to Know

♦ Modern prayer resources are only as good as what they are based on.

♦ The Bible is *the* resource on prayer.

♦ Jesus Christ is *the* teacher on prayer.

♦ The Lord's Prayer is *the* prayer to start all prayer.

Chapter 5

The Prayer to Begin All Prayer: Part 1

In This Chapter

- ◆ More about the God we're praying to
- ◆ How prayer helps us experience community
- ◆ How prayer allows us to have intimacy with God
- ◆ What the obscure phrases at the opening of the Lord's Prayer mean

There's a lot—I mean *a lot*—going on in the Lord's Prayer. It's like an army of ideas ready to overwhelm us, so we're wise to divide and conquer.

The Lord's Prayer can be divided into two parts. The opening ("Our father, who art in heaven, hallowed be thy name") helps us understand the setting of prayer. The seven phrases after that are requests, sometimes called "the seven petitions." In this chapter, we'll look at the opening and the first three petitions.

Our Father

It doesn't take long to find something meaningful in the Lord's Prayer. Take the first word: *Our*. By using this little pronoun, Jesus is trying to clear up three matters right off the bat.

You Never Pray Alone

I've made a point of saying that prayer is about personal communication with God; it's an intimate relationship, one on one. But it's also about much, much more. For one thing, prayer is about being connected with other pray-ers.

Let's take an example. I like to fly fish, and when I do, I have to spend a lot of time alone. Even when I go on a trip with my son, we usually split up and take different parts of the river we're fishing. We come back in a few hours and swap stories. Even when I'm casting by myself, though, alone in front of a gentle riffle, enjoying some solitude with nature, I never feel alone. I know my son is fishing with me, even though he's not fishing *with* me.

> **Prayer Pearls**
>
> After we have made our requests known to him, our language should be, "Thy will be done." I would a thousand times rather that God's will should be done than my own.
>
> —D. L. Moody, nineteenth-century evangelist

That's how it is with the Lord's Prayer. Even though we might say it alone, it reminds us that we're *not* alone. That's the point of the words *our* and *us* that run all the way through it. Even when you pray it alone, you are reminded that you're part of a community—in particular, a group that honors Christ, that prays to him regularly, and also, from time to time, that says the prayer he taught.

Prayer Is Learned Together

If I want to improve my golf game, let's say, I need to spend time on the practice tee, alone, flailing away at the ball. But if I'm serious about getting better, I find a group to play with regularly, and I take lessons from a pro. In other words, I get together with other golfers.

With this little word *our*—and the use of *us* throughout this prayer—Jesus is simply reminding us that if we really want to learn about prayer, we need to get together regularly with other pray-ers.

Jesus assumes prayer is first something done in the community of believers and by the community of believers.

This goes against conventional wisdom, of course (as does much of what Jesus has to say, by the way). For the longest time, when I heard the word *prayer*, I conjured up an image of a solitary individual, with bowed head and/or kneeling in a bedroom—alone.

Of course, this *is* prayer; prayer is something people do by themselves a lot. And, certainly, prayer expresses an individual's personal relationship with God. But if that were the only thing true about prayer, Jesus would have said to pray, "*My* father."

But he didn't. And one reason is that he wanted to suggest that if we want to learn how to pray well, we need to get together with others to learn. (More on this in Part 3.)

> **Prayer Pearls**
>
> Work as if everything depended upon your work, and pray as if everything depended upon your prayer.
> —Gen. William Booth, founder of the Salvation Army

God Is Bigger Than My Ideas About God

This is really good news. A lot of times I think I've got God figured out, and I couldn't be bothered with what other people think. But then I find that I pretty quickly get bored with the God I've figured out.

Fortunately, God is much bigger than my mind or my heart can capture, and for that reason God is a continual surprise. When I pray in the context of a larger prayer community, I can be sure that there will be times when the community teaches me how to expand my understanding of God. For example, my three children each know something about me that the others don't know. As they talk about me with one another, they sometimes discover things: how to get their way with me, what line not to cross, and so on.

God is not just "my" God, he's also "our" Father—the God of the entire community of prayer. So, as I become a part of that community, I'm going to have my understanding of God expanded.

> **Snapshots of Answered Prayers**
>
> In Luke 22:31 Jesus prays that Peter will not desert him at his trial and death. Though Peter initially failed, see John 21:15–19 for Peter's restoration.

Our *Father*

This word *Father* is the most radical word in this prayer—and maybe in the history of religions. Even the most skeptical New Testament scholars—some of whom believe that hardly anything in the New Testament is original—admit that calling God "Father," as Jesus did, is a fresh idea in the history of religions. Until then it was common to call God all sorts of things: Lord, Master, Creator, King, Holy One, Majestic One, Lawgiver. But not "papa."

I'm not being disrespectful here. We know that Jesus, in introducing this radical word, used the Aramaic word *abba*, which is equivalent to our "dad" or even "daddy." This has profound implications for the life of prayer.

We Can Have Intimacy with God

This gets back to what I was saying in Chapter 2: Prayer is a key means to experiencing God. And it also gets back to what I said in the Introduction: This word *Father* is not about God's maleness.

Admittedly, the Bible mostly uses masculine images for God. But it doesn't hesitate to use feminine ones as well to show the intimacy we can experience with God. One of my favorites is found in Psalm 131, where prayer is compared to a child nursing at a mother's breast:

> Lord, my heart is not proud;
>
> my eyes are not haughty.
>
> I don't concern myself with matters too great
>
> or awesome for me.
>
> But I have stilled and quieted myself,
>
> just as a small child is quiet with its mother.
>
> Yes, like a small child is my soul within me.

So *Father* is not about fathers or mothers, or males or females. It's about the meaning of prayer: intimacy with God.

We Become God's Children

Of course, if God is our Father, then we are his children. The apostle John put it this way: "See how very much the heavenly Father loves us, for he allows us to be called his children, and we really are!" (1 John 3:1) This takes some getting used to, but once you do get used to it, it's pretty incredible.

When I first got married, I thought it the strangest thing when my wife introduced me to others as her husband. I had never been a "husband," and it just sounded strange. But the more we've grown together and immersed ourselves in the mystery of being husband and wife, the more I've gotten used to the word. I've also grown to relish it, for it carries with it not only responsibility, but also a sense that I have a deep connection with my wife as no other man has.

It also has taken me a while to get used to being called a "child" or "son" of God. In fact, I never addressed God as "Father" for the longest time in my spiritual journey. And then one day I did. It's difficult to describe, but at that moment I felt immediately that I had become more intimate with God.

The apostle Paul wrote, "You should not be like cowering, fearful slaves. You should behave instead like God's very own children, adopted into his family—calling him 'Father, dear Father.' For his Holy Spirit speaks to us deep in our hearts and tells us that we are God's children." (Romans 8:15–16)

> **Prayer Pearls**
>
> Hurry is the death of prayer.
> —Samuel Chadwick, Puritan preacher

Indeed.

We Can Come to God with Confidence

I've quoted it once in another context, but this is such an important saying of Jesus that it bears repeating: "You parents—if your children ask for a loaf of bread, do you give them a stone instead? Or if they ask for a fish, do you give them a snake? Of course not! If you sinful people know how to give good gifts to your children, how much more will your heavenly Father give good gifts to those who ask him." (Matthew 7:9–11)

This doesn't mean we can assume that everything we request of God will be granted. God loves us a little more than that. It *does* mean that every prayer is heard and that God will give us what we most need (which doesn't always correspond to what we *think* we need).

The great theologian Augustine put it this way: "Our Father: At this name love is aroused in us ... and the confidence of obtaining what we are about to ask .... What would he not give to his children who ask, since he has already granted them the gift of being his children?"

Who Art in Heaven

If you haven't figured it out already, prayer is pretty hard to figure out. First it's one thing and then it's another. Here's another case in point: If the words *our Father* teach that God is intimate, this phrase—*who art in heaven*—suggests that God is distant. This doesn't sound very good until you understand what Jesus is driving at.

He doesn't mean to say that God is physically distant; "heaven" is not a place. It is a way of being—existing in perfect love—and that way of being is so perfect that it is unlike life as we know it (which, to put it as nicely as possible, is not perfect in love).

Heaven in the Bible is usually contrasted with *earth*, as in the phrase we're about to look at: "Thy will be done on earth as it is in heaven." This suggests that the one sphere, earth, has a long way to go to become like the other sphere, heaven.

The Bible usually uses the word *holy* to talk about this. *Holy* doesn't mean "perfectly good in a religious sort of way," but "set apart." In this sense, I could say my best suit is holy because it's set apart in many ways: It's the most expensive, finest tailored piece of clothing I own. And I've set it apart to wear only on the most special occasions.

 From the Good Book

May your eyes be open toward this temple night and day, this place of which you said, "My name shall be there," so that you will hear the prayer your servant prays toward this place. Hear the supplication of your servant and of your people Israel when they pray toward this place. Hear from heaven, your dwelling place, and when you hear, forgive.

—Solomon, 1 Kings 8:29, 30

In calling God holy, we're saying that he is set apart, distinct, utterly different than human beings. God is nothing like us: He is infinite, and we're finite; he is all-knowing and present everywhere, and we are not; he is pure goodness and love, and we are not. And here's the kicker for philosophical types: We participate in being, and he transcends being (let's not get into that here).

The practical point is this: The Lord's Prayer reminds us that we can never put God in a box, mold him into our image, or make him more acceptable to our sensibilities.

In her book *Amazing Grace*, Kathleen Norris talks about this dimension of faith:

> One so often hears people say, "I just can't handle it," when they reject a biblical image of God as Father, as Mother, as Lord or Judge; God as lover, as angry or jealous, God on a cross. I find this choice of words revealing, however real the pain they reflect: If we seek a God we can "handle," that will be exactly what we get. A God we can manipulate, suspiciously like ourselves, the wideness of whose mercy we've cut down to size.

As intimate as God becomes, he always remains himself, utterly distinct from us, someone we hold in awe, someone who continues to shape us—as well it should be if we don't want to narrowly confine the wideness of his mercy.

On to the first petition.

Hallowed Be Thy Name

To keep a name hallowed means to respect the name and what stands behind it. It's like having a great family name with a profound heritage and a long-standing reputation for honesty in business. Then along comes a son who dishonors the family name by lying to clients and embezzling funds. It's a disgrace to the family name, we say, and the family's name is tarnished.

Hallowed here, then, literally means to "keep holy," or to "honor and esteem."

Name here is not a reference to a convenient label, like those we put on people when they are born so we don't get them confused. In the Bible especially, a name often means something, usually describing unique characteristics of the person: Jesus means "savior," Barnabas means "encourager," and so on. That's even more true when it comes to names for God: Holy, Redeemer, Creator, and the like. It's especially true for the most revealing name of God: Father. (If you skimmed the section "Our *Father*," you'd better go back and read it now.)

> **Prayer Pearls**
>
> I have been driven many times to my knees by the overwhelming conviction that I had nowhere else to go. My own wisdom, and that of all about me, seemed insufficient for the day.
>
> —Abraham Lincoln, American president

It wouldn't seem that we would have to ask God to make sure his name is never disgraced; you'd think he'd be interested in maintaining his honor as well. He is, but we're not—at least, not always. This petition is just a roundabout way of saying, "Lord, help me never to do or say anything to dishonor your name and what you stand for."

This is a tall order because it doesn't take much to do something stupid to dishonor that name. I do it every day: being impatient with a co-worker; ignoring the street person asking for a handout; not helping my wife at home; and so on. This wouldn't be so bad if I didn't wear the family name, Christian, and if I hadn't prayed the Lord's Prayer last Sunday to keep the Father's name hallowed.

Because this is hard to do, I need God's help. And so I continue to pray, "Hallowed by thy name."

Thy Kingdom Come

This is a prayer for everything to turn out right in the end. It is, of course, another "useless" prayer, like so many others in this prayer: God is going to bring history to a glorious end. What he promised long ago he will fulfill.

There will come a day, according to the Book of Revelation, when: "[God] will live with them [meaning us], and they will be his people. God himself will be with them. He will remove all of their sorrows, and there will be no more death or sorrow or crying or pain. For the old world and its evils are gone forever." (Revelation 21:3–4)

The promise is sure, and it reminds us that this life isn't as good as it gets. One member of one congregation I served had lost a son in childhood. She was in her 70s by the time I knew her, and she had a great sense of humor and was not hesitant to share a smile with the rest of us. But she also carried with her a touch of sadness from this early loss, as well as from the loss of her husband a few years earlier. As much as she enjoyed her life, and as much as she contributed to the lives of others, she told me, "I'm looking forward to seeing my son and husband someday."

She understood this part of the Lord's Prayer. As good as this life can be, it's not good enough. There is something better we await and upon which we can pin our hopes and our lives.

Thy Will Be Done on Earth as It Is in Heaven

This is a deceptive little petition that seems so harmless and well intentioned at first. Henry Ward Beecher, a nineteenth-century Protestant preacher said, "You read, 'Thy will be done,' and you say to yourself, 'O, I can pray that'; and all the time your mind goes round and round in immense circuits and far-off distances; but God is continually bringing the circuits nearer to you, till he says, 'How is it about your temper and your pride? How is it about your business and daily life?'"

To pray to do God's will, then, is no small prayer. It encompasses about everything we do. This is not a prayer to do God's will on Sundays or when we feel religious. Nor is it a prayer to do God's will as best we can or according to our interpretation. No, the prayer is to do God's will "as it is done in heaven."

For a serious writer, heaven is *The New Yorker* magazine. If an aspiring writer were to write in such a way that someone would say, "That sounds like something from *The New Yorker*"—well, that's about as good as it gets.

For the person of prayer, we want to live life as it's lived in heaven. Again, heaven is not a place so much as a way of being, a way of existing, and that way is described as love. To say our friends who have died are "in heaven" is to say that they exist in a state of love, loving each other and God in ways that are unimaginable to us now.

That qualification, "as it is in heaven," is what saves this prayer from becoming an oppressive burden. The temptation is to begin to catalogue all the ways we fall short of doing God's will—impatience, ungratefulness, selfishness, gluttony—and vow to do better in the future. That we should do better goes without saying. But God's will is not a list of do's and don'ts as much as it is living in love. Someone once asked Jesus what the greatest commandments were, which essentially asked what God's will ultimately is. Jesus replied that we should love God with everything in us, and we should love other people as we love ourselves.

According to the first three petitions, then, to pray is to turn our lives completely over to God so that we may be shaped and guided by his loving hands. In some respects, this is a frightening idea; there's no getting around that. But it's also true that to give yourself to God is the most exciting (and exacting!) adventure a person can go on.

> **Prayer Pearls**
>
> Prayer is the gymnasium of the soul.
>
> —Samuel M. Zwemer, missionary to Islam

By this time, it should be more clear than ever that prayer is not a religious activity that we add to our lives to make them a little nicer; prayer is something that will transform our lives, inside and out.

What to Do if You Hate the Term "Father"

For people who have been verbally or physically abused by their fathers, this word causes all sorts of discomfort. Others reject the name *father* in prayer because they deeply resent the patriarchal assumptions that have oppressed women through the centuries. These powerful emotional reactions are understandable, and I agree with spiritual advisors who suggest that such people place a moratorium on using the word—if that's the thing that's keeping them from praying.

Because intimacy is such an important feature of Christian prayer, though, attempts to substitute another name for God have repeatedly failed. Some have suggested, for example, that we pray, "Our Creator." God is certainly our creator, and powerful, and the origin of all things in heaven and earth—as the title "Creator" implies—so it is good to address God as such from time to time.

> **From the Good Book**
>
> And Elisha prayed, "O Lord, open his eyes so he may see." Then the Lord opened the servant's eyes, and he looked and saw the hills full of horses and chariots of fire all around Elisha.
>
> —2 Kings 6:17

But to do so on a regular basis undermines the most interesting thing about Christian prayer: its ability to bring us closer to God. You just can't get as close to a creator as you can a father.

We have to remember that people were abused by fathers in Jesus' day, and that in his time, there were goddesses galore in the larger Roman and Greek cultures, to whom a lot of people preferred to pray. Jesus knew using the word *father* would create all sorts of problems for some people. But he still used it because he knew, in the long run, that it would do more spiritual good than psychological harm.

Prayer Hotline

When we object to the word *father* because it reminds us of our male parents, we are getting things backward. Jesus introduces the term not because he wants us to shape our understanding of God into the image of our earthly fathers. In fact, just the opposite is true: He wants us, among other things, to shape our understanding of fatherhood—and parenting—in light of who our Heavenly Father is.

So even if we are uncomfortable using this word in prayer (as I was for a time), we should come back to it now and then, until we come to the point when we can use the name freely. Then we can begin to shape our own parenting, not by our past, but in light of our Heavenly Father who loves us in unimaginable ways.

God Is Not a Lonely Father

As the *Catechism of the Catholic Church* puts it, "When we pray to the Father, we adore and glorify him together with the Son and the Holy Spirit." In other words, in the Christian tradition, the Lord's Prayer assumes that God exists as a Trinity: as Father, Son, and Holy Spirit.

> **Prayer Pearls**
>
> God is not a cosmic bellboy for whom we can press a button to get things.
>
> —Harry Emerson Fosdick, American pastor and author

This is not the place to discuss why this is central to Christianity, nor will we go into detail explaining how God can exist as a Trinity. Suffice it to say that the centuries-long Christian understanding is that God exists as one "essence" in three "persons," equal in power and glory. It's not a committee of three or one being with three "faces," but three in one and one in three. You can see that we've reached the limits of human language here.

This is not a merely theoretical matter for Christians, either. It arises out of our experience of God: We experience God as the creator of the world; we experience God as he walked among us as Jesus Christ, the Son; we experience God inwardly as the Holy Spirit.

The Trinity also demonstrates for us at a deep level why love is so central to Christian faith. Not only is it commanded by God, but God himself lives in an eternal relationship of love, as Father, Son, and Holy Spirit. Because we are created in God's image, it is vital for us to be in relationships of love.

The Trinity also helps us recognize what is going on in prayer. Author and scholar C. S. Lewis put it this way in his classic *Mere Christianity:*

> An ordinary Christian kneels down to say his prayers. He is trying to get into touch with God. But if he is a Christian, he knows that what is prompting him to pray is also God: God, so to speak, inside him. But he also knows that all his real knowledge of God comes through Christ, the man who was God—that Christ is standing beside him, helping him to pray, praying for him. You see what is happening. God is the thing to which he is praying—the goal he is trying to reach. God is also the thing inside him which is pushing him on—the motive power. God is also the road or bridge along which he is being pushed to that goal. So that the whole threefold life of the three-personal being is actually going on in that ordinary little bedroom where an ordinary man is saying his prayers.

The Least You Need to Know

- We learn to pray as a family of believers with one Father—we are not alone.

- Through prayer we establish community with others.

- The Lord's Prayer primarily shows us that we can be intimate with God and have confidence in him.

- God as Trinity means that he is one being in three distinct persons, equal in power and glory.

Chapter **6**

The Prayer to Begin All Prayer: Part 2

In This Chapter

- ◆ Prayer is concerned with the most mundane of matters
- ◆ Prayer as the most spiritual of things
- ◆ Praying for forgiveness, for ourselves and others
- ◆ The meaning of the last four petitions of the Lord's Prayer

The first part of the Lord's Prayer ascended the lofty heights of heaven and spoke of grand ideas such as the will of God: "Our Father who art in heaven, hallowed be thy name; thy kingdom come, thy will be done, on earth as it is in heaven." Those are large, transcendent concepts.

The next part of the prayer brings us down to earth: "Give us this day our daily bread; forgive us our trespasses as we forgive those who trespass against us; lead us not into temptation, but deliver us from evil …" The matters mentioned in this part, though few, actually cover nearly everything we need and want to pray about day by day.

Give Us This Day Our Daily Bread

You can't get any more basic than this: praying for your three squares a day. Praying for food, of course, makes some people nervous. It did me for a long time because it seemed, well, so pedestrian. Praying for God's will, for world peace, for serenity—that's real prayer. But praying about spaghetti and sausage doesn't seem very spiritual.

Baloney. I mean to say, the prayer is *about* baloney and pasta and hamburgers and even broccoli. Jesus is teaching that there is nothing too basic or too mundane to pray about. Every one of life's gifts is a gift from God ultimately, and it isn't as if he created courage and faith and the desire for peace, and then somehow broccoli just came along. Every gift—whether it be spiritual, moral, or physical—comes from God's hand ultimately, and Jesus is telling us that it is the Great Giver to whom we should turn about such matters.

Snapshots of Answered Prayers
Christ's apostles had been timid followers at times, even after his resurrection. But in Acts 4:23–31 they prayed a prayer for boldness in the face of persecution that literally shook the building and later shook the world.

But why? This would seem to be one area where prayer has nothing to do with it. I work for my daily bread by taking a job. And a lot of work by others goes into getting bread to my table: planting seeds, irrigating land, harvesting crops, shipping by railway, displaying in a supermarket, and so on. We can pray until the proverbial cows come home, but unless someone takes the trouble to get up at 4:00 A.M. and milk them, no one's going to have anything to put on their cereal. What does prayer have to do with all this?

Everything. This is exactly the point of this prayer: To remind us that the journey of food from planting to dinner table is a complex process that requires the efforts, skills, and faithfulness of countless people. Every time we eat, we receive a gift that comes to us through many hands. It is not merely *our* efforts that secure our daily bread. This is not the type of thing we ought to take for granted.

Then there's this little unpleasant fact: A few too many days without bread, and we die. Christian prayer is not about ethereal spirituality; it is no mere consciousness raising into airy transcendence. Prayer is about survival. This petition is a stark reminder of how close we are to not being, of how fragile our world really is, of how little it takes (a shipper's strike, a hurricane, a cancer cell) to disrupt everything we take for granted, of how vulnerable we really are. In other words, this is a prayer about dependence, utter dependence upon God for everything.

It is also about *daily* dependence. Ongoing trust is emphasized by Jesus: "Give us *this day* our *daily* bread." It's like he's saying, "Get it?" This is not a once-in-a-lifetime admission or an annual renewal of vows. It is a day-by-day looking to God as the giver of every gift.

It's also about looking to God for gifts sufficient only for the day, not anxiously praying to God to meet an entire lifetime of needs, or praying that we would have so much that we never need worry again. That's called greed, and it's not exactly the type of attitude Jesus approves of. Instead, our prayer should be, "Give us enough to sustain us today, Lord, to help us meet the challenges this day. And then tomorrow, we'll worry about tomorrow."

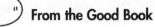

From the Good Book

Wash away all my iniquity and cleanse me from my sin. For I know my transgressions, and my sin is always before me. Against you, you only, have I sinned and done what is evil in your sight, so that you are proved right when you speak and justified when you judge.

—David, Psalm 51:2–4

This doesn't mean you can't plan or pray about the future, such as for retirement. Planning and putting money aside is something we do today, and as such it is something we can do with this prayerful attitude of daily dependence. We can plan retirement with a sense of anxiety and fear, or with a thankful, dependent heart: "Lord, help me plan my future wisely, to make good decisions this day, and help me to trust in your loving care over all of my life, no matter what happens." We would be negligent if we did not notice one other aspect of this petition: "Give *us* this day *our* daily bread." Again, the community makes itself known. This is not merely a prayer about our own needs, but also the needs of others. German theologian Dietrich Bonhoeffer says, "It is not God's will that his creation should be despised. The disciples are told to ask for bread not only for themselves but for all men on earth."

We needn't spend much time demonstrating that a lot of people in the world today are not getting their daily bread, and not because there isn't enough food to go around. With inefficient distribution systems, unjust governments, political bureaucracies, greed, and human stupidity, a lot of people are starving as I write this. It nearly goes without saying that those who pray this little petition, "Give us this day our daily bread," are committing themselves in some way, small or large, to help answer this prayer for those who lack bread this day.

From the Good Book

Jabez was more honorable than his brothers. His mother had named him Jabez, saying, "I gave birth to him in pain." Jabez cried out to the God of Israel, "Oh, that you would bless me and enlarge my territory! Let your hand be with me, and keep me from harm so that I will be free from pain." And God granted his request.

—1 Chronicles 4:9

And Forgive Us Our Trespasses ...

If the former petition was about physical survival, then the next three petitions are about spiritual survival.

First, let's make clear what the key word in this petition means. *Trespasses* is a legal image and refers to those acts by which we cross a boundary that God has set. In fact, a lot of commentators have talked about the Ten Commandments as a fence. We are free to do anything within these 10 boundaries, but once we commit adultery or steal or profane the Sabbath, we step outside the ordered life God intends for us. At this point we trespass into forbidden land.

In the other principle version of the Lord's Prayer, the image used here is economic: "Forgive us our *debts* as we forgive our *debtors*." Here the idea is that the moral law is like a bank account. Every time we break the law, we draw on this moral account and we owe God. It's like drawing upon the goodwill of a friend—let's say he gives you a ride to the airport—and then you saying, "I owe you one."

With God, though, we find that we owe him so much that we can never quite pay him back. There is something about human nature that makes it impossible for us to pay back our moral withdrawals. We just sink deeper and deeper into debt. Anyone who is morally sensitive understands what the apostle Paul is writing about when he says, "I don't understand myself at all, for I really want to do what is right, but I don't do it. Instead, I do the very thing I hate. I know perfectly well that what I am doing is wrong .... No matter which way I turn, I can't make myself do right. I want to, but I can't." (Romans 7:15–18)

We're talking big debt here: moral bankruptcy. It's like owing the Visa people so much money that the minimum payment you can afford cannot even cover the monthly interest.

Trespasses and *debts* are metaphors for the more abstract word *sin*. To put the matter most bluntly: Without forgiveness, we can have no relationship with God. That's not because God gets petty and self-righteous and wants nothing to do with us when we do something bad. To sin is to break the very relationship we have with God. It's like adultery in marriage: This is not a petty little indiscretion; it breaks the bond between husband and wife, and if the betrayed spouse does not forgive, the relationship cannot continue.

Anyone who has thought deeply about who God is—perfect in love and goodness—recognizes that every sin is an act of unfaithfulness, that is, spiritual adultery. (In fact, one book of the Bible, Hosea, says that Israel was acting like a husband lying with a prostitute when it forsook the laws of God.) The very relationship with God is ruptured—and without God, life quickly spirals into chaos and death and eternal loneliness. Unless God forgives, that is.

> **Prayer Pearls**
>
> It is quite useless knocking at the door of heaven for earthly comfort; it's not the sort of comfort they supply there.
>
> —C. S. Lewis, writer and Christian apologist

The point of this petition is to assure us that God *does*, in fact, offer his forgiveness. This is the *gospel* (that is, "good news") of the New Testament. That God offered forgiveness freely and fully was not completely clear until the coming of Jesus Christ. It is through Christ's death and resurrection that forgiveness—essentially, a restored relation with God and, thus, freedom from chaos and death and eternal loneliness—is given.

You can spend your life pretending this isn't true, either living in denial about the spiritual bankruptcy of your life or living in constant anxiety and guilt about your moral indebtedness. Or, you can claim the gift of forgiveness that Christ offers. To pray this petition is to claim that gift.

... As We Forgive Those Who Trespass Against Us

Now comes the hard part. Forgiveness is a package deal. It's not about *me* getting *my* sins forgiven so I can feel self-righteous and holy. The phrase is "Forgive *us our* trespasses." This is about seeking God's forgiveness for the sins of my neighbors, too—and even the sins of my enemies.

Yes, that includes even the sins of the friend who has betrayed you, the boss who overworks you, the neighbor who slanders you—all those people who owe you big-time and who have trespassed over you.

In some ways, then, the second part of this petition—"as we forgive those who trespass against us"—is redundant. We can hardly be praying for their forgiveness unless we have already forgiven them, can we?

Well, not exactly. Resentment and bitterness have a way of planting themselves deeply within our hearts, and it is mighty difficult to uproot them. I still remember an unkind remark of a (former) friend made some 20 years ago—and I'm still bothered by it. But prayer goes a long way toward softening such resentment. Praying for one's enemies, in fact, is a tried and true method for beginning to love and forgive even enemies.

When I'm angry with someone, or when I find myself resurrecting a long-standing resentment, I start praying for the person who has offended me. "Lord, please help Steve become successful in what's he doing; keep him and his family safe from disease …" and so on. This has a remarkable effect on my heart.

Jesus put it this way, "You have heard that the law of Moses says, 'Love your neighbor' and hate your enemy. But I say, love your enemies! Pray for those who persecute you! In that way, you will be acting as true children of your father in heaven." (Matthew 5:43–45)

The corporate nature of forgiveness is so crucial that this is the only petition of this prayer that Jesus comments on when he's done teaching it. He told his disciples, "If you forgive those who sin against you, your heavenly Father will forgive you. But if you refuse to forgive others, your Father will not forgive your sins." (Matthew 6:14–15)

This is not a *quid pro quo*, a deal God makes with us, let alone a threat. It has to do with the internal logic of prayer and forgiveness. As we noted, you can't very well pray, "Forgive *us our* trespasses" without including your neighbor and enemy in the prayer. Jesus is saying we shouldn't pretend that this prayer is only concerned about us. Forgiveness is the plea of the community; if you think you can receive it without seeking the forgiveness of others, you just don't get it.

From the Good Book

Then Moses and the Israelites sang this song to the Lord: "I will sing to the Lord, for he is highly exalted. The horse and its rider he has hurled into the sea. The Lord is my strength and my song; he has become my salvation. He is my God, and I will praise him, my father's God, and I will exalt him."

—Moses and the Israelites, Exodus 15:1–2

This doesn't mean that you have to *feel* forgiveness for others before you ever pray this prayer or that you have to be free of all resentment before you can ever hope to go before God. It does mean that when we enter into prayer, we recognize that our resentment and anger toward others needs to be a part of our prayer. In seeking to deepen our relationship with God, we are at the same time seeking to heal our relationship with others.

The promise of Jesus is that prayer is about the most effective way of doing both.

And Lead Us Not into Temptation

You have to wonder about this petition. We've just gotten through praying for forgiveness for succumbing to temptation, and now we're told to pray that God would not lead us into temptation. As if God wanted to do that; as if he tried to make us sin.

Not quite. In fact, the Bible is pretty clear about that: "Remember, no one who wants to do wrong should ever say, 'God is tempting me.' God is never tempted to do wrong, and he never tempts anyone else either." (James 1:13)

So if God never tempts, why should we pray that he would not lead us into temptation?

Frankly, the Bible is a little confusing at this point because it uses two terms—*trials* and *temptation*—interchangeably, though it is clear from its teaching that those are two different things.

From the Good Book

"'And give my son, Solomon, the wholehearted devotion to keep your commands, requirements, and decrees and to do everything to build the palatial structure for which I have provided.' Then David said to the whole assembly, 'Praise the Lord, your God.' So they all praised the Lord, the God of their fathers; they bowed low and fell prostrate before the Lord and the king."
—David, I Chronicles 29:19

Temptation is something that comes from the Evil One (see the next petition) or from within our own dark hearts. To be tempted is to be enticed to do something contrary to God's will, to deny or work against God's love. We are tempted to lie to the government on April 15. We are tempted to act with prejudice toward people who are different than us. We are tempted to commit adultery. These are not the kinds of things God is into.

Trials, on the other hand, are ordeals we undergo that, for all their misery and hardship, can actually strengthen our faith: the loss of a job, a child going wayward, the news of cancer. Such events, if lived through with faith, become opportunities to decide what is really important in life, to learn patience and humility, and to become closer to God and others.

One of my co-workers recently got the news that she had breast cancer. Being a human being, she was not just a little anxious about the news. Over the next few days, before she could see the doctor again, she researched and wondered and worried and, no doubt, cried. But she also prayed, as did all her friends. As a result, she said, she slowly regained her composure.

One day as she drove, she was listening to a song on a Christian radio station. In the song was a line about God's light shining on us, no matter how cloudy our lives seem. Just then she turned the corner, and ahead was one spectacular sunset; it seemed as if the rich colors of the light were shining down just on her. She could hardly continue driving for the tears that clouded her vision. To make a long story short, she came through her ordeal with a stronger sense of God's presence in her life and a greater courage to face whatever came her way.

This is why the Bible can be pretty upbeat about trials: "Whenever trouble comes your way, let it be an opportunity for joy. For when your faith is tested, your endurance has a chance to grow. So let it grow, for when your endurance is fully developed, you will be strong in character and ready for anything." (James 1:2)

But let's be clear about this: Trials can make us bitter and unloving and faithless. Along with every trial comes the opportunity to sin. If they didn't cut both ways, they wouldn't be real trials and they wouldn't have the possibility of doing any good. The point is not that we're supposed to figure out if we're being tempted or if we're undergoing a trial. Sometimes, from our perspective, both look pretty much the same.

The point to remember is that God can help us whenever we're assaulted. The apostle Paul put it this way: "Remember that the temptations that come into your life are not different from what others experience. And God is faithful. He will keep the temptation from becoming so strong that you can't stand up against it. When you are tempted, he will show you a way out so that you will not give in to it." (1 Corinthians 10:13)

This phrase "Lead us not into temptation" also means "Save us from the time of temptation." This other meaning is more literal: "God: Don't even let us be tempted." Though God helps us in times of temptation, and though trials can strengthen faith, we should never ask God to give us trials or lead us into temptation. Some Christians want to be heroes for God because they want to prove to him how strong they really are. I've done this myself. In youthful enthusiasm, I've prayed, "Lord, send me a trial so that I can endure it and become even stronger for you." As heroic as that sounds, I've discovered that it's just a form of pride—and stupidity.

> **Prayer Pearls**
>
> Prayer is not a convenient device for imposing our will upon God, or bending his will to ours, but the prescribed way of subordinating our will to his.
>
> —John R. W. Stott, Anglican preacher

Once you've been through a few ups and downs of the spiritual life, one thing becomes perfectly clear: We are terrible judges of how strong we are, and we have no business telling God when to put trials in our lives. Those matters are best left in his hands. The wise prayer is always, "Lead us not into temptation." We'll have more than enough opportunities to deal with temptations and trials, as Dietrich Bonhoeffer notes in a nice bit of understatement: "Many and diverse are the temptations that beset the Christian." In other words, there's no need to go looking for trouble.

But Deliver Us from Evil

If you were to read this petition in Greek, the language in which the New Testament was written, you would see that this petition literally means, "Deliver us from the Evil One." This little petition introduces us into the reality of spiritual warfare.

This is a part of the teachings of Jesus that makes us modern souls a tad uncomfortable. The recent fascination with angels is all well and good because it reminds us that there is a spiritual world of goodness and love that parallels and intersects with our own world. It is less comforting, however, to consider a spiritual world with personal beings who work against God's purposes. But this is the clear teaching of the New Testament, and especially of Jesus.

It is easy to mock such a worldview, although it's becoming harder and harder to do so. People all over the spectrum are recognizing the presence of personal, spiritual evil in the world. Scott M. Peck, a respected psychologist and author of the bestselling book *The Road Less Traveled*, wrote a sequel, *People of the Lie*, in which he describes his encounters with patients that he finally concluded were possessed by demons.

Exorcisms—prayers to deliver people from demon possession—have been a part of the church's prayer life since the beginning. Jesus cast out demons—read Mark 5:1–20 for perhaps the most dramatic instance of such. By the Middle Ages, the church had even created a liturgy for such. Today we associate such prayers with wild Pentecostals, but in fact, most mainline denominations still recognize that such prayers are indeed called for from time to time.

Modern psychology has helped us see some distinctions—we know now not to chalk up every dysfunction to demonic activity. But some "dysfunctions" are indeed spiritually based. This takes wisdom and discernment, but some people—your local priest or pastor, or perhaps a layperson—have such gifts. But it is always wise to get more than one opinion in the matter before laying hands on someone. As they say in TV stunt shows: Don't try this at home—meaning this is an aspect of prayer that shouldn't be entered into without a great deal of spiritual preparation and guidance from other Christians. I don't want to dwell on this type of direct confrontation with evil because that would be a mistake. To paraphrase English scholar C. S. Lewis, there are two mistakes made in regard to the devil: One is to naively refuse to believe in him; the other is to spend too much time thinking about him.

The point of this petition is simple: Prayer is not a way to enjoy warm, spiritual fuzzies. To pray is to step into a spiritual world where good and evil battle for supremacy. Though the outcome is never in doubt, the battle is real—and hard. There will be moments in our prayer lives when we will feel assaulted by an unknown power of such evil. It will frighten us, and we'll know at that point why we've been praying "Deliver us from evil."

And we'll also know that God will save us.

For Thine Is the Kingdom ...

The phrase at the end of the Lord's Prayer—"For thine is the kingdom, and the power, and the glory, forever and ever. Amen."—was probably never spoken by Jesus. As some ancient scribe copied the Lord's Prayer in the Gospel of Matthew, ending with "and deliver us from evil," he may have thought, "What a downer." So he composed this ending.

This ending got copied by other scribes, and over time it became inserted into the Lord's Prayer as it was used in worship. In the nineteenth century, as more and more ancient copies of the New Testament were unearthed, scholars discovered that in the earliest copies of Matthew, this ending doesn't exist. That's why you won't find it in recent translations of the Bible.

But you'll still find it in the church's liturgy. Though it doesn't come from the lips of Jesus, it does sum up quite nicely everything that is going in the Lord's Prayer. It acknowledges that the basis of prayer is the power of God. This simply reminds us once more—just in case we've not gotten it by now—that it is not our faith or our prayers or our religiosity or our goodness that makes prayer "work."

It is God, as king, who is in charge of everything that goes on in prayer. It is God who has the power in prayer. It is God who deserves the glory for everything that comes out of prayer. And this has been and always will be true, forever and ever. Amen, as they say.

The Least You Need to Know

- Prayer is about physical and spiritual survival.

- We can pray about anything.

- Seeking God's forgiveness, for ourselves and others, is an essential aspect of prayer.

- By praying, we enter into moral and spiritual warfare that tests us to the limits.

- God will, in fact, help us in times of trial and temptation.

Chapter 7

The Greatest School of Prayer

In This Chapter

- Why church is the ideal place to pray
- What we learn by praying in church
- How we can hear God during worship
- Objections to attending church—and why you shouldn't let them stop you

Before we dip into the real dynamics of prayer—the really practical stuff—we need to talk about the place where, more than any other place, we learn about Christian prayer. Books help. Talking with others helps. But if you really want to learn about prayer, you are wise to spend time with others who pray. And that means going to worship, or church.

This may be more than you bargained for in buying this book. You may have just wanted a little guidance on how to pray by yourself. If that's the case, just skip this chapter and move on to Part 4. But I have to warn you: Anyone *really* interested in growing in Christian prayer will need to explore what it means to worship—and in this chapter I explain why.

Why Go to Church to Pray?

In many circles these days, "going to church" is socially incorrect, something only old ladies and the feeble-hearted do. Sophisticated people don't need that sort of "crutch" to get through the week. Then again, more Americans go to church each and every weekend than watch the Super Bowl. Why? Church certainly isn't as entertaining as the Super Bowl—or the Super Bowl commercials.

And it isn't as if anyone in the community is going to look down on them, like people used to do. No, some go to church because they want to be with friends. Others actually believe all that church stuff, or at least want to. Still others go because they really want to learn how to pray. But how exactly? Let's find out.

> **From the Good Book**
>
> Though we are slaves, our God has not deserted us in our bondage. He has shown us kindness in the sight of the kings of Persia: He has granted us new life to rebuild the house of our God and repair its ruins, and he has given us a wall of protection in Judah and Jerusalem.
>
> —Ezra, Ezra 9:9

We Learn from Others

This is something I mentioned a couple of chapters ago, so I won't spend a lot of time with it here. Simply put, if you're serious about learning anything—golf, carpentry, cooking, or whatever—you spend time with others trying to learn the same thing. You take classes, you find a mentor, you try to get around people who know what they're doing. Why should it be any different in prayer?

We Get Stretched

One thing I've noticed about taking classes when I'm trying to learn something new: At some point, the teacher always pushes me to do something I didn't think I was capable of. When I took a class in creative writing, I expected to get weeks of lectures about various techniques. After we had studied all that, I figured we'd get to try our hand at putting it all together and writing a short story.

No way. We wrote stories from day one. I didn't know exactly what I was doing a lot of the time, but I was learning pretty quickly.

The same is true of prayer in church: It challenges us to stretch ourselves. For example, one key practice in Christian prayer is to pray for political leaders (I told you, prayer can be challenging). During my day-to-day existence, I don't give a whole lot of thought to government leaders—and when I do think about them, it's often in disgust. I end up cursing them a lot more than praying for them.

But in my church, we pray for "our president, our governor, and those in authority in communities comprising Saint Mark's parish." There are some weeks I'm pretty unhappy with the president, and yet there I am being called upon to pray for him so that he would manage the office well and make decisions that are just. Some weeks it's a stretch to really mean it— but that's one of the points of praying in the church.

> **Prayer Pearls**
>
> Prayer enlarges the heart until it is capable of containing God's gift of himself.
>
> —Mother Teresa, founder of the Order of Missionaries of Charity

We Hear God in Special Ways

Prayer is a two-way conversation, and one of the best places to tune in to what God is saying to you is in church. This happens to me in one of three ways.

First, there is the reading of Scripture. This is, after all, the "word of God," which means in some sense that it is God's speech to us. As common as many biblical teachings are—like "Love one another," "Do not bear false witness," and "God so loved the world"—I can never hear them enough because I always need reminders of what the world is really like.

On top of that, as I hear the Scripture read, often I hear not just a general word but a message *for me*. I don't know how to explain it (theologians call it the influence of the Holy Spirit), but sometimes when I hear a passage read—let's say it's Jesus saying, "Love your neighbor as yourself"—the image of a relative who has been irritating the bejeebers out of me will pop into my head. I know at that moment that someone is trying to tell me something.

The second way I hear God in church is through the sermon. In fact, I've *never* failed to hear some message for me in any sermon when I'm leaning forward trying to hear something for me. And I've heard some pretty lousy preachers. But even the worst preacher I've ever listened to always had at least one sentence or one phrase that caught my attention. And when it did, I would often have to stop listening to him as I considered what that little bit might mean for me.

The third way I hear God is less rational and more intuitive. God's word sneaks up on me in a service when I least expect it. One Sunday it was a sentimental song of the children's choir that helped me sense God's forgiveness. Another Sunday, I was overwhelmed with the breadth of the Christian community as I watched people—young and old, male and female, wealthy and modest, liberals and conservatives, and so

---

Snapshots of Answered Prayers

After hearing that she would be the mother of Jesus, and being honored by her cousin Elizabeth, Mary sang a prayer of praise in Luke 1:46–55—later to be known as the Magnificat.

on—all file forward and kneel to receive communion. Another Sunday still, it was a couple of children whispering in the pew in front of me that caused me to reflect more deeply about God's love.

Just when I've gotten bored or irritated with the routine and what seems superficial in church, God will surprise me like that with another bit of grace from him. And it wouldn't have happened had I not been present.

We Learn to Pray in Community

This is the heart of Christian prayer. As we noted in Chapter 5, a key to Christian prayer is found in the pronouns *we, us,* and *our.* So when we gather with others to worship and pray, we are experiencing the most profound form of Christian prayer.

Prayer Pearls

Prayer travels more strongly when said in unison.

—Petronius, Roman satirist

Certainly, we can enjoy moments of private prayer that blow us away. But it's like, excuse the analogy, the difference between cheering for the Chicago Cubs (or whomever) from your living room or rooting them on from a box seat at Wrigley Field. It's great to watch the team on TV, but there's nothing like being in the stadium with other fans.

The Bible paints a variety of pictures about what heaven will be like, but, invariably, the images all involve lots of people, enjoying new life and praising God together. One classic scene in the Book of Revelation, for instance, speaks of thousands upon thousands of people and angels standing around the throne of God: "And they fell face down before the throne and worshipped God. They said, 'Amen! Blessing and glory and wisdom and thanksgiving and honor and power and strength belong to our God forever and forever. Amen'." (Revelation 7:11–12)

Some Christian traditions (including the Eastern Orthodox) go so far as to say that when we attend worship, we are getting a glimpse of heaven. Some Sundays, I'm not so sure; other Sundays, I pretty much believe it.

Objections to Going to Church

There are lots of good reasons not to go to church. I've been going to church now for some 35 years—believe me, I've seriously considered every one of them.

"The Church Is Full of Hypocrites"

Agreed. Lots of them. The problem is, I can't think of an organized group that *isn't* full of hypocrites. I've known Christians who pray to a God of love on Sunday and then act like the devil on Monday. But I've also known liberal-minded professors who don't exactly act liberally toward conservatives. I've seen managers of health clubs who are overweight. And I've yelled at my children for not picking up after themselves, only to discover five minutes later that I left my coffee cup on the TV.

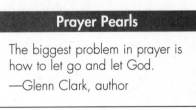

Prayer Pearls

The biggest problem in prayer is how to let go and let God.
—Glenn Clark, author

It seems that all sorts of institutions—educational, fitness, even the family—are full of hypocrites, and I have to count myself one. Which means to say, for me, it's always been a lame excuse not to go to church.

"I Don't Need the Church, I Can Pray by Myself"

Agreed again. As we've noted, prayer is about personal communion with God. Not only *can* I pray by myself, but I *should* pray by myself.

The only problem I've found is that when I skip church, I don't spend as much time in prayer. I may go off to a secluded setting, beneath a full red maple on a quiet patch of land on a local forest preserve. But it's pretty tough to worship there for an hour, and it's pretty tough to keep my focus for long.

This is a pretty common experience. When I was a pastor, people used to say to me, "I don't come to church, but I worship God on my own." At that point, I'd ask them how much time they had actually spent worshipping God on their own in the last month. Invariably, it was only a few paltry minutes.

This is not to say that the quality of prayer is determined by the quantity. That's hardly the case. But it's also silly to say that it's only quality time that matters. I've tried telling my boss that I'm going to give him 20 hours of quality time this week. He doesn't buy it. If I'm serious about prayer, then I can't be squeezing it in between the margins of a busy life. And in my experience, that means devoting some time to it.

The empirical fact is that most people don't pray as much—quantity or quality—when they depend on themselves to pray.

"Church Is Boring"

Indeed. Then again, when I find myself saying this regularly, I start feeling pretty juvenile. It drives me crazy when my teenagers say they're bored; they act like boredom is the ultimate existential crisis. I guess I'm hoping that I have evolved from teenagehood.

> **From the Good Book**
>
> Then I commanded the Levites to purify themselves and go and guard the gates in order to keep the Sabbath day holy. Remember me for this also, O my God, and show mercy to me according to your great love.
>
> —Nehemiah, Nehemiah 13:22

The difference between teenagers and adults is supposed to be this: As an adult, once you decide that something is important, you take the trouble to figure out why you're bored and then do something about it. You don't hang around waiting for others to entertain you.

In the case of church, I may be angry at God, or I may not really want to be there, or I may just find the minister dull. Well, I can deal with my anger, or figure out why I'm there. As a last resort, I could change churches.

"The Church Is Not My Kind of Place"

I hope not. If the church becomes a place where you feel pretty comfortable, you're probably no longer experiencing God. For all of the comfort, grace, hope, and other nice things God gives us, he also is in the business of helping us mature and grow. And that means he's going to make us decidedly uncomfortable at times.

When it comes to the church, an extended quote by the writer C. S. Lewis, one of the leading scholars of English literature in his day, is worth quoting. It sums up my experience, anyway:

> When I first became a Christian … I thought that I could do it on my own, by retiring to my room and reading theology, and I wouldn't go to churches …. I disliked very much their hymns, which I considered to be fifth-rate poems set to sixth-rate music. But as I went on I saw the great merit of it. I came up against different people of quite different outlooks and different education, and then gradually my conceit just began peeling off. I realized the hymns (which *were* just sixth-rate music) were, nevertheless, being sung with devotion and benefit by an old saint in elastic-side boots in the opposite pew, and then you realize that you aren't fit to clean those boots.

Prayer is not just about feeling closer to God and feeling better about the world. It's about allowing God to transform us into the people he has created us to be. For most of us, that means learning to respect and love people who are starkly different than us. One place we meet such people is in church, which is a ragtag collection of people who have little in common but this: They've gathered to worship Jesus Christ. With all that discomforting diversity, it's an awfully good place to be transformed by God into someone who actually can love all manner of people.

"Churches Make Things Too Complicated"

If I haven't yet made it clear that prayer is a complex and mysterious event, then I've not done my job. To step into the world of prayer is the easiest of things—a simple sigh to God is enough to get you started. But if we're interested in growing in prayer, then we're going to be challenged. Granted, churches can make things more complicated than they really are. On the other hand, if they're going to be honest about prayer, the way churches pray and talk about prayer is going to sound a tad complicated sometimes.

Prayer Pearls
Pray to God in the storm—but keep on rowing. —Danish proverb

"Churches Are Always Fighting and Splitting"

No question about that. Back in 1500, you could say there were two "denominations"—Roman Catholic and Eastern Orthodox. Today there are over 20,000, and despite the best efforts of ecumenists (people trying to bring denominations back together), the number of denominations simply grows every year.

Churches, full of selfish and sinful people as they are, will sometimes split over the silliest things: whether to sing classical hymns or contemporary music; whether to use the King James Version Bible or a modern translation. We have plenty of repenting to do on this matter.

But churches also split because people are passionate about their faith, and they long to keep that faith pure and vital. Naturally, we each have a limited perspective, and sometimes we can't see eye to eye on what are significant matters. Rather than spend life fighting one another or compromising on some point that each feels is vital, it is sometimes better to go our separate ways. I don't know that I'd want to be a part of a church that isn't passionate about its beliefs and practices. Naturally, sometimes that passion

Prayer Hotline

When it comes to matters of eternity—God, prayer, spiritual life—it's better to be a part of the enthusiastic group that is trying wholeheartedly to deepen its life than to stand on the sidelines watching and criticizing all the mistakes others make.

pushes people apart, but that is the risk one takes for caring deeply, no matter the organization one belongs to.

"I Don't Believe All That Church Nonsense"

I don't either, a lot of days. The church is indeed a miserable little institution sometimes, but it also happens to be a place where Jesus said he promises to make himself known. And, for all its flaws, I've not found a better place, week in and week out, to learn about Christian prayer.

In summary: If after reading this chapter, you're convinced about the value of going to church, you may also want to look at Chapters 34 and 35, about prayer in the free church and liturgical traditions.

The Least You Need to Know

- ◆ Church is one of the best places to learn about Christian prayer.

- ◆ Public worship teaches us about prayer in a way that solitary prayer never can.

- ◆ Worship is not only about speaking to God, but listening to him as well.

- ◆ Despite all the reasons you may have to not go to church, go anyway—you'll be glad you did.

Part 3

Just Doing It

Okay, enough background material. It's time to get practical and answer some burning questions:

- ◆ What are the different ways to pray?

- ◆ What exactly should I pray?

- ◆ What types of problems might I run into?

- ◆ Can things like fasting really help my prayer life?

- ◆ What if God doesn't seem to answer my prayer?

In this part, we take a look at some of the specifics of prayer—so let's get started.

Prayer Options

In This Chapter

- ◆ The many ways you can pray
- ◆ Listening to God: listening prayer
- ◆ Finding a style of prayer you feel comfortable with
- ◆ The benefits of recording your prayers in a journal

If I want to communicate with a friend, I have options galore these days. I can phone him, fax him, e-mail him, or send him something by snail mail (or two-day mail or overnight mail). I can page him or call his cell phone. Or, I can do it the old-fashioned way: I can go and see him and talk to him face to face. And then I've got all sorts of options on how to travel.

Likewise, though we tend to think that prayer consists of one or two activities, there are all sorts of ways to communicate with God.

Rational and Beyond

Let's begin with the big picture. There are two ways to break down our options.

First, there is what I call "rational" prayer. That is to say, we use our usual logical abilities, our reason, to form sentences and express thoughts to

God. We use language, which has structure and meaning, to express those thoughts. This is the type of prayer we usually think of when we think of prayer, and it is the primary subject of this book. Rational prayer is, after all, something you can talk about in a book.

But there is another way to approach prayer, what I'd call "experiential prayer." Here the idea is not so much to tell God something, or even to hear God say something back. The idea is simply to allow yourself to experience God's presence.

Again the analogy of husband and wife is helpful. Most of the time, my wife and I use reason to communicate with one another. We use words—talking, whispering, shouting—to tell each other what we're thinking. Other times, though, we just want to be together.

I remember when I realized how important this aspect of our relationship had become to me. We were driving somewhere one evening, and we were both silent for a long time when my wife broke in, "Are you angry with me?"

"No," I replied, wondering what she was talking about.

"Well, you're not speaking to me," she said. "You said you wanted to spend time with me, and now you're not speaking to me."

I examined myself to see if I was angry. I was not. I just didn't feel like talking. But I also didn't want to be alone. I just wanted to be with her. That's it.

We'll look at this more in Chapter 11; for now, it is enough to know that not all prayer has to be jabbering away at God.

Listening Prayer

Another type of nontalking prayer is "listening prayer." Here the idea is to shut up for a while, to lean forward, to turn our ears to God, and to really listen to what God might be saying to us.

Listening can be a rational experience. Some people—not many, mind you, but some—literally hear a voice. During a high school church retreat I attended, we were asked one evening to go off by ourselves and spend some time in prayer, and to spend some of that time listening to God. For me it was the usual experience: praying for a couple of minutes, then thinking about the baseball game I was missing, then thinking about a girl, then praying for a couple of minutes. And so on.

But suddenly I heard some shouting coming from the center of camp. I rushed over, and in the excitement I finally figured out what was going on. One of the girls was saying that she had heard a distinct voice, which she was sure was from God: "You will be my missionary."

This was electrifying to a lot of the kids, though at the time I was pretty skeptical. I don't know if the girl ever became a missionary, but in the years since, I've become less skeptical about such matters. Not that I believe every report—hardly. There are a lot of confused people out there who think God has told them all sorts of strange things. But I've read enough history now to know that, indeed, sometimes God speaks to people as in a voice.

At other times people experience God's voice as explicit thoughts. Other times still, we just "sense" what God is saying to us.

> **Prayer Pearls**
>
> We can do nothing unless divine aid supports us. This divine aid is at hand for all who seek it with truly humble and devout hearts. To seek thus is to sigh for divine aid in prayer. Prayer then is the mother and origin of every upward striving of the soul.
>
> —St. Bonaventure, Franciscan theologian

As a favor to a friend, I phoned a man 2,000 miles away who was offering me a job. I was pretty happy doing what I was doing—pastoring a church—but I thought I'd at least do my friend the courtesy of phoning his boss and finding out what the job—in journalism—was all about.

It was a typical conversation about a job. We talked about qualifications, range of pay, and so on. We ended the conversation simply saying we'd take the next step: He'd send me application forms and I'd think about it.

But when I hung up the phone, I suddenly was aware of something I hadn't been aware of: I knew I was going to not only get accepted for the job, but I was going to take it. I hadn't talked to my wife. I hadn't even decided to do it yet. But I had this "sense"— some people call it a premonition—that it was all going to work out. It did. To this day I believe that "sense" came from God.

> **From the Good Book**
>
> "At this, Job got up and tore his robe and shaved his head. Then he fell to the ground in worship and said: 'Naked I came from my mother's womb, and naked I will depart. The Lord gave and the Lord has taken away; may the name of the Lord be praised.'"
>
> —Job 1:20, 21

There's more about listening prayer in Chapter 11.

Praying Aloud

When I was taught to pray as a kid, I just assumed that if I were praying by myself, I'd *think* my prayer to God. I'd basically think sentences to God. Then one evening I walked into my cousin's room, and my idea of prayer expanded. She was living at our home at the time, and she had recently become a Christian. That night, she was on her knees beside her bed, head bowed, and she seemed to be saying something aloud to no one in particular.

"Judy, what are you doing?" I asked. She lifted her head to look at me. "I'm praying." There was an awkward pause as I tried to take in this new idea. "Did you need me for something?" she asked. "Uh, no." And I stumbled back to my room wondering why someone would say her prayers aloud when no one was in the room.

> ### Prayer Pearls
>
> I fancy we may sometimes be deterred from small prayers by a sense of our own dignity rather than of God's.
>
> —C. S. Lewis, writer and Christian apologist

Since that time, of course, I've learned about how people have different learning styles: Some need things diagrammed; others learn best by listening; others by manipulating objects.

The same is true in prayer: Some people don't feel like they're praying unless they are actually using their vocal chords. And there have been times—in fact, a lot of times, for some reason, when I'm driving in the car—when I pray aloud. It's just another way to pray.

Hodge-Podge Prayer

I come out of a tradition in which linear prayer is the ideal. By linear prayer, I mean praying in a logical sequence, sticking with one topic until you move on to the next.

Growing up, we were so linear that we had prayer *lists*, which mostly contained names of people, categorized by relationship (family, extended family, friends, co-workers), to make sure that we prayed for everyone who needed to be prayed for.

I'm not knocking linear prayer—as you'll see in Chapter 10, I suggest a linear model for guiding prayer. Linear is good because it can help us stay focused.

But linear isn't everything. In fact, most conversations are not linear, if dinner table conversation is any indication. We move from what happened in school to what's on TV to who's got a game on Thursday to who's baby-sitting on Saturday—all in about 18 seconds.

If conversation with loved ones is like that, why couldn't prayer be like that? Well, it can be. It doesn't have to have a plan of attack, an outline, or a goal. It can simply be a hodge-podge of thoughts or words directed in no particular order to God. It can be, well, like a conversation with a loved one.

Short and Sweet

And another thing: Free yourself from the stereotype that a good prayer is a long prayer. That's no truer than saying that a good speech is a long speech. Let's never forget that the most famous and most moving speech in American history, the Gettysburg Address, is a mere 265 words.

Sometimes the best prayers are the short ones. In fact, if I waited around until I had a large block of time in which I could really get into prayer, I'd probably hardly ever pray. That's why many people make use of "arrow prayers." Here are single-subject, single-sentence prayers:

◆ "Thank you, God, for this sunset!"

◆ "God, give me wisdom in this meeting."

◆ "God, help!"

Don't get me wrong. We need to have times when we spend a lot of time with God, when we pray long and hard. But our prayer lives can be enriched immeasurably if we can learn to punctuate our days with short prayers as well.

On the Fly and on the Page

You've probably guessed that I'm an advocate of extemporaneous prayer, prayer that comes from the heart and that is spoken freely at the moment. But I'm also taken with formal, written prayers—though this was not something I appreciated for a long time.

For years, as I attempted to pray each morning, I fashioned my own prayers. I said what was on my mind in the best words I could think of—a lot of mornings those probably weren't the best words. In fact, I realized slowly that they were pretty mundane words and that they just didn't express exactly what I was trying to say. For instance, I'd want to pray that I would trust God for his guidance during the day. On one day I'd pray, "God, help me to trust you today." And then the next day, "Lord, help me to be open to your guidance today and to trust it." Or, I'd pray for forgiveness: "Lord, I've sinned again. I don't know what is the matter with me. Please forgive me."

Certainly, God hears such prayers because they come from the heart. The problem was not with God—it was with me. I got tired of what I was saying, and I wasn't saying what I wanted to say.

Then I ran across the Episcopal *Book of Common Prayer,* the church's prayer book. There I found prayers for trust and guidance, like this one:

> Heavenly Father, in you we live and move and have our being. We humbly pray you so to guide and govern us by your Holy Spirit, that in all the care and occupations of our life, we may not forget you, but may remember that we are ever walking in your sight; through Jesus Christ, our Lord. Amen.

And I found prayers of confession, like this:

> Most merciful God,
>
> We confess that we have sinned against you
>
> in thought, word, and deed,
>
> by what we have done and left undone.
>
> We have not loved you with our whole heart;
>
> we have not loved our neighbors as ourselves.
>
> We are truly sorry and we humbly repent.
>
> For the sake of your son, Jesus Christ,
>
> have mercy on us and forgive us;
>
> that we may delight in your will,
>
> and walk in your ways,
>
> to the glory of your name. Amen.

When I first read that, I said to myself, "That's what I've been trying to say!" And that's what I often say when I come across a well-crafted prayer. Using written prayers isn't for everyone, but it is another way to pray. (See Chapter 29 for more on *The Book of Common Prayer.*)

Journaling

One tactic I use when my prayer life gets boring is journaling. Instead of thinking or speaking my prayers, I write them in a journal.

I can't recall where I got this idea, but it is a long-standing tradition. The *Confessions* of Augustine of Hippo, one of the most remarkable books in Western civilization, is one long prayer journal. It begins, "Man is one of your creatures, Lord, and his instinct is to praise you," and God is addressed in nearly every paragraph throughout the book.

Prayer Pearls
It is what we are when we pray our prayers that counts with God. —James Philip, author

I don't know that I've ever tried to craft a formal prayer in my journal. It's more along the line of expressing my thoughts and feelings to God as they come to me. I also use it as a means to examine myself in the presence of God:

> Lord, this morning I'm anxious about my work. Part of it is the pressure of trying to get so much done in so little time. But part of it is this continual struggle I have: I want to prove myself worthy to others. I know I'm worthy. So why do I so want to please others? Is it that I don't really believe you think I'm worthy? Help me to think through this issue so that I can work with energy but without anxiety.

Writing is slower than speaking or thinking, of course, which means that I pray about fewer things. But it does help me focus in prayer, and for that reason it is one of the most meaningful ways for me to pray. It also helps me in two other ways:

- ◆ It helps me to pray when I can't find the words to pray. For some reason, when I can't think of anything to say, if I put pen to paper, the ideas start flowing. (By the way: When I said, "I put pen to paper," I meant it literally. I've tried to journal on the computer, but the clicking and pounding of keys, the in-your-face light from the monitor, the having to sit erect in a chair—all work against a prayerful attitude, at least for me.)

- ◆ I can monitor my spiritual growth. Every once in a while, I read through old journal entries. I'm usually surprised. I often run across a description of a dream I was trying to understand—a dream I had completely forgotten about but that came back in full force when I read about it again. Sometimes I'm surprised by my insights; I didn't know I had been thinking those thoughts way back then— I thought this was a new insight! Sometimes I'm amazed at how long I've struggled with certain sins or concerns.

Prayer Hotline

Most people like to write in their journal first thing in the morning. The mind is fresh, and often dreams from the night before are fuel for spiritual reflection. Some people like to type their journals on a computer, but others find the clicking of keys a distraction. If you stick with old-fashioned pen and paper, it's better to purchase a sturdy notebook, one that can stand some punishment. If you get into journaling, you'll be taking it with you on all sorts of trips. You'll also want the journal to hold up so that, years later, you can reread it to note your spiritual progress.

Now What?

By now I think you're getting the idea that there is no one right way to pray and that I've probably not covered every option. So how should you pray? Certainly, rational prayer is the dominant style, as it is in all human relationships. But our prayer lives are richer when we open ourselves to other ways of praying. So as time and interest allows, experiment!

The Least You Need to Know

◆ There are many ways to communicate with God, not just one right way.

◆ Listening to God is an essential part of prayer.

◆ Sometimes short is sweet when it comes to talking with God.

◆ Experiment with different types of prayer to find the one you feel most comfortable with.

Finding Your Rhythm

In This Chapter

- The importance of establishing a regular prayer routine

- Morning, evening, or noon prayers?

- Finding a comfortable place and position in which to pray

- The key elements in a prayer routine

When I was in high school and learning how to play basketball, I would set aside an hour each afternoon to work on my game. During that hour I had a routine. I'd stretch. I'd dribble for 10 minutes: right hand, left hand, switching hands, between the legs, behind the back. I'd shoot close in, maybe 50 shots. I'd shoot 10 shots each from different spots on the perimeter. I'd shoot 50 free throws. Then I'd work on moves.

Establishing a regular routine is key to improving in anything, including prayer, as you'll see in this chapter.

Why Regular Times for Prayer?

In some ways, it's hard to imagine that a regular routine is necessary in something as intimate, as personal, and as spontaneous as a personal relationship. But it sure helps.

That's why a lot of couples schedule times for one another. Some go to the Wednesday matinee every week. Others go out for breakfast every Saturday. Some make sure they have sex on Sunday morning. Others take a walk together every evening. Couples have learned that a serious relationship cannot be sustained by spontaneous moments alone. There needs to be some routine.

It's no different in a relationship with God—in fact, it's probably even *more* important. If I don't set aside regular times for my wife, well, I'm going to keep bumping into her anyway, and at some point she's just going to grab me and make me sit and talk with her. But God tends to be more of a gentleman and will not force us to spend time with him. The result? We can go weeks without praying, our awareness of God becomes dull, and our spiritual walk slows to a halt.

> **Prayer Pearls**
>
> Prayer is the chief exercise of faith.
>
> —John Calvin, French theologian and reformer

The need for a routine comes and goes. Sometimes I'm resolute about it: I'm determined to find a time and a place and a routine and then stick with it. I want to grow in prayer. I want to become more spiritually aware.

Other times, though, I rebel against the routine—and for good reason. Sometimes the routine itself turns into a god. I take pride in externals: Good for me—I spent time in prayer every day for a month! Big deal—since I was so anal-retentive about the whole thing, I never actually met God during the time. When I find myself in this sort of confused state, I back off from routine and let my prayer life become more spontaneous. But for most people most of the time, routine is a key element in a maturing prayer life.

Time to Pray

Routine starts with picking a time of the day to settle into prayer. What are your options? Let's take a look at each.

Prayer Hotline _____

Those who choose to pray in the morning will have to be realistic about their evenings! Praying for 15 to 30 minutes in the morning means going to bed that much earlier in the evening. This seems like common sense, but it is not commonly done at the beginning of prayer. We imagine we can just tack prayer on to the day somehow and still stay up for David Letterman. Eventually something will have to give if you're serious about prayer.

Morning

This can be a great time of day for prayer, especially for the morning person who is alert and chipper and ready to tackle anything—even prayer. Morning prayer allows you to think about the day ahead and to prepare and pray accordingly. But even the morning-impaired might want to consider early morning prayer. Let me explain.

In her book *Becoming a Writer*, Dorothea Brand tells would-be writers to make it a habit to rise early and write whatever comes to mind. It doesn't matter what you write; just do it immediately upon waking. She argues that when we awake, we're still partially in a dream state, a state that encourages creative, intuitive thinking, which is a key process for writers.

The same principle works in prayer. As mentioned in the last chapter, there is the rational side of prayer and an intuitive side. Praying immediately upon waking is one way to experience God in a more intuitive way. Because the morning-impaired are not exactly in touch with their rational faculties, morning may be the perfect time to experience the nonrational aspects of prayer. Assuming that you just don't fall asleep, that is! This can be a problem for the morning-impaired, which means you may want to consider other times.

Evening

For night owls, though, evening is the time when the brain is finally in gear, and prayer can become a time of keen reflection and insight. In evening prayer, you tend to focus on how the day has gone; in that sense, it's less a time of preparation (as in morning prayer) and more of evaluation. Then again, some people use evening prayer to think about the activities of the following day.

Even if you don't make evening prayer your main prayer time, it is a good idea to end the day with some sort of Scripture or devotional reading and prayer. I don't know that it is all that healthy, in the long run, to have the last thoughts of the day driven by a fast-paced novel or ESPN. Whatever we focus on last at night tends to shape our hearts and minds (and dreams) during our sleeping hours. It's not that novels or sports are evil; it's more a question of what you most want to be shaped by. Most of us would readily grant that as much as we enjoy the entertainment culture, we really want to be shaped by more profound things. Prayer at the end of the day is a simple but powerful way to do that.

> **Prayer Pearls**
>
> Many of us are familiar with the best-selling book *The Prayer of Jabez*. We know nothing about Jabez from the Bible but he did pray in 1 Chronicles 4:10 that God would expand his territory and protect him from evil. God granted his request.

Noon Hour

You can split the difference and have your main prayer time at noon, or sometime in the middle of the day. Some people like to just start their days with a bang and stop in the middle and reflect on how things are going. I, for one, have never found this helpful. Once I start into my day, which often moves at breakneck speed, it's hard to get into a frame of mind that allows me to pray more than an arrow prayer.

How long should you set aside for regular prayer? My advice is to take things easy at first. If you've never had a routine of prayer, 5 or 10 minutes will be seem like a lot. Once you get into it, though, it will hardly seem long enough. A few hardy souls spend up to an hour or two a day in prayer, but 15 minutes to a half-hour is probably what you can expect to work up to.

Finding a Place

Naturally, you'll want to find a place where you can be alone and undistracted, a room where you can shut the door. The bedroom has certain advantages: For one thing, you're right there—in the morning as you awake, and in the evening as you go to bed.

But there's a serious drawback, especially if you pray in bed. The temptation is to slump lower and lower until you're on your back and the eyelids close, and you move into that completely intuitive state called sleep. Another disadvantage if you're married and your spouse is in bed next to you: Snoring and prayer just don't seem to go together.

Prayer Hotline

Some people are too restless to sit quietly and pray for any length of time—so they *jog* and pray. I don't get it, myself. I just can't keep focused for more than a few steps. But I have a friend in Minneapolis who jogs summer and winter—and prays as he jogs his 30 to 45 minutes a day.

Some people set aside a room or a corner of a room for prayer. They'll set up a couple of candles and maybe a cross on a table next to their chair. Speaking of chairs—pick one that is comfortable. There are few things more distracting to prayer than your leg or butt going to sleep.

Then there's the outdoors. Especially in seasonal weather, sitting in your garden or under the branches of a towering pine or maple can be a splendid setting for prayer. Few things can bring out a sense of devotion better than being surrounded by the creator's handiwork.

Some people switch from one setting to another. Writer Kathleen Norris (*Dakota: A Spiritual Geography, The Cloister Walk,* and *Amazing Grace: A Vocabulary of Faith*) says she starts her day like this: "I meditate on Scripture while I'm walking. That really stimulates my body and my mind. Then I come back, and I'll sing hymns and read some Psalms. If I don't read the Bible for a couple of days, the world just seems a lot flatter and life a lot less interesting."

Again, this is a matter of experimentation and regular reappraisal. What works for one person doesn't for another—and what works for you at one time in your life may not work at another.

Posture Counts

The tongue and brain are not the only two parts of the body used in prayer. In fact, how we position ourselves when praying can change the nature of praying. Most people prefer sitting. They're used to it. It's comfortable. But for some it seems a bit too casual.

Some kneel. Kneeling may seem old-fashioned, but there's a reason it has been around since prayer has been around—that's a few thousand years. It does put one into a humble frame of mind, just the sort of attitude you want to have in prayer. Other people like to stand. They feel this better honors God, just as we stand when an important person comes into the room.

Some people employ prayer gestures. The classic gesture is to bow your head and to either clasp your hands or press them together with the fingers pointing upward. These are gestures of respect and supplication; another gesture of supplication is to open your arms and turn your palms upward. A gesture of praise is to raise one or both hands high with the palm pointing outward. Though most people pray with bowed heads, some like to tilt their heads back with their eyes closed, as if God's love is pouring down upon them, and as if they are opening themselves to allow God to fill them.

 From the Good Book

I will extol the Lord at all times; his praise will always be on my lips. My soul will boast in the Lord; let the afflicted hear and rejoice. Glorify the Lord with me; let us exalt his name together. I sought the Lord, and he answered me; he delivered me from all my fears.

—David, Psalm 34:1–4

As with so many other aspects of prayer, you'll have to see what works best for you. Even if none of this seems meaningful to you now, I'd encourage you to give each of these postures another try at another time. I used to feel too self-conscious to use them—I spent all my time thinking about how I looked (even though no one was looking). But now I use a number of them, depending on my mood, because they help me pray better.

Establishing a Pattern

In the next chapter, I'll discuss one method of prayer, but here I want to mention briefly how you might structure your prayer time. Here's a routine I've followed with success:

1. *Focus.* I begin by clearing my mind of all distractions, and I try to visualize that God is present. One method I've used is, in my mind's eye, to step outside the earth's atmosphere. I imagine that I am looking down on the earth, as God might. Then I zero on North America, then Illinois, then Chicago, then the suburb of Glen Ellyn, then on my street, then my home, then the room I'm sitting in. For some reason, this can help me realize that God is thinking of me and listening to me.

2. *Pray for guidance.* This is a simple prayer asking that God would help me during this time of prayer.

3. *Read.* This means a reading from the Bible or from a devotional classic or from a current booklet that includes a Scripture reading, an explanation, and a prayer.

4. *Meditate or write in journal.* I spend time reflecting on what I've read, and sometimes I note my thoughts in my prayer journal.

5. *Pray.* Now I turn to prayer. I might follow the outline from the next chapter, or I might just pray as the Spirit moves me. I might spend some time praying and some time listening. I might use the time simply to sit in the presence of God.

6. *Return.* This may seem silly, but it's important to move out of prayer slowly, especially if the time has been meaningful. It's jarring to simply jump up and rush into my day. So to end my prayer, I might, for example, turn my mind slowly from the room I'm in to the other people in my home, or to the people I'll be meeting in the day and the tasks I'll be doing.

> **Prayer Pearls**
>
> It is better ... that the hearers should wish the prayer had been longer, than spend half or a considerable part of the time in wishing it was over.
>
> —John Newton, Anglican priest and hymn writer

One advantage of a routine is that it helps keep my priorities straight. I'm always tempted to skip prayer, especially when I'm wrestling with some issue in my family or at work. I'd rather spend the time thinking the problem through, or rehearsing the great speech I'm going to give the person I'm angry with, or just ruminate on my many shortcomings. But to give in to this sort of thing is to remain trapped in myself.

I always find it better to enter into my prayer routine, and to go through the steps I've just outlined. There will certainly be time to pray and meditate about my current crisis, but the routine also pushes me outside of myself. It in a sense gives me the freedom to spend time focusing on God and on others who need my prayers. And that very act then puts my personal problem in a larger perspective, and helps me deal with it in a more healthy way.

I've hardly begun to explore the options you can use to establish a routine. Unfortunately, using the word *routine* suggests that you'll hit on one pattern that will really "work" for you forever. Not quite. As we grow and mature in prayer, our routine will change—sometimes within days. There is value in being consistent in prayer, but not necessarily in how you go about it.

The Least You Need to Know

- Prayer will be more consistent and meaningful if done with a regular routine.

- You can choose different times of the day or night to pray, based on your habits and preferences, but once a routine is chosen it should be consistent.

- Finding a comfortable place and a position in which to pray can enhance your experience.

- It's important to choose a structure or pattern that helps you transition into and out of your prayer time.

Chapter 10

ACTS Now

In This Chapter

- Learning to simply praise God for who he is
- How to get things off your chest in prayer
- Prayer is one way to count your blessings
- Prayer is not just about us

After they've prayed for a minute or so, those just beginning to pray sometimes wonder, "Now what?" They're not quite sure what they should be praying about or how to go about doing it. In this chapter, we'll look at one method.

Everything we pray about falls into one of four categories. And if we give these categories the right name, we can come up with an acronym, ACTS, that can guide our prayers:

A = Adoration

C = Confession

T = Thanksgiving

S = Supplication

Let's take a closer look at each of these actions.

Adoration: Praise God

To adore God is to praise him, to honor him for his greatness. To "bless the Lord" is a biblical way of putting it. There is a difference between adoration and thanksgiving. One way to think of it is like this: We praise God for who he is; we thank God for what he has done for us. Admittedly, the line can get fine: When we praise God for being our Redeemer, we're thanking him for redeeming us. Still, the emphasis in adoration is on God's greatness.

Another take on the difference can be put like this: We praise God for the big picture (creating the world, redeeming people, watching over history) and we thank him for his special gifts to us (giving us wisdom to handle a problem, keeping us in good health). Again, the emphasis in adoration is on God's greatness.

For me, this has always been the hardest part of prayer. It takes a poet's sensibilities to call forth words that can even begin to express praise and adoration. And a poet I am not. But the poetry of prayer I know, and I make use of it to help me praise God. Let me give one example from each of the three sources I rely on. First, there are the Psalms, which are littered with praise. Psalm 145 begins like this:

> I will praise you, my God and King,
>
> and bless your name forever and ever.
>
> I will bless you every day,
>
> and I will praise you forever.
>
> Great is the Lord! He is most worthy of praise!
>
> His greatness is beyond discovery!

And then the Psalmist goes on to praise God for his "mighty acts" and "wonderful goodness" and so on.

Another place I find great words of praise is in a hymnal. Again, let me pick something out almost at random (whose title is in the first line):

> Sing praise to God who reigns above,
>
> The God of all creation,
>
> The God of power, the God of love,

The God of our salvation;

With healing balm my soul he fills,

And every faithless murmur stills:

To God all praise and glory.

—Johann J. Schultz

The great prayers in the Christian tradition are another source of praise. A classic example comes from Francis of Assisi:

You are holy, Lord, the only God,

and your deeds are wonderful.

You are strong.

You are great.

You are the most high.

You are almighty.

You, holy Father, are

King of heaven and earth.

You are three and one,

Lord God, all good.

You are good, all good, supreme good,

Lord God, living and true.

You are love,

You are wisdom,

You are humility,

You are endurance.

You are rest,

You are peace.

You are joy and gladness.

You are justice and moderation.

You are all our riches,

And you suffice for us.

You are beauty.

You are gentleness.

You are our protector,

You are our guardian and defender.

You are courage.

You are our haven and our hope.

You are our faith,

Our great consolation.

You are our eternal life,

Great and wonderful Lord,

God almighty,

Merciful Savior.

Prayer Pearls

God loves to be consulted.
—Charles Bridges, author

Such prayers are enthusiastic with praise, overflowing with joy. This is not me—at least, not a lot of mornings. So, the question naturally arises: "Isn't it hypocritical to use such a prayer when I'm not feeling the way the Psalmist, or whoever, did?"

Yes and no. Some prayers of praise are really not me, and so I don't use them. But I would be foolish if I waited until I *felt* like praising God before I praised him. After all, I'm a pretty self-centered individual, and it might be a few years before I got around to it. But God is worthy of praise day in and day out.

I use prayers of praise not only to praise *God* but also to help *me* praise. I want to learn how to praise. I want to feel more "praiseful." Such praise prayers help me become the person I'd like to become, a person who is more aware of God's greatness.

One morning recently, I was in despair. The previous day I had lost my temper with a colleague at work, and I was feeling pretty miserable about my behavior. I knew I was forgiven—both by him and by God—but I was still deeply troubled at what the outburst had revealed about my character. I could clearly see that there was a lot of pride and arrogance still living in my soul, and that it was going to take a long time to clean this up. I was appropriately humbled, and felt pretty lowly going into prayer.

Then I came to the adoration and praise part of my morning routine. I certainly didn't feel like praying like that—I would have much rather wallowed in my discouragement. But it occurred to me that regardless of my inadequacies, God was still great and mighty and wise and loving and all the rest. So he deserved praise whether I happened to feel up to it or not. When I praised God for his greatness, it didn't take away the knowledge of my shortcomings, but it reminded me that who I am and what I am like is not as crucial to the universe as who God is and what he is like.

One preacher put it like this: "You don't learn to praise in a day, especially since you may have been complaining for years! New habits take time to develop. But you can begin today and practice tomorrow, and the next day, until it becomes a part of you."

Confession: God Will Forgive

There is a certain logic to putting confession after adoration. After reflecting on the absolute goodness of God, we become keenly aware that we are not all that good, that we fall far short of who he has created us to be, that we've failed him and failed ourselves. It's an easy step to move into prayers of confession.

Some people wonder why we should even dwell on our shortcomings. Won't that just drag us down? Shouldn't we just focus on the positive and what we've done right to help us move forward?

The problem is that thinking positive thoughts does not change reality, and part of reality is that we just don't live, act, or think as we ought. Another part of reality is that we feel bad about that. Yet another part of reality is that God is in the midst of reality and offers forgiveness and hope.

Besides, confession is not plaintive breast-beating, where we wallow in self-induced misery. There will be times when we are miserable, to be sure. We are capable of some terrible deeds. But when we confess to God, it is never with the question, "Will God forgive?" Instead, it is always with a sure hope: We have the courage to confess because we know we'll be accepted.

 From the Good Book

When David saw the angel who was striking down the people, he said to the Lord, "I am the one who has sinned and done wrong. These are but sheep. What have they done? Let your hand fall upon me and my family."

—David, 2 Samuel 24:17

Snapshots of Answered Prayers

James reminds us in his epistle (James 5:17,18) that although the prophet Elijah was human like us, God answered him when he prayed that rain would not fall for three years. Then he prayed for rain in 1 Kings 18:42 and 43, and immediately it poured.

One line from the Bible puts it succinctly: "If we confess our sins … God is faithful and just, to forgive us and to cleanse us from every wrong." (1 John 1:9)

It is always good to be specific when it comes to confession. It is much better to pray, "Lord, I shouldn't have yelled at my kids yesterday," than to say, "Lord, I've not acted like I wanted to act yesterday." A vague confession will only lead to a vague sense of forgiveness.

This doesn't mean that generic prayers of confession aren't useful. I mentioned in Chapter 8 how meaningful I find one prayer of confession in *The Book of Common Prayer*, which begins like this:

> Most merciful God,
>
> We confess that we have sinned against you
>
> in thought, word, and deed,
>
> by what we have done and left undone.
>
> We have not loved you with our whole heart;
>
> we have not loved our neighbors as ourselves.

But I use such prayers as a guide to elicit specific thoughts. I try to pause over each word or phrase and do a quick self-inventory: "… sinned against you in thought … word … and deed …, by what we have done … and by what we have left undone …." And so on. This prayer, in particular, has an amazing ability to help me do an honest and full self-inventory.

As you incorporate confession into your regular prayer routine, you'll find yourself acknowledging the same shortcomings: It may be pride, lust, temper, self-centeredness, or whatever. This can get discouraging, and you may wonder if God will continue to forgive this sort of thing and whether it does any good to continue mentioning such stuff. Yes, and yes. God's capacity to forgive is actually bigger than our capacity to sin, as hard as that is to believe some days.

And to acknowledge our habitual sins is simply a bit of housecleaning. For example, I try to keep my desk in order, but it regularly succumbs to chaos. I don't beat myself up when this happens, but I do acknowledge it. Then I set about straightening it up. I don't refuse to straighten it simply because odds are that it will become a mess again.

> **Prayer Pearls**
>
> God the Father understands prayers which are sighed rather than said, because he searches our hearts and can read our thoughts.
>
> —John R. W. Stott, Anglican preacher and writer

The same is true with confession: It's merely an acknowledgment that my soul is in a mess again and that it needs attention.

Thanksgiving: Count Your Blessings

Confession, in turn, naturally moves into thanksgiving because we tend to be thankful when we recall that God sticks with us even when we don't stick with him. This then leads us to think of other things God has done for us, and that usually leads into thanksgiving.

But that's not always the case. In fact, sometimes we get amnesia about our blessings and move right into pestering God for this and that. This easily can open us up to the spirit of ungratefulness, which is a close cousin of bitterness.

We've all met such people. Even when life grants them blessing after blessing, they manage to spend all their energy thinking about their handful of problems. They are not only a burden to themselves, they're also annoying to others around them.

On the other hand, there are people like Ben, who used to work in the mailroom at my office. Every day he was upbeat. He gave everyone a smile and a warm greeting. He never complained about his job, as menial as it could be. He not only asked about how others were doing, but he remembered what they said and followed up in later conversations. He was a grateful man—often mentioning his many blessings—and he lifted everyone around him.

I used to think it pretty corny and superficial when people would say, "Count your blessings." But when I was a pastor, I met people who had just endured some human disaster (the loss of a job, or even the loss of a spouse or child to sudden death), who pretty soon would start talking about their blessings and what they were still thankful for. They didn't deny their grief or loss, but it simply wasn't the total picture. Widows, for example, would lament their loss and then start talking about how thankful they were that they were able to have their husband as long as they did.

I don't want to be glib about this. Life sometimes can be truly horrific—famine, genocide, unspeakable acts of personal violence. Some people who have endured such things have found that, indeed, gratefulness is the immediate way out of despair—even many sufferers of the Holocaust have taken this approach. But others find it impossible to count their blessings because their blessings seem so paltry next to the disaster they've just endured. For them, *any* advice is probably inappropriate. Sometimes we need to honor the suffering of others by suffering with them in silence, letting God heal them how and when he would.

But aside from extraordinary circumstances, it's not bad advice to focus on those things for which we are grateful in our day-to-day life—and it's certainly better than counting your disasters.

This is one reason thanksgiving precedes petition in this and most prayer methods. So important is thanksgiving that it is often put before *and* after petition. Some would argue that gratefulness is *the* attribute of Christians: "Rejoice in the Lord always," wrote the apostle Paul—and then, to make sure his readers got it, he continued, "Again, I say, rejoice!" (Philippians 4:4, Revised Standard Version)

Prayer Hotline

Counting your blessings is not an act of denial or a superficial response to suffering; it's a realistic appraisal of the situation. Life deals us blows, but never so many as to completely wipe out the blessing. Thanksgiving in prayer is a key discipline to remembering the blessings: the gift of life, friends, family, vocation, freedom, the sun, the rain, flowers, music, silence, prayer, a hug, a joke, the comfort of the chair you're sitting in—and on and on it goes.

Supplication: Asking God for Help

Supplication is a long-winded word for asking God for help. Classically, these pleas for help fall into two categories: Requests for oneself, which are called "petitions," and requests for others, called "intercessions." Let's take them one at a time.

Petitions

Let me try to clear up a noble but dumb idea that the spiritually mature don't ask God anything for themselves. Two reasons are usually given.

First, we incorrectly assume that God isn't interested in our mundane concerns. I refer you back to the Lord's Prayer and that little petition, "Give us this day our daily bread." There are few things more mundane than eating, and yet Jesus thinks it is a topic worthy of prayer.

Furthermore, the Bible is littered with comments that suggest God is, in fact, concerned about the little things. He is said to count the hairs on our heads. He is said to care for us as a shepherd cares for lost sheep. He is said to be a heavenly Father who values us as children.

Parents care about the little things. My 9-year-old worries whether she'll do well on her science test. My high school son is bored on a Friday night. My high school freshman just played badly in a basketball loss. In the cosmic sweep of things, these are indeed petty issues, but I'm the father of these children, and I'm concerned about things they are concerned about. I can't help it. God can't help it, either.

Second, it's not always selfish to pray for yourself. Something can concern the self and yet not be selfish. Selfishness, on the other hand, occurs when we're inordinately concerned about ourselves. We've been created as individuals with yearnings, hopes, desires, dreams, wants, and needs—spiritual, emotional, mental, and physical. To seek these at the expense of others is selfish; to seek them, however, is not.

And to pretend that we don't have desires, or to say that we shouldn't have them, is subhuman. It is also sub-Christian. The Bible is a very human book, and it accepts people as they really are. For sure, people really are beings with desires. We want nicer homes. We want to be better people. We want attractive spouses. We want to be healthy. We want to grow spiritually. We want to be proud of our children. We want to eat well. And so on.

Jesus also speaks about this part of us nearly every time he speaks about prayer:

- "Ask and you shall receive." (Matthew 7:7, RSV)

- "You can ask for anything in my name, and I will do it." (John 14:13)

- "Listen to me! You can pray for anything, and if you believe, you will have it." (Mark 11:24)

Jesus assumes that prayer will very much be concerned about asking all sorts of things from God.

This doesn't mean that God will honor every request, of course, and neither does it mean that every request is equally valid. A vacation home in the Bahamas or a new Lexus is not quite on par with wanting more patience with your children.

But that also doesn't mean that there are some restrictions about what we pray for. Prayer is a process by which we discover which of our desires are truly selfish and which are not, and it's about learning to curb those selfish desires. We pray for this or that, unsure of our motives, and wait for God's response—in prayer, in Scripture, in life, in circumstances. In this give and take of prayer, we discover what we're supposed to have—and what we're not supposed to have.

From the Good Book

You want something but don't get it. You kill and covet, but you cannot have what you want. You quarrel and fight. You do not have because you do not ask God. When you ask, you do not receive, because you ask with wrong motives, that you may spend what you get on your pleasures.

—James, James 4:2, 3

Those who are suspicious of petition are partly right: Prayer is first and foremost about aligning our wills to God's will. But the way that happens is not by denying that we have a will; it's by expressing our will to God and letting him affirm or shape that will as is necessary.

Let's be clear: Selfish desires come in all sorts of disguises. The yearning for a 6,000-square-foot home may be selfish, but the prayer to be a good example to everyone around you can also be a form of selfishness. This prayer may arise out of spiritual pride: You may simply be wanting everyone to look up to you and praise you for your goodness.

The human heart is deceitful, and its motives are often difficult to fathom. But prayers of petition—telling God honestly what it is we're wanting—is about the best way to begin to discern what's really going on.

Intercessions

To intercede is to pray for others, and this is one of the most significant ways we can help others.

God has constructed reality so that there are a variety of ways to help others. For instance, let's say that my friend Tom comes down with a sore back and, after seeing the doctor, is ordered to stay in bed for a week. I'll naturally respond to this bit of news with words of encouragement. Perhaps I'll prepare some meals for Tom. Maybe I'll go to the video store to rent him some movies, or maybe I'll go to the library to check out some books. I'll take notes at a meeting he was supposed to attend. And so on.

I can also help Tom by praying for him. If he knows I'm praying for him, that will encourage him because he'll be aware at another level that I care about him. That is one of the psychological aspects of prayer. Here's another: My praying for Tom will help me reflect on how I can help Tom even more.

But prayer works at another level still. It unleashes a spiritual power that can do extraordinary things, everything from keeping Tom from frustration to actually healing his back. How exactly this all works remains a mystery, but it is the clear teaching of the Bible and the common experience of pray-ers through the centuries.

Some people like to systematically cover their bases when they pray. Here is one way to organize a prayer list:

- Sunday: Immediate family

- Monday: Extended family

- Tuesday: Neighbors and friends

- Wednesday: Co-workers

- Thursday: People in groups you belong to (church, running club, online chat room)

- Friday: The poor and needy

- Saturday: Your community, the nation

The Least You Need to Know

- We adore God by praising and worshipping him for how great he is.

- We need to keep our accounts up to date with God by confessing our wrong-doings, knowing that he will forgive us.

- Each of us receives daily blessings from God, and we need to acknowledge them by giving thanks.

- Supplication is both petitioning God for our needs and interceding for the needs of others.

Chapter 11

Listen Up

In This Chapter

+ The importance of listening in prayer

+ The difference between meditation and contemplation

+ How dreams can be a part of prayer

+ How daily events can bring messages from God

+ One method that will allow you to hear God

Nobody likes to be in a one-sided conversation, in which the other person just talks and talks and talks. Or just listens, listens, listens! Something vital is missing in the relationship if there is no back and forth.

If prayer is "conversation with God," then prayer is not just about talking to God. It's also about listening to God. In our rush to unburden our hearts, this aspect of prayer is easily neglected—to our misfortune.

Silence Is Golden

Ever since owning my first car, my habit has been to start the engine and, as I put the car in gear and pull away, to find a radio station. Then one day, years into this habit and many cars later, the radio broke. Because of the nature of the problem and the state of my finances, it wasn't going to be fixed for a while, so for a few months, I found myself driving in silence.

At first, it was a pretty uncomfortable experience. I kept reaching for the radio, only to remember that it wasn't working. I didn't know quite what to do with my mind if I didn't have a song to sing along with or a talk show or news segment to listen in on. I had to live with my own thoughts (a scary proposition, to be sure).

But in a few days, I found myself enjoying the experience. I realized there were few spaces in my life in which noise didn't bombard me. At home it was TV or radio or CDs. At work it was the hum of fluorescent lights and office chatter. In stores it was Muzak. At the library, of course, there was silence, but the library was a place where I filled my head with thoughts as I looked up this book or that article. Here, in the car, was one place where I could simply be quiet, with no verbal or mental agenda.

I began to actually mull over things in a way I'd never done before. And I began to hear things—not voices, but thoughts that had never had a chance to make their way into my consciousness. Whether these were from God or not, I don't know. I do know that I began to understand my life a tad better, and I found I was better able to manage it as a result. I liked that so much that I began carving out other places for silence.

Prayer Hotline

Prayer can become a habit that is filled with noise, namely the noise of one's own thoughts and words. But if that is all it is, then prayer becomes mere self-talk. Danish philosopher Søren Kierkegaard put it this way: "A man prayed, and at first he thought that prayer was talking. But he became more and more quiet until in the end, he realized that prayer is listening."

Prayer isn't *only* listening, but it is partly listening. And that part can have the most dramatic impact on the pray-er's life.

So how do you actually hear God? He interrupts our lives and speaks to us whenever and however he wants: through voices, visions, thoughts, experiences, and encounters with others. But this is a hit-or-miss proposition. For better results, we can actually cultivate a couple of practices to train our ears to better hear God.

Meditation

To meditate is to consciously mull over something—a passage from a book, a phrase, an object. It means to look at something from different perspectives, to understand the various parts of it, to weigh its meaning. In the context of prayer, to meditate is to do all this with one purpose: to try to discover what God might be saying to us.

For example, let's say I were to meditate on this saying of Jesus: "I am the vine; you are the branches. Those who remain in me, and I in them, will produce much fruit. For apart from me you can do nothing." (John 15:5) I'd begin by thinking about vines and branches, how branches grow out of the trunk of the vine, and how no fruit can grow on the branch if it isn't connected to the vine.

I'd move on to filling out the analogy: Christ is like the trunk, and I am a branch. And then I'd begin asking questions like these: What are the ways I "remain" in Christ? What more can I do to stay faithful to him? What more can I do to experience his presence in my life? What part of my spiritual life is lacking right now? Prayer? Worship? Loving others? What part needs the greatest attention?

After thinking in this vein, I might conclude that I've not been spending enough time actually reading the life and teachings of Christ, that I need to spend more time reading about the one whom I call Lord so that I can better understand how I might live my life.

Meditation may seem unspiritual because it seems so deliberate. But our thoughts, our reason, and our ability to discern insights are gifts from God, and are ways in which God speaks to us. Frankly, meditation isn't always as rational as it sounds, either. When I begin meditating, invariably my mind is forced down one path or another, and certain thoughts keep coming back to me over and over. I take this as movements of the Spirit, and I pursue such thought in my meditation.

> ### Snapshots of Answered Prayers
>
> Samson had been captured by the Philistines and was tied to two pillars in their temple. He prayed to "bring down the house" since he would die anyway. He pushed the pillars, and see what happens in Judges 16: 28–31.

Some days when I'm done, I have a specific "word" from the Lord. This could be something I'm more keenly aware of (that I'm forgiven, or that there is hope for a situation I face), or something I'm convinced that I'm supposed to do (phone a friend, give money to a charity, or be kind to a certain person at work).

Some days nothing specific comes to mind, and that's okay. I don't want to force these things. And some days, when I go about trying to do the thing I was so positive I was supposed to do, I find that it created more problems than it solved, or that it simply didn't work. I go back into prayer the next day and meditate on how I might have misheard or what I might do differently.

Meditation is not a formula, but an ongoing process, and learning to hear God—*really* hear—is a lifelong pursuit. It's something you never quite master (as if we could master God!), but it's something that we can get better at over time.

Contemplation

Many people use the terms *meditate* and *contemplate* interchangeably. In terms of prayer, however, it is helpful to think about each separately. These concepts teach us about two key ways to listen. If we employ our wills in meditation, then in contemplation we try to let go. Meditation is like the counselor who asks questions and probes to discover what another is really saying. To contemplate, on the other hand, is simply to listen without conscious probing; it is to let the phrase or object have its way with us.

When I meditate on the saying of Jesus in my previous example, I ask questions of it and of myself, and I try to figure out what God is saying to me. To contemplate that passage, I do my best to put aside the rational and simply try to experience the passage. That may mean, for instance, allowing myself to become a part of the metaphor and letting my imagination go.

> ### Prayer Pearls
>
> Prayer is the pulse of the renewed soul; and the constancy of its beat is the test and measure of the spiritual life.
>
> —Octavius Winslow, Baptist pastor

For example, I once did this with a story in the gospels during a time when I was struggling with the idea of grace. I had become a very busy person for God, chairing committees at church, teaching Sunday school, writing articles on spirituality, attending all my kids' sporting events, helping them with their homework, trying to spend time with my wife, working overtime at the office—and on and on. I felt that God had given me many opportunities to serve him and others, and I just kept piling them on until I found myself weary and discouraged.

I spoke about this with my spiritual director, and she suggested that I contemplate the following story and see what happened:

> One day some parents brought their children to Jesus so he could touch them and bless them, but the disciples told them not to bother him. But when Jesus saw what was happening, he was very displeased with his disciples. He said to them, 'Let the children come to me. Don't stop them! For the kingdom of God belongs to such as these. I assure you, anyone who doesn't have their kind of faith will never get into the kingdom of God.' Then he took the children into his arms and placed his hands on their heads and blessed them. (Mark 10:13–16)

I tried to become a part of this story by entering it as one of the children, as my spiritual director had suggested. And this is how the scene unfolded: Jesus lifted me upon his lap. We talked for a bit, and then he put me down and said, "Now go play."

I was so surprised by this that I was startled out of the contemplation. This was the last thing I had expected Jesus to say to me. "Now get back to work," yes. But not "Go play." This seemed so irresponsible of Jesus. Play was, well, such a waste of time.

> **Prayer Pearls**
>
> In prayer it is better to have a heart without words, than words without a heart.
>
> —John Bunyan, English preacher and writer

And yet as I ruminated on this and spoke about it with my spiritual director, it became clear that this was a word of grace from God. It wasn't good works or duty or responsibility that God was calling me to—he was calling me to joy, the type of joy a child experiences when he plays. Of course, I was called to serve God and others. But this isn't what he wanted of me most. First and foremost, I was accepted for who I was, a child of God; as a child, what God wanted for me more than anything was that I would enjoy life, just as a child enjoys play.

We can also contemplate a painting or a symbol or a sunset or a garden. Usually the voice of God is not a specific message, but just a larger sense of God's presence in the world or a more profound sense of God's presence in you.

 **From the Good Book**

> Praise awaits you, O God, in Zion; to you our vows will be fulfilled. O you who hear prayer, to you all men will come.
>
> —David, Psalm 65:1, 2

In practice, meditation and contemplation often merge in prayer. Sometimes I begin by probing a passage only to find that after a few minutes, it is probing me! Sometimes I begin by contemplating a vista, but then I find myself analyzing it for meaning. Still, it is helpful, I think, to recognize the two means of listening to God.

Dreams

I'm not going to spend a lot of time with this topic, partly because it has never been a meaningful part of my prayer life, and partly because I know little about it. But I do know this: To some people, God reveals his will in dreams.

Joseph, the adoptive father of Jesus, was such a man. The Gospel of Matthew says that it was by means of a dream that Joseph was told to flee from Herod and to take his wife and infant son to Egypt. In another dream, Joseph was told to return to Israel. The Bible, Old and New Testaments, have many such stories about other people influenced by dreams directly from God.

That also happens in life today. Some people fall asleep wondering about which college to attend or which job to take, and they have a dream. When they awake, they are sure what their decision should be.

Psychology chalks this up to the work of the subconscious, that in a dream state, certain parts of our minds can work more freely to solve problems. This strikes me as a reasonable explanation, though hardly complete. Many people awake with a sense not just that they've been talking to themselves, but that another has entered into their minds and spoken to them with words or images. Is it possible that it is not either/or—either psychology or spirituality—but both?

Dreams, of course, can be pretty wacky, and many are clearly the work of the subconscious: If I dream of having an affair with a neighbor, it's not likely that this is a voice from God. Other dreams are stories with amazing plot twists or striking symbolism. As such, they can be mighty difficult to interpret.

No matter: Whenever you have a dream in which you feel God may be speaking to you, you are wise to take advantage of your connection to the larger prayer community. In other words, get a second opinion. Talk with another who is seeking to know God better, and ask if what you "heard" really makes sense. It isn't a bad idea to check dreams against the plain teaching of Jesus, either.

Paying Attention to Daily Events

Sometimes one must be prepared to listen for God in the most humdrum circumstances of life. An acquaintance of co-author Jim Bell tells the story of the night she felt a sudden thump as she clutched her car's steering wheel. The car began to wobble, and it soon became clear that she had a flat tire. The road was deserted (and had been for some miles), and she knew little about changing tires. Given the rough day she had been having, all she could do was put her head on the steering wheel and cry.

And pray: "Heavenly Father, give me strength and courage for the task and show me; show me how to replace the damaged tire." She had hardly finished when she heard a rapping sound on her window. She looked up and saw a plump, middle-aged woman standing beside her car. When she rolled down her window, the woman said, "Looks like you're in trouble, so I've come to help you put on your spare tire."

Weak and trembling with relief and gratitude, the driver replied, "Thank you! I don't think I can change it by myself." Together they popped open the trunk, and the unannounced visitor found the jack and soon had the car up and the wheel changed.

The driver looked around and couldn't spot another vehicle. And when her helper started across the road into the darkness, she asked, "What is your name? Do you live nearby? How did you know I was in trouble?" The woman answered, "Everything is all right now. Don't be afraid. You can drive on safely." "But who are you?" "I'm your guardian angel," the woman answered, and then disappeared across the road.

The driver swears to this day it was a heavenly angel, God's messenger sent to help her. But whether an angelic being from heaven, or a human being who lived nearby and was being a good Samaritan—well, it doesn't really matter. God made his love and power present to her that night though one instrument or another.

We are wise, then, to listen and look for God's presence when we're not even formally praying. He can come to us at the strangest times.

> **Prayer Pearls**
>
> It is strange that in our praying we seldom ask for a change of character, but always a change of circumstances.
>
> —Anonymous

Lectio Divina: A Method to Listen

Let me conclude this chapter by offering one specific model of meditative/ contemplative prayer. It's a practice that goes back to the early centuries of the church and was made popular by Benedict of Nursa, the founder of the Benedictine monastic order. This method, called *Lectio Divina*, or Divine Reading, has three stages, each with its own Latin name. Let's look at each stage in greater detail.

Lectio: Reading

You begin by reading a passage from the Bible or some other spiritual book, prefer- ably one that you are already familiar with. This is not an exercise in reading some- thing for the first time as much as exploring at a deeper level something you've read. Read until you come to a sentence or a phrase that strikes you in some way. It may seem odd, or you may see something in it that you've never noticed before. It may fill you with a sense of peace or joy. When you come to that sentence or phrase, stop.

Meditatio: Meditation

Though called "meditation," it is really closer to contemplation, as I've spoken of it already (see what I mean about these two terms melding?). Read the phrase aloud, over and over, putting emphasis on different words. Read parts of the phrase with varying emphasis, almost chanting some parts.

Let's take this saying of Jesus': "Come to me all you who are weary and burdened, and I will give you rest." (Matthew 11:28) So you might say: "*Come* to me, all who are weary. Come *to me* all who are weary. Come to me *all* who are weary. Come to me all who are *weary*. Weary. Weary. Weary. Burdened. Burden."

And so on. The goal is not to grasp the line rationally, but to let the words soak into you.

Oratio: Prayer

Keep repeating words and phrases until you are ready to stop in silence and simply dwell on them in prayer. Then begin to probe their meaning, especially their meaning *for you*. "Lord, what burdens am I needlessly carrying? In what areas of my life are you ready to lift a burden from me, if I would only let you?" And so on. Pray a question or two, and then wait in silence for any thoughts. Then ask more questions, and wait for more answers.

End the time by simply sitting in silence, basking in the presence of God.

The Least You Need to Know

◆ An important part of prayer is listening, because God speaks to us in a variety of ways.

◆ Not every dream is a message from God, but some are.

◆ We shouldn't overlook everyday events as moments when God comes to us.

◆ In meditation, we use our minds and wills to look closely at a truth of God from different perspectives. In contemplation, we give our entire selves over to God and his truth and allow ourselves to fully experience his presence.

Sensual Prayer

In This Chapter

- ◆ How employing the senses can help deepen prayer
- ◆ Why a cross or crucifix has been so helpful to so many
- ◆ Using objects such as candles, incense, and icons to engage the senses
- ◆ How creation itself becomes a physical inspiration to prayer

We are rightly concerned when we meet someone who is blind, deaf, or has lost the sense of smell. What a loss to go through life and not be able to use all your senses—some of the richness of life will never be experienced.

It is also a loss to go through prayer and not use as many senses as possible. We've already talked about the difference posture and setting can make in prayer. In addition, many people of prayer have discovered that when they employ all their senses in praying, the act of prayer can be a richer experience.

How It Works

It seems only natural that when you want to pray with some seriousness, you find a quiet place and shut your eyes—that is, you try to disengage the two most active senses of sight and sound to focus on God. There are many pray-ers who find this the most meaningful way to pray.

Yet another approach has a long history as well. In this one, pray-ers go to some quiet place to get away from the usual sights and sounds that bombard them, but only to re-engage the senses in a new task and redirect them to a new focus.

God has created us as both spiritual and physical beings, and he has created a physical place in which we live. He also has given us five means to navigate his creation: sight, smell, hearing, touch, and taste. When someone is not able to use one of these senses, we say he is "handicapped"—or "impaired" or "challenged." Some pray-ers may be handicapping themselves because they are unaware of or deliberately avoid engaging all their senses in prayer.

To put it more positively, many pray-ers have found that when they engage all their senses in prayers, their prayer lives take on new meaning. Over the centuries, the use of certain objects in prayer has helped them engage their senses.

Crucifix/Cross

The cross has been a symbol in many religions. Egyptians thought the *tau* cross (which looks like a capital "T") represented life. For the ancient Greeks, the four points of the cross represented earth, air, water, and fire—what they believed were the four eternal elements.

But today in the West, the cross is associated with Christianity, and it is its most popular symbol, by far. This is surprising when you think about it. The cross was an instrument of torture and death in the Roman Empire, the equivalent to our electric chair. Perhaps if Jesus would have been executed in an electric chair, Christians would display electric chairs in churches and hang them around their necks.

Though the gruesomeness of crucifixion is nearly forgotten, the fact of Christ's death has not been. For Christians, that death has multiple meanings.

It shows God's love: "God so loved the world," says one biblical writer, "that he gave his only Son, so that everyone who believes in him will not perish but have eternal life." (John 3:16)

From the Good Book _____

Praise the Lord, O my soul; all my inmost being, praise his holy name. Praise the Lord, O my soul, and forget not all his benefits—who forgives all your sins and heals all your diseases, who redeems your life from the pit and crowns you with love and compassion, who satisfies your desires with good things so that your youth is renewed like the eagle's.

—David, Psalm 103:1–5

It shows grace: "While we were utterly helpless, sinners, Christ came at just the right time and died for us sinners." (Romans 5:6)

It shows God's paradoxical wisdom and power. The apostle Paul once explained it this way: "When we preach that Christ was crucified, the Jews are offended and the Gentiles say it's all nonsense. But to those called by God to salvation, both Jews and Gentiles, Christ is the mighty power of God and the wonderful wisdom of God. This 'foolish' plan of God is far wiser than the wisest human plans, and God's weakness is far stronger than the greatest human strength." (1 Corinthians 1:23–25)

A focus on the cross can also remind us of God's power in our weakness and temptation. The famous evangelist D. L. Moody tells this story. He once met a man in Scotland who had been bedridden for many years. He had fallen and broken his back when he was about 15 years old, and had lain in bed for some 40 years. He could not be moved without a good deal of pain, and not a day passed all those years without suffering.

When Moody first entered the man's room, he was startled by the atmosphere: "It seemed as though I was about as near heaven as I could get on this earth. I seldom see a face that shines as did his. I can imagine that the very angels when they are passing over the city on some mission of mercy come down into the man's chamber to get refreshed."

In the course of conversation, Moody asked the man, "My friend, does the devil never tempt you to doubt God and to think He is a hard master?" "Well, now," the man replied, "that is just what he tries to do. Sometimes, as I look out of the window and see people walking along in health, Satan whispers: 'If God is so good, why does He keep you here all these weary years? Why, if He loved you, instead of lying here and being dependent on others, you might now have been a rich man and riding in your own carriage.'"

"What do you do when the devil tempts you?" asked Moody.

"Oh," the man replied, "I just take him up to the cross; and he had such a fright there eighteen hundred years ago that he cannot stand it; and he leaves me."

It's a humorous picture at the end, but the point is serious. By pondering the cross of Christ, one gains a deep perspective into one's own suffering—that cross still has the power to chase away self-pity and doubt.

When it comes to the cross, on it goes, ad infinitum. It might be fair to say that every book written about the Christian faith has, in some sense, been an attempt to understand the meaning of the cross. This cross transcends human understanding, and thus it has become a key symbol of prayer.

You'll find crosses in two basic forms. The crucifix is a cross with Jesus hanging on it, designed to remind us of the sufferings of Christ on our behalf. The empty cross, though also acknowledging Christ's death, is said to recall his conquering death through his resurrection.

On top of that, you'll see a variety of patterns. Entire books are devoted to showing that variety, but here let me simply look at three:

◆ **The Latin Cross:** Simple and elegant, it is the cross in its most basic form. This is the cross you'll see more than any other.

> **Snapshots of Answered Prayers**
>
> Do you pray for big things? Joshua asked God to stop the sun! He needed more time for battle and God caused it to stand still in the middle of the sky for him that day. It says in Joshua 10:14, "Never before or since has there been a day like that one, when the Lord answered such a request for a human being."

◆ **The Celtic Cross:** Today Presbyterians think of this as their cross, but it was first used by Celtic Christians in Ireland, starting in the A.D. 500s to 600s. The circle in the middle is said to represent the earth, with Christ having authority over the whole world. It also represents the sun, as a circle of light, and therefore Christ as the light of the world. As a circle, a figure without beginning or end, it also signifies eternity.

◆ **The Jerusalem Cross:** Like most symbols, the four crosses within a cross can represent a variety of things: the four corners of the earth and Jesus' sacrifice for the whole world; the four Gospels; and so on.

And on it goes. Some books contain outlines of as many as 60 different styles of crosses, each with its own history and symbolism.

Candles

Candles have been a regular part of prayer in many religions for many centuries. The practice may have begun merely as a means to bring light to a darkened sanctuary, but it soon became a powerful symbol of hope. Though we have incandescent bulbs to light our way these days, candles remain an important element in worship and prayer—the gentle flickering, the shape and color of the flame, and the soft light all lend themselves to a prayerful mood.

In Christian circles, candles represent Christ as the light of the world, the one who brings light into our spiritual darkness. Candles are also lit as a prayer, especially before shrines or in memory of someone who has died: The idea is that, though our words and body may cease praying, the candle continues to burn as a kind of ongoing prayer. In another sense, the candle continues to burn until it burns out as a symbol of our desire to give ourselves fully to Christ until we die.

Many people set up candles where they pray each day. Sometimes it's a single candle, sometimes two, or three, or seven. Nearly every number has some sort of symbolism, though in practice the numeric symbol seems to be less important than the power of the light itself.

Incense

So far we've been talking about objects that affect sight: This is one that affects the sense of smell as well. The burning of incense has been a feature of religious cere-monies since ancient times. It is mentioned as early as 1530 B.C. on an inscribed tablet near the Sphinx at Giza, Egypt, and it was used in early Jewish religion and later by the Romans, in both religious and civic ceremonies. In Christian circles, incense is widely used in Anglican, Roman Catholic, and Orthodox churches.

Some people burn incense in their homes as they pray. The rising smoke is a symbol of prayers going up to God, and the scent of the incense used tangibly sets a person in the context of prayer. In fact, the sense of smell is one of the most powerful at get-ting us to associate one thing with another. When I smell motor oil, for instance, my mind immediately conjures up images of working on my car. When I smell tur-key cooking, I'm instantly transported to one of the many Thanksgiving Day get-togethers I've enjoyed. After you've experienced the use of incense in worship or prayer, you begin to become more prayerful when you inhale its scent.

Icons

Though all manner of paintings, sculptures, woodcuts, and the like can be used to aid prayer, I'll mention here the type of image most associated with prayer: icons.

Icons are the special contribution of the Eastern Orthodox churches. The Orthodox believe that icons are not just human pictures or visual aids to contemplation and prayer. Icons are sometimes called "windows to heaven," or "witnesses of the presence of the kingdom of God to us, and so of our own presence to the kingdom of God in the church." That is, icons may help us see the reality of God more clearly in the here and now.

In terms of content, icons are depictions of biblical and church saints and angels. They are not meant to be realistic depictions of natural features but spiritual depictions that seek to illuminate the transcendent qualities of the subject. There are strict rules about creating icons (for example, they cannot be 3D because that might tempt the viewer to think of icons as an attempt at physical realism, or as mere paintings).

Though icons are not just aids to prayer, they are at least that. It's not that people pray *to* them, but *through* them. By focusing on the saint and his or her spiritual qualities, we can be transported to that which lies beyond the saint—namely, God.

> **Prayer Pearls**
>
> Surely he who feeds the ravens when they cry will not starve his children when they pray.
>
> —Joseph Hall, Anglican bishop

Natural Objects

Since God is the creator of the earth, it only makes sense that his glory and will can be made known through the various objects of creation. The apostle Paul says that together they constitute a proof of God, so much so, he argues, that those who deny God after looking at creation, have no excuse for not seeking after God. Be that as it may, the larger point, and one felt instinctively by people of faith over the centuries, is that the natural world has a great deal to teach us about God and his ways.

The great American theologian Jonathan Edwards could wax eloquent about the glory of God as revealed in the natural world. Many hymns extol God's wonder as found in creation. And some have found that by focusing on one little aspect of that creation, God can be heard.

Julian of Norwich, the celebrated mystic of the 1300s, gives us probably the most famous example. It comes from her classic, *Revelations of Divine Love*. Julian was struck one day by a very small object. She tells it like this:

And this he showed me a little thing, the quantity of a hazel nut, lying in the palm of my hand, as it seemed. And it was as round as any ball. I looked upon it with my eye of my understanding and thought, *What may this be?* And it was answered generally thus, 'It is all that is made.' I marveled how it might last, for I thought it might suddenly have fallen to nought for littleness. And I was answered in my understanding, 'It lasts and ever shall, for God loves it.' And so have all things their beginning by the love of God.

She went on to note that God made it, loves it, and keeps it, and likewise God made, loves, and keeps her.

As with all objects, the insights we gain need to be shaped by something more than our imaginations. In Julian's case, her perceptions of the hazelnut were shaped by her profound reading of Scripture. And when we meditate on the natural world through the lens of the Bible, God can speak to us in wonderous ways sometimes.

> **Prayer Hotline** _____
>
> The objects we use don't need to have immediate religious associations. Sometimes common objects can become powerful symbols. In one church, a large, rugged nail was passed out to each person attending. The service concerned the crucifixion of Christ, and people were encouraged to think about the pain and sacrifice that Christ's crucifixion entailed. People were then encouraged to take the nails home and hold them during their prayer times for the weeks leading up to Good Friday and Easter.

Odds and Ends

The objects I've just discussed are the most common and traditional aids to Christian prayer, but they hardly limit what can be done. In one worship service, we each received a nail, and we used that during prayer to remind us of Christ's crucifixion. Certainly music can help deepen prayer. We are limited only by our fortitude: To remind themselves of Christ's death and their own mortality, many medieval saints meditated on skulls!

Then again, you may not be a tactile person, and the whole idea of using anything physical to pursue the spiritual just seems like a big distraction. You have a strong tradition behind you. But so do those who feel that they have to employ as many senses as possible to fully enter into prayer.

The Least You Need to Know

◆ Using more of your senses can enrich your prayer life.

◆ The spiritual symbolism behind physical objects such as the cross allows us to enter more deeply into God's presence.

◆ Because we are both physical and spiritual beings, we can engage our senses as we seek God. Including objects such as candles and incense in prayer helps us to do that.

◆ The created world can be an almost infinite source of metaphors and physical images by which faith is deepened.

13

Fasting and Prayer

In This Chapter

♦ How fasting helps one's prayer life

♦ How different Christian traditions view fasting

♦ The main reason to fast

♦ Reasons *not* to fast

♦ Insights from major-league fasters

Other than saying grace before meals, prayer and food seem to have little to do with one another. Nothing could be further from the truth, biblically speaking. Eating, in fact, seems to be very much tied to who we are as human beings. In one sense, the Bible agrees with the German materialistic philosopher Ludwig Feuerbach, who was the first to say that we are what we eat.

From beginning to end of the Bible, food plays a key role. In the opening pages, the man is put in a garden and told that every plant and fruit-bearing tree has been given to him for food. The end of history as portrayed in the Bible, the kingdom of heaven, is often depicted as a great banquet. And at the pivotal moment in biblical history—the death of Jesus—stands a meal, the Last Supper. And for Christians, this becomes the most important way, week by week, to remember Christ's death and participate in his life, by eating bread and drinking wine at the meal we call Communion or the Eucharist.

Oddly, abstaining from this special gift of God, food, becomes an important feature of the spiritual life and is very much tied to prayer. In this chapter, we'll explore why and how that is so.

Why People Fast

Fasting is not a uniquely Christian practice. Most religions use fasting, usually as a form of self-discipline or self-purification. Some people have fasted as a sign of mourning; others use it to commemorate a catastrophe.

In the past, national rulers would periodically declare national days of fasting as a path to humility and to seek God's blessing. In the United States, even with our political system that separates religious activity from government activity, presidents Madison, Lincoln, and Wilson each approved national days of prayer and fasting during wartime.

> **Snapshots of Answered Prayers**
>
> Have you ever asked God for a sign in prayer? Gideon asked God to make a lamb's fleece wet with dew to prove he would be used to rescue Israel from the Midianites. Read all about it in Judges chapter 6.

Some religions fast because their adherents believe that the body and material existence is essentially evil, and that fasts are a key way to deny the body the destructive pleasure it craves. This is not the Christian worldview, which affirms the essential goodness of the body and of food.

Nonetheless, even the different Christian traditions come at fasting from slightly different perspectives. Let's take a closer look at some of these views.

Mainstream Protestants

Mainstream Protestants (Presbyterians, Methodists, Congregationalists, for instance), have never put much of an emphasis on fasting. When they do fast, it is often mostly a means of identifying with the poor and the hungry. Sometimes individuals are encouraged to take the money they would have normally spent on food and give it to some worthy charity. Fasting is mostly left up to the discretion of individual believers.

Evangelicals

The same holds true for Evangelical Protestants, especially that part about leaving it up to individuals. They also have not given much emphasis to fasting in the past (it reminds some of them of a religion of works, in which people try to earn God's favor). But in the last decade or so, some leading evangelicals, such as the late Bill Bright, the founder of Campus Crusade for Christ, have begun advocating the practice as a means of spiritual purification and to promote national revival.

Liturgical Traditions

Fasting has been a key feature for Roman Catholics and the Eastern Orthodox. Catholics are supposed to fast on Ash Wednesday, all Fridays in Lent, and Good Friday. The main purposes of Catholic fasting? It helps control fleshly desires; it's a way to do penance for sins. For many centuries, Catholics were forbidden to eat meat on Fridays, but since the mid-1960s, Friday fasting has been a matter of local discretion. On Ash Wednesday and Good Friday, two small meals and one regular meal are allowed; meat is forbidden. On Fridays in Lent, no meat is allowed. For the optional Friday fast, some people substitute a different penance or special prayer instead of fasting.

> **Prayer Pearls**
>
> No horse gets anywhere until he is harnessed. No steam or gas ever drives anything until it is confined. No Niagara is ever turned into light and power until it is tunneled. No life ever grows great until it is focused, dedicated, and disciplined.
>
> —Harry Emerson Fosdick, American pastor

The Orthodox are the major-league fasters of Christendom. They fast many more times a year, including Lent, Apostles' Fast, Dormition Fast, and the Nativity Fast, and several one-day fasts. In addition, every Wednesday and Friday is considered a fast day (Orthodox Christians fast on Wednesday in remembrance of the betrayal of Christ and on Fridays, like Catholics, in remembrance of His crucifixion and death). The Orthodox believe that fasting strengthens resistance to gluttony and other sins, and thus helps open a person more and more to God's grace. In general, meat, dairy products, and eggs are prohibited. Fish is prohibited on some fast days and allowed on others (fasting can get very complicated for the Orthodox, as they are the first to admit!).

How Now?

There are all manner of fasts, from skipping one meal to not eating for a week. Usually when people fast, it is for one day. For some that means skipping all meals in a 24-hour period: That can mean eating dinner one night, but not breakfast or lunch the next day, and only having dinner after 24 hours is up. Or, it can mean simply skipping breakfast, lunch, and dinner one day and not eating until the next. Some fast by only eschewing solid food: They feel free to drink fruit juices during the day to keep up their energy.

The Ultimate Reason to Fast

Despite the long and varied history and practice of fasting, all Christians would agree on the ultimate purpose of fasting. Fasting is primarily about God and not about us. As the founder of the Methodists, John Wesley, put it, "First, let [fasting] be done unto the Lord with our eye singly fixed on Him. Let our intention herein be this, and this alone, to glorify our Father which is in heaven."

> **Prayer Pearls**
>
> Who is the greatest saint in the world? It is not he who prays most or fasts most; it is not he who gives the most alms, or is most eminent for temperance, chastity, or justice; but it is he who is always thankful to God, who wills everything that God wills.
>
> —William Law, Anglican author

It is for this reason that fasting is very much connected with prayer. It isn't primarily about self-denial or self-discipline to make us better human beings. It is about self-denial and self-discipline as a means of focusing more on God.

Father Ted Stylianopoulos, a professor of the New Testament at the Holy Cross Greek Orthodox School of Theology in Brookline, Massachusetts, has helped me understand three dimensions of fasting that key off this main insight. They can be gleaned by looking at Jesus' 40 days of temptation in the wilderness, during which he fasted.

It's About God

When Jesus was tempted to make bread out of stones, he replied to the devil, "Man shall not live by bread alone but by every word that proceeds from the mouth of God." (Matthew 4:4) Thus, fasting is a way to demonstrate ultimate reliance on God, rather than on material goods, including food. When done with prayer and in a spirit of prayer, fasting declares God as our priority, and that we are ultimately and totally dependant on him.

It's About Godly Character

The devil's second temptation was to ask Jesus to leap from the pinnacle of the Temple so that angels would come and save him from destruction, thus proving his special relationship to God. Jesus recognized this as nothing but a temptation of religious exhibitionism. He answered: "You shall not tempt the Lord your God." (Matthew 4:7) Fasting is not about piling up brownie points before God, showing off to God and others what a religious person you are. It is a self-discipline that aims to root out such religious pride, as well as correct all undesirable character traits.

St. Basil said, "True fasting consists of driving out evil, controlling the tongue, abstaining from anger, giving up evil desires, slander, lying, false witness against others, and the like." St. John Chrysostom taught that those who fast "ought most of all to keep their anger in check, learn the lesson of mildness and kindness, have a contrite heart, banish the flood of unworthy passions, and keep before their eyes the all-seeing presence of God."

It's About a Godly Attitude Toward Others

In the third temptation, the devil promised Jesus the whole world and its glory if he would only bow down to Satan. But Jesus replied, "Be gone, Satan! You shall worship the Lord your God and him only you shall serve." (Matthew 4:10) Fasting shapes one's view of the world. We learn not to try to control and dominate others, but to live in humility with others.

> **From the Good Book**
>
> So we fasted and petitioned our God ... and he answered our prayer.
>
> —Ezra 8:23

Not a Spiritual Bribe

I should make clear that, indeed, fasting is sometimes combined with prayer in order "get" God to answer a petition. We see examples of this throughout the Bible, and even Jesus himself admitted as much. His disciples had been thwarted in their own efforts to heal a young man who had symptoms of epilepsy. When Jesus came upon the scene, he quickly healed the boy. His disciples later asked him why they couldn't heal the young man. Jesus replied that this sort of healing required "prayer and fasting."

The context here and elsewhere in the Bible is clear. Fasting is not a spiritual bribe to God—as if our fasting somehow makes us more worthy in his eyes. He knows what's still going on deep in our usually very selfish hearts. Instead, fasting both shows our passion for the issue at hand, and it shapes our character to see and submit to God's will. This means it teaches us to pray aright, so that we tend to ask for things that are in line with God's will in the first place.

It's About More Than Food

Food is not the only thing that can prompt gluttony or greed or covetousness. Many people also practice fasts of alcohol, tobacco, television viewing, and other activities that can start to dominate our lives.

In addition, the great teachers of the church have said that true fasting is not only a matter of abstaining but also of acting creatively and positively to help others and alleviate suffering, oppression, and ignorance in the world. Again, to quote St. John Chrysostom: "This is the essence of fasting: that along with abstinence from food, we should practice abstinence from whatever is harmful, and should give close attention to spiritual duties and do good."

When Not to Fast

Fasting, then, is an incredible spiritual discipline that can reap tremendous spiritual rewards. But it isn't for everybody, and it isn't for every time. If you are pregnant or ill, or if you have a special medical or health condition, fasting should be discouraged. Check with your doctor if you have any questions. God is not interested in making us physically ill! Even for those who are physically able, there are still occasions when fasting should be avoided.

Not During Party Times

Don't fast when it's time to feast. For Christians, Easter commemorates the resurrection of Jesus, the most joyful event ever. So between Easter and Pentecost is not a time to fast, but to celebrate. For this reason, every Sunday is considered a "feast day," even during the season of Lent. The same goes for the birth of Jesus, so the days between Christmas and Epiphany are for celebrating.

Indeed, many Christians prepare for these feast days and seasons by fasting. Some don't let any food touch their lips from Saturday evening until they receive the bread and wine of Communion on Sunday. This what the season of Lent is about—preparing for the feast of resurrection. But when the day of feasting comes, enough fasting, already.

As a Way to Lose Weight

You also shouldn't fast merely as a way to diet. It's not a divine weight-loss plan. If one gets into that frame of mind, it could easily turn into anorexia with spiritual justification. If you're overweight only because you have no self-discipline (versus because of a medical issue), better to learn the discipline of proper diet first, or at least alongside periodic spiritual fasts.

Prayer Hotline

Some people find fasting brings them such spiritual benefits that they are tempted to "go for it." They may try fasting for days at a time. But it's not a good idea to fast to the extent that you make yourself a burden to others because you've made yourself sick. Nor should you fast so severely that you can't keep up at work and others have to carry part of your load. That's a form of spiritual selfishness.

To Teach Yourself a Lesson

Fasting should not be used as a form of self-punishment. You overeat one day, despise yourself, and decide to teach yourself a lesson by fasting the next day. This subverts the ultimate purpose of fasting—to focus on God—by focusing on yourself. It also moves fasting from a positive self-discipline to enhance one's character to a practice that demeans oneself.

From the Good Book

When you fast, do not look gloomy like the hypocrites, for they disfigure their faces that their fasting might be seen by others.

—Jesus, Matthew 6:16

One can burden other people with excessive fasting in more subtle ways. If you find that fasting makes you particularly grouchy, rude, or short-tempered with others—well, you either need to focus on that, or cut back on your fasting in some way. As the Reformer Martin Luther put it, "[God] wants nothing at all to do with you if by your fasting you court Him as if you were a great saint, and yet meanwhile nurse a grudge or anger against your neighbor."

Some Insights from Major-League Fasters

Even though I don't practice fasting in the way the Orthodox do, I do find their thinking on the matter very instructive and sometimes inspiring. I also find it unnerving sometimes. Be that as it may, I end this chapter by outlining some of the features of Orthodox fasting.

When to Fast

Here are the specific seasons of fasting for the Orthodox (in addition to the weekly Wednesday and Friday fasts!):

◆ The Christmas Fast is from November 15 to December 24.

◆ The Great Fast of Lent, including Holy Week, begins seven weeks before Easter.

◆ The Fast of Saints Peter and Paul, whose feast is on June 29, lasts from a few days to six weeks, depending on the date of Easter and Pentecost.

◆ The Fast of the Falling Asleep of the Virgin Mary (August 15) is from August 1 to August 14.

And then there are additional specific days of fasting, such as on the Beheading of St. John the Baptist (August 29), the Exaltation of the Cross (September 14), and the Eve of Epiphany (January 5).

What to Abstain From

It isn't as draconian as it first seems. The Orthodox only abstain from certain foods; basically meats, eggs, dairy products (milk, cheese, butter, etc.), as well as fish with backbone. (Such things as shrimp, crab, and octopus are permitted.)

Strict fasting is usually reserved for monastic communities, and this would include days of eating nothing at all or only "dry eating" (xerophagy), meaning fruit, nuts, bread, and vegetables. The details of the calendar and food prescriptions are quite numerous, and vary according to local tradition. So the expert is likely to be the Orthodox priest in your town or neighborhood.

Prayer Pearls

Jesus has many who love his heavenly kingdom, but few who bear his cross. Many want consolation, but few desire adversity. Many are eager to share Jesus' table, but few will join him in fasting.

—Thomas à Kempis, German monk

Keeping It Real

In the Orthodox tradition, there are some real legalists who think nothing but strict adherence to the fasting rules will do. Fortunately, most priests and parishes understand that following the letter of the law sometimes subverts the meaning of the law. If one denies oneself meat only to pig out on a meal of shrimp and crab—well, he's missed the point.

In addition, if fasting starts to control us—if we spend hour upon hour reading every ingredient label and planning our menus down to the last detail—then we're missing the point in another way.

What some call "the substitution syndrome" can be another temptation. For example, some Orthodox Lenten cookbooks warn that margarine should be used instead of butter on the lobster tail recipe, since butter is a dairy product. Again, the point of fasting—attending to a discipline of self-denial to open oneself more fully to God— is being subverted.

Little by Little

I am basically a coward when it comes to fasting. I haven't done it much, because the idea of giving up food for some reason unnerves me. I am asking God for strength to make fasting a more regular part of my spiritual regimen. It's funny that I feel this way, because there have been times when I have fasted and I've definitely experienced the presence of God.

Skeptics might chalk this up to delusion brought on by lack of sustenance, but those who have actually had the experience know otherwise. I remember one prayer time in particular that came after a day-long fast. As I went into prayer, I felt God's presence as tangibly as I feel the chair I'm sitting on now. I've fasted enough to know the difference between hunger that toys with my emotional state and the presence of something beyond emotion.

There are no hard-and-fast (excuse the pun) rules here, nor are there any guaranteed experiences that result. But it is nonetheless discipline that millions of Christians past and present have found enhances their prayer life, and their relationship to God, in powerful ways.

The Least You Need to Know

- ◆ Fasting has been practiced by Christians for centuries, and practiced for varied reasons and in various forms.

- ◆ Ultimately, fasting is about focusing on God.

- ◆ As good as fasting is, there are times when you shouldn't fast.

- ◆ A legalistic approach to fasting can get in the way of the spiritual meaning of fasting.

Chapter 14

Healing Prayer

In This Chapter

- ◆ The healing power of prayer
- ◆ Real-life stories about physical healing through prayer
- ◆ How psychological healing can be equally necessary
- ◆ Clearing up some misconceptions about healing prayer

In many churches from Presbyterian to Pentecostal, just before the morning prayer, people are asked to mention concerns they would like the rest of the church to pray for. What you'll find is that most prayer requests are for healing, sometimes emotional healing but mostly physical healing. Everything from colds to cancer are mentioned.

Whatever their tradition—or even lack of tradition—people care about their physical and emotional well-being, and healing naturally becomes a topic of prayer. Yet a lot of misconceptions circulate about healing prayer, and we are wise to clarify some matters before we enter into this type of prayer.

Healing Happens

Let's deal with the doubters first, those who wonder whether prayers of healing are a waste of time.

Because we live in a rationalistic age, in which science and medicine do "miracles," it is tempting to think that healing prayer is pointless. In other ages, when people had no other recourse, they prayed to God for healing. Today, the argument goes, we shouldn't pray to God for healing; we should see a specialist.

It doesn't have to be an either/or situation. We can pray for healing *and* go see a doctor. And we should; prayer should not be a substitute for medical care. Most of the time God heals through natural means, through the work of able physicians and through the body's healing capacity. But sometimes God goes beyond natural means to bring healing, even today.

A quick search on the Internet turns up dozens of healing ministries in the United States alone. It doesn't take long to find stories like this one: "I had breast cancer with metastasis to the spine, pelvis, lungs, and lymph nodes around the heart. After … receiving the laying on of hands, I am now cancer free. A bone scan and blood work show no traces of cancer."

Or this: "I had been diagnosed with MS [multiple sclerosis] …. I had been confined to a wheelchair. I also fell and broke a bone in my leg …. With the laying on of hands, I have received strength to walk, and I can stand pain-free. I am no longer in a wheelchair, and my reflexes have improved in walking."

Are these people deluded? Perhaps, but the number of stories of healing keeps mounting, and one cannot dismiss every single one of them out of hand. Even if 99 percent are imaginary or fakes, the 1 percent left would amount to thousands of stories.

Another common doubt is this: Sometimes we're tempted to think that prayers for healing are nothing more than a form of positive thinking, of visualizing. In other words, we might think that prayer is psychologically useful, but not necessarily spiritually powerful.

Again, it's not a matter of either/or. Of course, prayer *is* psychologically powerful. After all, God has created us in such a way that almost anything we do has a psychological effect on us. But in prayer, more than psychology is at work—God is at work, too.

How can we "prove" this? Well, healing prayer is not subject to proof in a scientific sense. In fact, the most important things of life can't be "proved." For example, my wife loves me. Though there are lots of indications that this is true, none of them is absolute proof: She could be lying to me and putting on an act for some ulterior motive. Then again, I *know* she loves me, and I know that as surely as I know that I'm typing at a computer now.

Healing prayer works like that. You can't prove it, yet you know it's real. The only way to talk about it sensibly is through stories. Let me tell you about the experiences of two people, one who was healed physically and one who was healed emotionally. I picked them not because they are unusual, but because they are so typical. You'll find such stories in many Christian books and periodicals, including *Guideposts* (the source of the second story) and *Christian Reader* (the source of the first).

Physical Healing

As he sat in his Phoenix, Arizona, home in late November 1996 (the Tuesday before Thanksgiving), Rich Payton began shivering unexpectedly. Chills ran through his body so hard that his teeth rattled. Rich, an administrator of the Boys and Girls Clubs, thought to himself, "This is the worst possible time for me to be coming down with the flu."

It became increasingly clear, however, that the problem wasn't the flu: Rich didn't eat or sleep much for the next three days, and he began feeling pain in his right arm and left leg. When his right arm swelled and became hot and sensitive to touch, his wife, Heidi, rushed him to the emergency room.

After running tests, the doctor announced to Heidi that Rich had a rare disease, a group A strep bacteria called *necrotising fascitis*, also known as "flesh-eating" bacteria. This bacteria had already entered his bloodstream, and it was killing off muscle and heading toward his vital organs. If it reached them, he had no chance of survival. As it was, the mortality rate was 70 percent, despite aggressive treatment. In any event, his leg and arm would have to be amputated.

Doctors rushed him to the operating room and tried to clean out or "debride" the affected tissues. They stalled on the amputation as they became increasingly convinced that Rich's chances of survival were nil. They told Heidi to contact Rich's parents and to prepare for the worst.

For Heidi, preparing meant prayer—not only her prayers, but those of friends and church members. For the next two weeks, she sat with her husband—who was so drugged on morphine to kill the pain that he remembers little of that time—and tried to encourage him. "Sleep sound in Jesus," she whispered, quoting a line from their daughter's favorite lullaby. Heidi struggled with grief, but her shock and mourning slowly turned to peace as she became assured that God was in control.

And then things began to turn for Rich, so much so that by the middle of December, the doctors announced that somehow the bacteria had disappeared from his body. They said they had no idea why it was gone, but it *was* gone. They said that Rich was a walking miracle.

> **Snapshots of Answered Prayers**
>
> When Miriam complained that Moses wasn't the only spokesperson for God, she was struck with leprosy. Moses prayed and it was removed in Numbers 12:6–15.

Doctors don't completely understand how this bacteria works normally, and there's no question that the medical procedures helped. But those involved directly in the event seem to agree with Heidi, who says, "I knew that heaven had been bombarded with prayer and had retaliated with volleys of peace, strength, and healing."

Psychological Healing

This is an older story, but one of my favorites. You'll see that it parallels so many stories of addiction that we hear about these days. Harold Hughes was a man who would go on to become governor and then a senator from Iowa, but in his early years he was addicted to alcohol, and drinking was ruining his life. Harold drank on the job (he ran a small association of truck drivers), and on top of that he was in the habit of verbally abusing his wife and children at home. He promised his family dozens of times—after each binge of drinking and abusive behavior—that he would quit drinking, but he never managed to break his addiction.

One night, when his wife had scheduled them to attend a dinner party, Harold stopped into a bar on the way home to have "just one drink." When 11:00 P.M. rolled around, he was drunk and depressed. He came home to an empty house and lay down on the couch, his head pounding with nausea—and guilt. The years of abuse and lack of control suddenly assaulted him. A sense of shame and self-loathing sank deep into him as he lay there.

"What's the point of living?" he thought. "I've failed everyone who has ever meant anything to me; I'm a disgrace to my town. I'm a hypocrite. I can't do anything right. I am an evil, rotten drunk, a liar. And what should happen to evil men? They deserve to die."

He got up and went to the closet where he kept his shotgun. He slid three shells into the magazine and pumped one into the chamber. With tears streaming down his face, he lay down again and put the shotgun on his chest and the muzzle into his mouth. He then got up and moved to the bathroom because, as he remembered thinking, it would be easier to clean up.

An even more terrible sadness now filled him, and the thought came to him that he should explain all this to God, who could then at least forgive him for this final sin.

He knelt and prayed, "Oh God, I'm a failure, a drunk, a liar, and a cheat. I'm lost and hopeless and want to die. Forgive me for doing this," and then he broke into sobs. "Please take care of Eve and the girls. Please help them forget me ...." He slid to the floor, convulsing and sobbing. He was totally exhausted, and he lay drained and still.

He didn't know for how long, but in the quiet, something happened: "A warm peace seemed to settle deep within me, filling the terrible emptiness, driving out the self-hate and condemnation." Harold felt that God was reaching down to him, and joy suddenly filled him.

He looked back at that as the moment when the healing of his alcoholism had begun. He still had to regain the trust of his wife and children. He had to change his patterns of behavior. He had to learn not to run from but to deal with his crises. He began attending Alcoholics Anonymous and reading his Bible. And he began praying.

> **From the Good Book**
>
> I cannot carry all these people by myself; the burden is too heavy for me. If this is how you are going to treat me, put me to death right now—if I have found favor in your eyes—and do not let me face my own ruin.
>
> —Moses, Numbers 11:14, 15

> **From the Good Book**
>
> Search me, O God, and know my heart; test me and know my anxious thoughts. See if there is any offensive way in me, and lead me in the way everlasting.
>
> —David, Psalm 139:23, 24

Two Misconceptions

Such stories are sometimes criticized for their predictable plot and for their superficial treatment of the human condition. I'm not suggesting that such things happen all the time, or that they'll happen to everyone who prays. But if we accept them for what they are—simple testimonies of people who have been remarkably changed by healing prayer—then they speak volumes.

Many people have tried to determine the key to healing. They want to figure out what they have to do to guarantee, or at least improve the chances of, their healing. This has led to two misconceptions about healing prayer that I would like to clear up. As is the case with so many things, there is some truth in each, but there's also a lot of misunderstanding.

You Have to Have Enough Faith

It is clear that faith is a key to healing. Jesus himself told people he had healed, "Your faith has made you well." But many people take this insight a step too far: They think they are responsible for manufacturing this faith, that they must work up some sort of supreme inner confidence in God. Furthermore, such teaching implies that if they are not healed, the fault lies with them: They simply didn't manufacture enough faith.

> **Prayer Pearls**
>
> Today any successful and competent businessman will employ the latest and best-tested methods in production, distribution, and administration, and many are discovering that one of the greatest of all efficiency methods is prayer power.
>
> —Norman Vincent Peale, American clergyman

This is patently false. There was no person with more faith and confidence in God than Jesus Christ. And he prayed to God that he would not have to be crucified, but God didn't answer his prayer. We can hardly chalk up that "failure" to Jesus' lack of faith.

The type of faith that leads to healing is not a form of positive thinking that we work up, it's the receiving of a gift that comes from God. Sometimes when people face a personal crisis, immediately a sense of peace overtakes them. They are confident from that moment on that everything will work out. This is not faith working up to peace, but a gift of peace that brings faith.

You Have to Pray in the Right Way

That means praying "in Jesus' name" and/or anointing with oil and/or the practice of laying on of hands and/or whatever. In this case, a prayer *help* has become a prayer *requirement*, almost a magical formula.

Let's be clear: All these practices can certainly help. To pray "in Jesus' name" simply means to pray by his power and in his will. The laying on of hands in prayer is an ancient practice, in which people place their hands on your head, shoulders, or arms and pray for you. Anointing with oil (a symbol of abundance and blessing) is also an ancient practice: One person wets his thumb with oil and makes the sign of the cross on the forehead of the person who is being prayed for.

Such practices speak to us in inexplicable ways, deep into our souls and psyches. This is why God has ordained their use. But healing prayer is not a magic formula. Healing does not *depend* on such practices. Healing is a gift that can come through prayer, but as a gift it is not something we control.

Instead, healing is something we can open ourselves up to. That means always being open to the possibility of miraculous healing, and even praying for it. It might also mean arguing with God when he doesn't heal. It means, as you might have guessed, entering into a conversation with God about even those parts of your life that need healing, looking for his blessings, thanking him when it comes, and still trusting him when it doesn't.

Trusting God when there is no answer, of course, is not always easy. People who are not healed wonder if God really exists. Others begin to doubt that he cares about them. Still others become bitter at him. You'll find these and other reactions all through the Bible, and you'll discover some fuller explanations for unanswered prayer in Chapter 16. For now, suffice it to say that when God denies a request, even a request in which life hangs in the balance, it does not mean he no longer cares or does not exist. The one who felt utterly abandoned—Jesus at Gethsemane, the night before his crucifixion, when he prayed to be delivered from death—was still God's "beloved Son." It is a mystery, this business of suffering (including unanswered prayer), but it is a mystery finally bathed in love.

The Least You Need to Know

- There are unexplainable cases of healing that go beyond science into the realm of supernatural miracle.

- Physical healing through prayer is rare but attested to time and again.

- Healing of psychological wounds is often more necessary than physical healing.

- We can't work up our own faith in God to be healed, and we can't achieve healing with a specific formula.

Chapter 15

Handling the Seven Distractions

In This Chapter

◆ How to keep your mind from wandering

◆ Dealing with feelings of boredom, restlessness, or irritation

◆ Working through "pray-er's block"

◆ What to do if you disagree or feel uncomfortable with certain prayers

If it's easy to get started in prayer, then it's also easy to get distracted during prayer. This is true of any new habit we're seeking to form, but it is especially true of prayer. We're trying to engage in an activity that can transcend normal human experience, and yet human nature keeps getting in the way.

In one way, it's surprising that our minds so easily wander. Prayer is conversation with God, after all. You'd think there would be nothing more interesting than talking with the creator of heaven and earth. And yet, though we can stay riveted on a cheap novel for hours, we often can't give more than a minute to spiritual things without our minds wandering. Let's take a look at the seven common distractions of prayer and how to deal with them.

"My Mind Wanders"

The most common distraction is the wandering mind. You start to pray, let's say, about your 10-year-old who just started school, and as you do, you remember how hard it was when you started fifth grade when your family moved to Chicago. But you also remember that your dad took you to a Cubs games in late September that year, and you liked the Cubs right away, and you wish Ron Santo were still playing because he was a better player than he is a radio announcer. That reminds you that the car radio needs to be taken in to be repaired, but you think you're going to try someone else this time, because the last time ....

And then you remember that you're supposed to be praying, but by this time you can't remember where you were in the prayer.

When we're distracted repeatedly during the same prayer time, and when this happens day after day, we're tempted to give up. But if we can put this in perspective, we won't get so easily discouraged.

First, when it comes to any activity that demands a lot of the mind, we get easily distracted. I try to stitch into my reading routine a "blast from the past" once in a while, anything from Plato's *Republic* to Dostoevsky's *Crime and Punishment*. Invariably, there are passages where the mind just doesn't want to stay focused. That's because it's being challenged; just like a muscle resists when first being asked to lift a weight, so the mind resists when it faces a new challenge.

> ### Prayer Pearls
>
> God communicates or talks to us through the Bible, the circumstances of life, and the inward persuasion of his Holy Spirit. But we can communicate with him through the single means of prayer. There is no other medium by which men can converse with God.
>
> —Harold Lindsell, American theologian

Second, the wandering mind is a problem for beginners and experienced pray-ers alike. John Bunyan, who wrote the spiritual classic *Pilgrim's Progress*, articulated this frustration as well as anyone: "None knows how many by-ways the heart hath, and back lanes, to slip away from the presence of God." The biography of every spiritual giant contains lines like these.

Third, the wandering mind is a problem intrinsic to prayer. We are required to engage our entire humanity—heart, mind, soul, and strength—in prayer. We are told to bring to God all our cares and concerns, all our thoughts and questions. When we're in his presence—especially if we feel comfortable in God's presence—we are going to tend to wander over landscape that is important to us. Prayer is not a rigid routine we practice in the presence of a bureaucratic God who wishes that our prayers would be more orderly. It is a conversation—and a messy one, at that—with someone we love and who loves us.

It is this insight that can give us a practical way to deal with the wandering mind. Our temptation after a bit of wandering is to abruptly halt, mentally chastise ourselves, and get back to "real" prayer. Instead, we might simply admit that our minds have wandered into an area that, in fact, really interests us—that's where the mind usually goes, after all. As such, instead of casting it out of our prayer, we can incorporate that wandering, and even use it to take us back to what we began praying about in the first place. Taking the example I mentioned earlier, I might do this:

> ... that reminds me, I need to take in the car radio to be repaired, but I need to take it to someone else, because last time that jerk at Robinson's Car Stereo ... Oops! Where was I, Lord? Okay, I pray for my attitude toward that guy; it's obvious that I'm still angry with him. Forgive me, and help me to forgive him. I do love the simple pleasure of listening to the radio while I drive, and I thank you for such good gifts—like the game of baseball, which is really a silly sport in a lot of ways, but for some reason it brings me great pleasure. Thank you for that. And that first year in Chicago—well, it was difficult, though my dad really helped me get through it. Help me to be a good father to my daughter when I get home this evening, especially because this is her first day at a new school.

This is where complete honesty in prayer is vital. We may put ourselves into a pious mood and try to pray about others and about spiritual things, but when our minds keep wandering back to our own concerns and "petty" things, there's no sense in trying to fool God. Our mind wanders to those things that really are important to us. We might as well admit that and make them a part of our prayer. We may wish that we weren't so selfish and petty, but the fact is, we are sometimes. And that frustration, too, can become a topic of prayer.

 From the Good Book _____

... He will swallow up death forever. The sovereign Lord will wipe away the tears from all faces; he will remove the disgrace of his people from all the earth. The Lord has spoken. In that day they will say, "Surely this is our God; we trusted in him, and he saved us. This is the Lord, we trusted in him; let us rejoice and be glad in his salvation."

—Isaiah, Isaiah 25:8, 9

"I'm Bored"

There are many reasons we might find ourselves bored in or with prayer, and the first thing to do when bored is to try to find the source of our boredom.

We may simply be stuck in the rut of routine—same thing, same way, every day. The solution for this, of course, is simple: Do something different. This may include one of the following ideas:

- Pray during a different time of the day.
- Change locations.
- Try different postures.
- Change the order of your routine.
- Change the book you're reading.
- Try different styles of prayer.

Then again, boredom may not be so simple. Sometimes we're bored precisely because the book we're reading or the prayer routine we're trying is challenging us to go deeper. Let's say I've just added praise and adoration to my prayer routine, but I find praising and adoring God pretty boring. It may be that I'm bored because, well, I'm ungrateful. I just don't care about God's greatness as much as my day-to-day life.

The solution here is two-fold. First, I must admit to God my lousy attitude. Second, I must continue my routine right through the boredom until some of my ungratefulness is cured.

Finally, boredom may be the product of sheer selfishness. I may be seeking some experience in prayer, or I may be demanding that prayer do something for me; when it doesn't do that immediately, I become bored. I may be approaching prayer as I do a television show: If it doesn't hook me in a couple of minutes, I flip channels.

When this is the case, I find it helpful to remind myself that prayer is not about me. Though I'm going through a time when prayer seems to be doing nothing for me, I can still be praying for others. And there isn't a time when those I love don't need prayer: Right now, I have teenage children who are trying to figure out adolescence, a wife who is trying to fulfill the demands of both work and home, a friend who is struggling to figure out what he's supposed to do with his life, another who has cancer—and on it goes. To deny them my prayers because I'm bored—well, I may be selfish, but I hope I'm not that selfish (all right—sometimes I am).

While we're on the subject, let's examine this business about prayer not seeming to do anything for us. We do well to remind ourselves that many experiences in life don't *appear* to be doing anything for us when they are actually changing us profoundly.

School is just such an experience. It was a rare day growing up when I'd come from school and feel as if I'd learned something new. It all seemed so routine and boring; so much of it was stuff I already knew—or so I thought.

And yet, by the time I finished sixth grade, I knew a heck of a lot more than I did when I entered kindergarten. When exactly that happened is hard to say. But all the time I thought school wasn't doing anything for me, it was doing a whole lot. The school of prayer is very much like that.

> **Prayer Pearls**
>
> A person who reads a book on prayer but does not put its suggestions into practice may possibly find the book interesting, but he will not find the great spiritual adventure which prayer can give him.
>
> —Donald J. Campbell

"I Feel Restless"

I get into moods when prayer seems like such a waste of time. I'd rather be getting something done: write another chapter, fix the drip in the kitchen sink, wax my car, prepare a flower bed. I'm a person who likes to stay busy, and I get a great deal of satisfaction from accomplishing things. When I am overtaken with this spirit, I find it very difficult to sit down to pray because a lot of the time prayer doesn't feel very "useful."

In such moods, I probably need to pray more than ever. Work has a way of filling the time allotted to it. There is always more to be done, and if I let my to-do list run my life, it will run my life right into the ground. If man does not live by bread alone, neither does he live by work alone.

This is why God created the Sabbath—one day a week in which work is discouraged and worship and play and relationships are encouraged. This is not just a divine suggestion, but one of the Ten Commandments: "Remember to observe the Sabbath day by keeping it holy." That was written for accomplishment junkies like me.

The reasoning behind the commandment is probably the most interesting part of it: "Six days a week are set apart for your daily duties

> **Snapshots of Answered Prayers**
>
> Have you ever tried to negotiate with God? Though Sodom was a wicked city, Abraham bargained with God to spare it. He talked God down from the need for 50 good people to only 10 in order to hold back his judgment. Find out what happens in Genesis 19.

and regular work, but the seventh day is a day of rest, dedicated to the Lord, your God …. For in six days the Lord made the heavens, the earth, the sea, and everything in them; then he rested on the seventh day." (Exodus 20:11) If it's good enough for the Lord, it ought to be good enough for me.

Prayer is a mini-Sabbath stuck into our daily routines. It's a time to step back from activity, thank God for the goodness of life, pray for others, and put our own lives in perspective. If I don't have time for that, I'm way too busy.

"I Don't Know What to Pray For"

Writers get writer's block. Pray-ers get pray-er's block. Some days I bow my head and my mind goes completely blank. I just can't think of anything to pray.

Fortunately, the problem is easily cured. One of four methods works for me:

- **Pray about it.** I start praying about the fact that I don't know what to prayer for, about my frustration, boredom, and so on.

- **Start reading.** I stop praying and pick up my Bible or devotional material and just start reading. This gets my mind focused on things spiritual, and soon it starts me thinking about areas in my own life that need attention; it may also get me thinking about others' needs as well.

- **Write it down.** When my mind goes blank, I put my pen to work. I start entering my thoughts into my journal, even if I have to begin with: "Lord, I don't know what to pray for. I don't know why I go through periods like this …."

- **Create a prayer list.** Here's one adapted from Chapter 10:

  - Immediate family

  - Extended family

  - Neighbors and friends

  - Co-workers

  - People in groups you belong to (church, running club, online chat room)

  - The poor and needy

  - Your community, the nation

"I'm in a Bad Mood"

Sometimes I come to prayer irritated. I'm feeling rushed or angry or just out of sorts—I'm certainly not in any mood to pray. Two courses of action present themselves immediately:

1. **Don't pray.** Sometimes I just need time to settle down. I walk into the house some evenings pretty grumpy. I'd like to be able to talk with my wife and children, but if I do, I just start snapping at them. It's better if they just leave me alone for a few minutes until my equilibrium is restored.

2. **Make the bad mood part of your prayer.** You probably guessed this one, because by now you've seen that it is a pretty standard way I attack problems in prayer. I just cannot emphasize too strongly that prayer is not about getting into some pious state of mind or having some euphoric spiritual experience. It's about an honest conversation with God. It's about getting in touch with who we are at any given moment—the good, the bad, and the ugly—and expressing that to God.

Prayer Hotline

Sometimes it's wise to simply sit for a few moments, have a cup of coffee, remind yourself why you pray, and figure out what's bugging you before you enter into prayer.

"I Disagree with What I'm Reading"

Good! It means you're reading material that doesn't merely reinforce your current thinking. Prayer is meant to stretch us, and the material we choose to read should do the same. The Bible is notorious for busting our myths about the way life works, which is one reason reading it is standard issue in a prayer routine.

When you find yourself disagreeing, ask yourself some questions to discover the source:

♦ Do you disagree because you're being asked to change some behavior you enjoy? Should you change?

♦ Do you disagree because you can't buy into this concept of God? If so, why not?

♦ Do you disagree because life doesn't work that way in your experience? Should you broaden your understanding?

♦ Do you disagree because it doesn't agree with what the Bible teaches? Or does it at a deeper level?

You get the idea. I don't feel right simply dismissing the passage, because one purpose of prayer is to expand my heart and mind. That usually involves the uncomfortable process of confronting opinions and ideas that don't seem right to me. As you can imagine, a lot of the "dumb" ideas of others turn out to be pretty wise.

Wisdom and common sense are called for here, of course. You shouldn't blindly trust every prayer you read and every devotional book you study—not even this one. If you do find yourself uncomfortable with a passage or idea, you should first see how it stacks up against the teachings of Jesus, Paul, and the other biblical teachers. Yes, a lot of times the most uncomfortable ideas come from these very biblical writers. ("Love your enemies"!?) Then again, a lot of spiritual advice is plainly unbiblical (for example, "If you give money to God, you'll get more in return!"), and should simply be ignored.

"I Just Can't Pray Certain Prayers or Use Certain Expressions"

Then don't. Pray in a way that allows you to be sincere. Then again, I sometimes wonder if I should continue to pray those uncomfortable prayers. If prayer is about stretching the spiritual self, maybe I should practice calling God "Father" or using a prayer that says I'm a "miserable sinner." Perhaps expressions such as these—precisely because they irk me—speak about areas in my life where I most need to grow.

Or, perhaps I should explore the prayer or the expression that troubles me, asking the same sort of questions I'd ask of a passage that I disagree with.

" " From the Good Book

Yes, Lord, walking in the way of your laws, we wait for you; your name and renown are the desire of our hearts. My soul yearns for you in the night; in the morning my spirit longs for you. When your judgments come upon the earth, the people of the world learn righteousness.

—Isaiah, Isaiah 26:8

Or—you guessed it—perhaps I should make this stumbling block a part of my prayer. "Lord, this prayer I just prayed says, 'To you all angels … cherubim and seraphim, sing in endless praise.' The phrase means absolutely nothing to me, and I don't even know if I believe in angels. Lord, are there angels? And if there are, what is their purpose? Help me to understand what I'm to understand by this phrase."

Remember that prayer is a conversation with God about the real things going on inside us. That includes the myriad concerns and problems that distract us from prayer. Co-opt your distractions, and put them to good use: Pray about them and pray through them.

The Least You Need to Know

- ◆ We can use distractions, moods, or questions as part of our prayer process and thus work through them.

- ◆ When our mind wanders in prayer, we shouldn't fret or jerk it back into line— easy does it!

- ◆ Boredom is a very common problem, even among the most devout.

- ◆ We should be honest with God about our struggles and not put on false piety.

Chapter 16

When God Doesn't Seem to Answer

In This Chapter

- ◆ Why answers are promised in the Bible but not always granted
- ◆ How God answers prayers in a variety of ways: yes, no, wait, and try again
- ◆ What God may be teaching you by not answering your prayers
- ◆ How to stick it out when your prayers aren't answered

If the life of prayer is made difficult by distractions, it can be completely destroyed by doubts. Doubts begin pestering us early on in prayer, especially if our prayers aren't answered as we imagine they should be answered. We wonder if we've prayed correctly, or if we've done something to displease God, and so on.

As we mature in our faith, we realize that God is not waiting for the perfect prayer from the perfect person before he'll grant our wishes. That takes some of the burden off our spiritual shoulders. But it still leaves us with a troublesome question: Why doesn't God answer many of our prayers?

The Contradiction of Prayer

On the one hand, the Bible is full of great promises about prayer, most of them coming from the lips of Jesus himself:

- "Keep on asking and you will be given what you ask for." (Matthew 7:7)

- "If two of you agree down here on earth concerning anything you ask, my Father in heaven will do it for you." (Matthew 18:19)

- "Listen to me! You can pray for anything, and if you believe, you will have it." (Mark 11:24)

The apostle James put it most bluntly: "The reason you don't have what you want is that you don't ask God for it." (James 4:2)

And then you have all those wonderful examples of answered prayer: Moses prays for deliverance from Egypt, and it's done. King David prays for victory over his enemies, and it happens. Jesus prays that Lazarus will rise from the dead, and here comes Lazarus out of his tomb. And so on. (See the Snapshots of Answered Prayers sidebars throughout this book for more examples.)

If that were the end of the story, however, the Bible would not be a very interesting book. The Bible never gives a promise without at the same time being brutally honest about the way life works. And the way life works sometimes is this: Prayers are not always answered:

- "Every day I call to you, my God, but you do not answer." (Psalm 22:2)

- "I cry to you, O God, but you don't answer me. I stand before you, and you don't bother to look." (Job 20:30)

- "How long, O Lord, must I call for help? But you do not listen!" (Habakkuk 1:2)

Prayer Pearls

Prayer is ... a treasure undiminished, a mine never exhausted, a sky unobstructed by clouds, a haven unruffled by storm. It is the root, the fountain, and the mother of a thousand blessings.

—John Chrysostom, early church father

And then you have these depressing examples: Paul prays that a "thorn in his flesh" will be taken away, but it never is. Jesus prays that he will not have to face the cross, but he ends up there anyway. And so on.

This is the contradictory nature of prayer. Rather than leave it at that, though, we are wise to explore the three ways God answers prayer. If we do, we'll end up with a richer prayer life.

God Sometimes Says "Yes"

This book is premised on this truth, as are all books on prayer throughout time. If you didn't hope this was true, and if I didn't believe it was, you wouldn't be reading this right now.

Nearly everyone, in fact, has experienced an answer to prayer. Many times the prayer and answer are more commonplace. "Lord, help me to stay calm and be myself in this job interview." And we find an unusual peace settling in as we meet our prospective employer. Some seem downright miraculous. "Oh God, I don't know how I'm going to have enough money to last the month. Please help!" and within a week, an unexpected check from a friend arrives in the mail, with a note that says, "Finally am on my feet again, and I haven't forgotten the $300 you lent me a few years ago. Here you go, with interest."

Co-author Jim Bell tells such a story from his own life: "When my wife and I were returning to the States after my study in Ireland, we had just enough money in our bank account to pay for two tickets back to New York. We were going to live with my parents and I would then trust God for a quick job. When we got to the airport they discovered that Margaret was still an Irish citizen and she would need her visa stamped by the American embassy. She frantically went into Dublin on this early Sunday morning to make it happen. But by the time she got back to the airport the flight had left and the next one with open seats didn't leave until three more days. Worse yet, the flight fare had increased by 55 Irish pounds.

"I panicked and asked her what family member of hers could lend us the money. She said that instead we should pray, tell no one of our need and wait on the Lord. I thought she was crazy but agreed. The next day we got a phone call from a dear older woman who had been a spiritual mentor to us. Auntie Elsie said the Lord had spoke to her and asked us over for tea.

"As we were leaving she handed us a packet. Inside was exactly 55 pounds! She told us the Lord led her to the Bible in Isaiah chapter 55 (of all numbers!) where it begins: 'Is anyone thirsty? Come and drink—even if you have no money.' We learned at an early stage in our marriage that God knows our needs and if we pray in faith we don't need to take matters into our own hands."

Some answers end up changing your life. My mother was battling with my older brother when he was in junior college and living at home. She was not even a believing Christian at the time, but at her wit's end, she prayed, "Lord, if you'll just get Michael to join the military, to give him some direction and discipline, I'll give my life to you." That very afternoon, my brother walks in the door saying he had been to the Air Force Recruiter and has signed up for a stint. My mother started going to church the next Sunday. She never looked back.

It's funny the age we live in, because sometimes a prayer is answered, and then explained away "logically." In the movie *O Brother, Where Art Thou?*, Delmer and his friends are about to be hung by state police in the backwoods. Delmer, who has been a rational atheist throughout the movie, now pleads to God in desperation to save them, the first humble and loving sentiment he's expressed in the movie. As soon as he finishes, a flood of water inundates the area, and Delmer and his friends escape unharmed. When one of his friends tells Delmer that God had answered his prayer, Delmer denies it, chalking the whole thing up to coincidence, to the government's flooding the valley to bring electricity to the region.

> **Snapshots of Answered Prayers**
>
> Even the prayers of demons are answered in Luke 8:26–31. They begged Jesus not to be sent to the bottomless pit and he sent them into a herd of pigs instead.

To be sure, sometimes it is hard to tell when coincidence ends and an answer to prayer begins. Then again, the distinction is often artificial. In fact, God uses the laws of nature and the actions of people to bring about his answers, so that every answer to prayer is in some sense disguised. It takes the eyes of faith to see beneath the coincidence to a deeper reality governing the universe.

God Sometimes Says "No"

If answers to prayer are one reality we experience, unanswered prayer is another. We often pray for something to happen, something to change, something inside us to feel different—and it's as if we haven't prayed at all, or as if God is simply not listening. What is going on with that? It could mean, for one, that God is simply saying, "No." And there are many reasons for that.

The Answer Would Cause More Problems Than It Would Solve

The poet Longfellow once said, "What discord we should bring into the universe if our prayers were all answered! Then we should govern the world and not God."

I'll admit there are times I imagine I could run the universe better than God—it does appear to be mismanaged at times. Then again, I know what a mess I've made of my life.

One petty example will suffice: I'm anxious to have a friend over for dinner—so anxious that I pick the first available opening in his and my schedule. That means a dinner that starts at 8:00 on Thursday night. Not a problem, except that I have to get up at 3:00 on Friday morning. So not only does the dinner feel rushed, but the next day I'm exhausted. And I won't even tell you about some of the biggest life decisions I've blown.

Rather than me running the universe, then, I'm wise to let God decide which prayers to answer. Sometimes it's clear in retrospect that it's better they weren't answered. I remember interviewing for a church in San Pedro, a suburb of Los Angeles. I liked the senior pastor, and the church and setting sounded great. I prayed to get the job, but I didn't even make it past the initial interview. Naturally I was disappointed—until another job offer came my way to serve in a church in Mexico City. Speaking from a purely selfish point of view (what the job did for me), it was a much better fit and a much better experience. I'm glad my prayer wasn't answered regarding the church in San Pedro.

We're Getting in the Way

Sometimes we don't hear from the Lord because we've created so much spiritual noise within us that we can't hear God speaking to us. The Bible calls this "sin" and recognizes that it is a common problem when it comes to prayer.

The Psalmist put it this way: "If I had not confessed the sin in my heart, my Lord would not have listened." (Psalm 66:18) It's not that God won't listen to us if we don't confess every sin. That's impossible, because we're not even aware of all the ways we fail before God. Nor is it true that God turns away from us in disgust until we say we're sorry. God is a little bigger than that.

But there is a dynamic at work that must be respected if we want to have functioning prayer lives. I can't go before God harboring some sin—cheating on taxes, or carrying on an affair, or refusing to forgive a friend, or whatever—and expect that I can have a healthy relationship with God. It ain't gonna happen, as they say. I have to allow God to cleanse my heart and my life before I'm going to have a meaningful prayer life again.

Sometimes sin has a much more direct effect on prayer. The apostle James said, "Even when you do ask [in prayer], you don't get it because your whole motive is wrong—you want only what will give you pleasure." If we treat God as Santa Claus, we can expect to hear a lot of silence.

This does not mean that we cannot ask God for anything that would give us pleasure. We can pray to enjoy a fine meal, good sex, a sunny day, a good book—and so on. But the motive cannot be a greedy grabbing for hedonistic pleasure; it must be a simple desire to enjoy God's good gifts. What's more, it must always be in the context of God's will so that when the answer is no, we don't pout, but simply move on to what God would have us do next.

Prayer Is Only Part of the Answer

Sometimes no answer means that God's part is only part of the answer. The other part of the answer must be supplied by us. Prayer is not a substitute for action. Let's say I pray that a friend, who just lost her husband, might be comforted in her grief.

Prayer Pearls

Never give up prayer; and should you find dryness and difficulty, persevere in it for this very reason. God often desires to see what love your soul has, and love is not tried by ease and satisfaction.

—St. John of the Cross, devotional writer

Prayer Hotline

Prayer is not a substitute for action, but neither is action a substitute for prayer. As the old saying goes, "Pray as if everything depended on God; act as if everything depended on you."

But maybe part of that answer requires my doing some jobs that her husband normally did: mowing her lawn, changing the oil in her car, and so on. You get the idea. Along the same lines, my son prays that he might do well on the SAT. The answer to that prayer, however, has a great deal to do with the amount of time he studies.

But some get the wrong idea: They think that prayer is useless and what really matters is their own action. A lot of people who don't pray do well on the SAT, after all. Yes, and a lot of people go through life alone, but that doesn't mean it's the best way to do it. God may not miraculously give my son answers when he takes the SAT, but to know that as he takes the test God is present, and to know that God is working in and through my son's experience, wisdom, and knowledge, through his body and mind— it lifts the whole experience to a different dimension. This is what prayer is meant to do: to help us see that our mundane lives are not so mundane, that we do, in fact, live in a different dimension than our five senses reveal.

Sometimes God Is Saying "Wait"

Sometimes God's silence does not mean "No" as much as it means "Wait." My daughter recently asked me if she could watch a certain television show. I thought about my 10-year-old, and I thought about the show (decidedly adult in nature), and said no. What I really meant was "Wait. In a few years, you'll be old enough to handle such a show. Until then, you'll have to watch something else."

In the same way, some of our prayers are not answered because we're not ready for them to be answered. This can be a great comfort when you're really anxious.

When I was in college, I recall feeling a great amount of pressure about some matter (which says something about how ultimately important it was—today I can't remember exactly the reason!). I became so upset about it that one evening at dinner, I found myself getting irritated with a friend, snapping at him, and bolting up from the table in disgust.

I went to my room and opened my Bible to see if I could find some guidance in the matter. What my Bible opened to was this: "Wait patiently for the Lord. Be brave and courageous. Yes, wait patiently for the Lord." (Psalm 27:14)

I felt as though God was speaking to me personally, and the tension inside me released. I realized that it wasn't the right time for the issue to be resolved; instead, I was required to wait.

Sometimes we have to wait a very long time—sometimes a lifetime. Jim Bell, in pursuing a project on the power of prayer, was e-mailed countless stories. One man wrote that by the time he entered college, his churchgoing youth was "buried in the dust of atheism." He became a successful attorney, married a beautiful woman, and was living the good life. Then his mom was diagnosed with breast cancer, and when he realized she was not going to make it, he began attending church again—for her sake. He still didn't believe in prayer or God, but he thought this act would be a comfort to his mother.

Slowly, the messages of the sermon and Scripture and teaching began to settle in, and, as he put it, "Much to my surprise, I began to discover Christianity was the answer, after all."

His mom died two years after his conversion, and shortly after her passing, he was sorting through her things when he discovered her notebooks and journals. He noticed that she had been praying for him his entire life.

Sometimes God Is Saying "Try Again"

Finally, sometimes no answer means that a better answer is on its way or has already arrived. Or it can mean you need to rethink your request and go deeper into prayer.

When I became pastor of my own church, I had visions of glory for the church—and for myself. I was going to make that little church (150 members) a growing, dynamic congregation that impacted the city (Sacramento) for Christ. I had dreams of a large Sunday school program, an active youth program, ministries to families, outreach to the poor, and so on. And I prayed that God might make it so.

He didn't. At the end of six years of ministry, we still had a congregation of 150, and we still "muddled along." I can take a lot of the "blame" for that—I simply didn't have the gifts to lead the church as my dreams dictated.

On the other hand, I learned that our little congregation was, in fact, impacting the city of Sacramento. Our members were bringing the love and grace of Christ to neighbors and friends simply by being good neighbors and caring friends. And we were ministering to many families who found life in a small church much more to their liking. What I learned was that it wasn't size or programs that made a church, but people who loved God and cared for one another. And that was a much better answer to my prayer than if the church had tripled in size. It also taught me to focus my prayers in this more meaningful way.

There is no better way to sum up this idea than to quote the famous prayer of an unknown Confederate soldier:

> I asked for strength, that I might achieve;
>
> I was made weak, that I might learn humbly to obey. I asked for health, that I might do greater things;
>
> I was given infirmity, that I might do better things. I asked for riches, that I might be happy;
>
> I was given poverty, that I might be wise. I asked for power, that I might have the praise of men;
>
> I was given weakness, that I might feel the need for God. I asked for all things, that I might enjoy life;
>
> I was given life, that I might enjoy all things. I got nothing that I had asked for, but everything that I had hoped for. Almost despite myself, my unspoken prayers were answered;
>
> I am, among all men, most richly blessed.

Dealing With Discouragement When God Seems Silent

All well and good—at least the mind can take all this in and "understand" what the silence or the definite "no" is about. But the heart is not so easily convinced. We still sometimes feel deeply disappointed or even abandoned by God when a prayer isn't answered, or isn't answered as we wished.

This is especially true when the issues are big: a spouse has cancer and after many prayers for healing, she still dies. All your applications to medical schools have been rejected, and years of college prep seem to be going down the drain. Your business is failing after much effort and prayer, and you don't know how you are going to feed your family. At such times, we may theologize that God has some better plan for us, but in the meantime, we're left groping just to survive.

Nobody's asking you to have a stiff upper lip, to suck it up, to move on stoically. As noted elsewhere in this book, the place to begin is by telling God honestly how you feel—disappointed, angry, disillusioned, or whatever. There's no sense in pretending you are feeling anything different. And there's no sense in abandoning God or prayer—because this is the only lasting way out of your despair. You can "drug it" by drinking, or going on a spending spree, or indulging in a long vacation, even taking a vacation from God. But if you want to deal with your feelings at a deeper level, sooner or later you'll have to come back to prayer. The sooner the better.

The Least You Need to Know

- God answers prayers in a variety of ways: yes, no, wait, and try again.

- We don't always get what we ask for, but God runs things better than we do and knows what is best.

- When we pray, we still have to do our part to cooperate with God as he provides the answer.

- Sometimes God answers our prayers in unusual and better ways than we had anticipated.

- Deal with the discouragement of unanswered prayer with continual and honest prayer.

Chapter 17

Dealing With Doubts: No God

In This Chapter

◆ Why people experience God's absence

◆ The role physical fatigue plays in the spiritual life

◆ The importance of self-examination

◆ How to pray during such times

Doubts about God's willingness or ability to answer prayer are one thing; doubts about the very presence of God in prayer is another. This can be a frightening experience; if God is not present—or if he doesn't even exist— the structure and meaning of our life would collapse around us.

But experienced pray-ers know this is not a time to panic. They know that in the normal ebb and flow of prayer, there are times when God's absence is about the only thing they experience. Still, it can be unnerving, and so it's a matter worth spending some time thinking about.

"Dark Night of the Soul"

This is one of the strange aspects of prayer: Although prayer is designed to help us experience God, one experience of it is the experience of God's absence. In fact, the longer we pray and the more spiritually mature we become, the more likely it is that we will experience not just days, but even weeks and months when we feel that God is more absent than he is present.

This has been the experience of the great pray-ers of history. Look at the writings of any one of them—Teresa of Avila, John of the Cross, Madam Guyon, John Bunyan—and you'll find passages in which they describe "long periods of privation" where they find themselves locked out by God and "insensible to his mercies." It was even experienced by Jesus himself, whose intimacy with his heavenly Father can hardly be questioned: On the cross he cried out, "My God, my God, why have you forsaken me?"

The sense of God's absence is accompanied by other negative feelings: despair, hope-lessness, discouragement, listlessness, and so on. This is such a common experience, and such an integral part of the prayer life, that many prayer books devote an entire chapter to it. One writer, John of the Cross, wrote a whole book about it, which became a spiritual classic; its title has become the name by which many people call the experience: *The Dark Night of the Soul*.

Why do pray-ers—who, after all, are giving themselves to God sacrificially—have to endure such an experience? It can mean a number of things, but we'll cover the three most common.

From the Good Book

From inside the fish, Jonah prayed to the Lord, his God. He said: "In my distress I called to the Lord, and he answered me. From the depths of the grave I called for help, and you listened to my cry. You hurled me into the deep, into the very heart of the seas, and the currents swirled about me; all your waves and breakers swept over me. I said, I have been banished from your sight; yet I will look again toward your holy temple."

—Jonah, Jonah 2:1–4

Too Tired to Feel Anything

Let's start with the most common, the most overlooked, and the most easily solved cause: fatigue. We recognize early in life that fatigue has detrimental effects on us.

Irritability is the first sign that I've been pushing myself too hard and haven't been getting enough sleep. I'm impatient in grocery checkout lines; I drive hurriedly (and carelessly); I snap at my children; I yell at the dog; I scold myself for the simplest mistakes (such as forgetting my lunch or leaving the lights on).

Sometimes I can ride through the irritation and even get it under control, only to then be attacked by a low-grade depression. I lose energy. I don't have a lot of optimism about projects I'm working on. I just feel like vegging all day.

I used to spend a lot of time analyzing why exactly I was irritable or depressed. I'd write in my journal, explore my past, examine my current situation, pray for healing, and so on. I'd bludgeon myself for not being a good father and husband, for being slothful, for not living up to my beliefs.

Then one day I discovered that the problem wasn't always spiritual or emotional or moral. Sometimes it was physical: I was tired. I needed to get more sleep. I can pray until I'm blue in the knees, but it won't make a dent in irritation or depression until I get eight hours of sleep a night. The dark night of the soul is often brought on by too many late nights for the body.

Secret Sins

Another cause of the dark night of the soul is darkness within the soul. We cannot very well expect to have an ongoing experience of God while we're angry or resentful, or participating in some destructive habit, or harboring some sin. We cannot experience God if we're living in a way that is "un-Godly." You cannot enjoy the game of basketball, for instance, if you're trying to play it with a football. It just won't work.

It's not that God doesn't want to have anything to do with us unless we're perfect. Far from it. But we cannot simply wallow in anger and sin and try to pretend it doesn't matter—which usually means not even mentioning it in prayer. We don't have to wait until we're morally unstuck before we can experience God in prayer. We simply have to acknowledge in prayer what a mess we've made of things.

Affliction

Simone Weil, a twentieth-century writer and mystic, put it this way: "Affliction makes God appear to be absent for a time, more absent than a dead man, more absent than light in the utter darkness of a cell. A kind of horror submerges the whole soul. During this absence there is nothing to love."

It doesn't take much to get us spiritually off-center. A project at work fails. A friend moves far away. An argument erupts with your spouse. At such times we realize afresh how we depend on an orderly and good life to bolster our spiritual feelings. When things go wrong, we just don't feel spiritual.

And when we're dealt a major blow—unemployment, death, disease, severe depression—we can really sink into profound spiritual discouragement. Though some people feel God's presence more than ever during a crisis, others feel completely abandoned and ask, "Why, God, have you abandoned me?"

So What's Going On?

In truth, God cannot abandon us any more than we can be abandoned by the air around us. But the experience of pray-ers suggests that he does at times withdraw a sense of his presence—which, from our point of view, is devastating enough. Yes, I'm saying that although we bring this upon ourselves sometimes (through fatigue and sin), there are times when God allows—and perhaps even arranges—this experience.

So why would God, who has designed prayer so that we might become intimate with him, sometimes withdraw himself from us as we pray?

Philosopher Søren Kierkegaard had this take on the experience: "He who dreams must be awakened, and the deeper the man is who slumbers, or the deeper he slumbers, the more important it is that he be awakened, and the more powerfully must he be awakened." In other words, our lives fall into easy patterns, and this is also true of prayer. Sometimes the only way to deepen our intimacy with God is to experience the distance of God. Again, let's listen to Kierkegaard in his *Christian Discourses*, who was very wise on this point:

> Then comes affliction to awaken the dreamer, affliction which like a storm tears off the blossoms, affliction which nevertheless does not bereave of hope, but recruits hope. Affliction is able to drown out every earthly voice, that is precisely what it is to do, but the voice of eternity within a man it cannot drown .... When by the aid of affliction all irrelevant voices are brought to silence, it can be heard, this voice within.

Sometimes the experience of God can be so pleasurable that we imagine that the joy we experience is God himself. When that happens, God withdraws himself to show that he is more than the emotion we experience, and that he is to be loved beyond and behind the emotion. Evelyn Underhill called this the "great negation," and said it was "the great sorting house of the spiritual life."

> **Snapshots of Answered Prayers**
>
> A synagogue ruler had great faith when he stated that Jesus could resurrect his daughter who had just died. Jesus, in turn, raised her from the dead in Matthew 9:18–26.

The Way Back

So what is to be done when God seems absent and the idea of loving God or pursuing the life of prayer is about the last thing you feel like doing?

The advice of the great men and women of prayer seems to be this: Keep loving, keep praying. This is not cheap advice as much as it is spiritual survival.

In terms of love, Simone Weil, in her book *Waiting for God*, said it best:

> What is terrible is that if, in this darkness, where there is nothing to love, the soul ceases to love, God's absence becomes final. The soul has to go on loving in the emptiness, or at least to go on wanting to love, though it may only be with at infinitesimal part of itself. Then, one day, God will come to show himself to this soul and to reveal the beauty of the world to it …. But if the soul stops loving, it falls, even in this life, into something almost equivalent to hell.

Sometimes this means persevering in praise and adoration, as strange as that may seem at such times. Joni Eareckson Tada was paralyzed in a swimming accident in her teens. She's a woman who knows affliction and the absence of God, and in her book *Secret Strength for Those Who Search* she writes eloquently on the need to persevere at such times:

> We will be compelled to voice our words of praise firmly and precisely, even as our logic screams that God has no idea what he's doing. Most of the verses written about praise in God's word were penned by men and women who faced crushing heartaches, injustice, treachery, slander, and scores of other intolerable situations.

This loving of God during affliction will take some unusual forms. It doesn't necessarily mean a quiet and humble acceptance of anything that comes your way. This is certainly not the way the Psalmist went through such a period:

O Lord, I cry out to you.

I will keep on pleading day by day.

O Lord, why do you reject me?

Why do you turn your face away from me?

I have been sickly and close to death since my youth.

I stand helpless and desperate before your terrors.

—Psalm 88:13–15

There is an Old Testament story about Jacob wrestling all night with God (see 32:24–31). In the same way, sometimes we are called upon to wrestle with God to "force" him to bless us.

Of course, we can never actually force God to do anything. He's all powerful and we're not. Nor do we have to overpower him in order to get him to love us. But just as a human father sometimes asks a child to do more work before rewarding her, so God sometimes asks us to dig deeper into our souls and emotions—requiring more fervent prayer—before he will reveal his love to us. The difference is this: many human fathers make their children *earn* their reward; our heavenly Father is merely helping us identify those issues that really are important for us—those we really wrestle with inside and with him. He also wants us to recognize how utterly gracious his love is—not something one can take for granted nor order up with a snap of the fingers.

Missionary Gracia Burnham, who was held captive by terrorists in the Philippines for more than a year and whose husband was killed during the rescue, wrote in her book *In the Presence of My Enemies* about her ongoing questions: "Sometimes I wonder, *Why did Martin die when everyone was praying he wouldn't? Why does Scripture lead you to believe that if you pray a certain way, you'll get what you pray for?* People all over the world were praying that we'd both get out alive, but we didn't."

She hasn't had all her questions answered, but by perseverance, she has gained some peace about the most important issue. She wrote, "I used to have this concept of what God is like, and how life's supposed to be because of that. But in the jungle, I learned I don't know as much about God as I thought I did. I don't have him in a theological box anymore. What I do know is that God is God—and I'm not. The world's in a mess because of sin, not God. Some awful things may happen to me, but God does what is right. And he makes good out of bad situations."

Hanging On

Through all this, we will discover more of God and more of ourselves. When we come to the other side, our intimacy with God will be that much deeper.

A trivial example from everyday life can illustrate this. I love to dabble in computer programming, at least at a modest level. I'll write little routines that allow me to do repetitive functions with a keystroke. For instance, at work I have a program that allows me to instantly call up addresses. The process used to take 10 to 15 keystrokes; now it takes three.

But just when I'm feeling pretty confident about my abilities and feeling pretty good about computers, I'll mess up. I'll write the program incorrectly, and the routine simply will not run. I'll go through all the usual checks to see what's going on, but nothing will fix the problem. This is the dark night of the computer programmer— it's very frustrating and discouraging.

What it forces me to do, though, is to go deeper. I have to take out a manual and read more closely and carefully than ever about what certain commands do and in what order they need to be written. Invariably, I learn more about programming and gain an even deeper appreciation of my computer.

Prayer is a tad more complex and rich than computer programming, and lessons learned from a dark night of the soul sometimes are not so easily discerned. But the same fundamental dynamic is at work: Frustration and loneliness are often the paths of deeper peace and joy. Perseverance and love—the continued pursuit of God— are not the happiest of paths to have to trod sometimes, but they are the most trustworthy.

From the Good Book

Though the fig tree does not bud and there are no grapes on the vines, though the olive crop fails and the fields produce no food, though there are no sheep in the pen and no cattle in the stalls, yet I will rejoice in the Lord, I will be joyful in God, my Savior. The sovereign Lord is my strength; he makes my feet like the feet of a deer, he enables me to go on the heights.

—Habakkuk, Habakkuk 3:17–19

The Least You Need to Know

◆ Negative feelings accompany God's perceived absence, but he only wants to draw us to a new level of closeness to him.

◆ Sometimes doubts about God's presence can be dealt with simply by getting a good night's sleep.

◆ God seems absent sometimes because we, by our sins, are blocking him out.

◆ As we hang on in the midst of discomfort, we learn more about God and ourselves and find the path to peace and joy.

Part 4

The Big Book on the Big Issues

Through the centuries, people of prayer have discovered that man does not live by extemporaneous prayer alone. They have also discovered that certain books and practices do wonders for one's prayer life. In this part, we'll take a look at the most important and enduring resources in *the* prayer book for Christians: the Bible. We'll look at how to pray two of the most important types of literature in the Bible, and we'll look at some of the most important prayers of the Bible, which happen to be about the most important issues facing human beings.

Chapter 18

Praying the Psalms

In This Chapter

♦ The origin and purpose of the Psalms

♦ How the Psalms are organized

♦ How to read a Psalm intelligently

♦ How to pray the Psalms

You wouldn't imagine that prayers and songs written 2,000 years ago could have relevance today. They were written by men (literally) living in a pre-industrial, agriculturally based, authoritarian monarchy (often militaristic and vengeful) and, naturally, who had no comprehension of life in a fast-paced, technological, egalitarian, democratic, and relativistic age. Yet people continue to discover—as they have discovered in each century—that the Psalms are by far the most meaningful and relevant prayer resource we have.

Jesus often quoted or referred to Psalms; for instance, at his temptation (Matthew 4:6), in the Sermon on the Mount (Matthew 5:7, 35, 7:23), and at the crucifixion (Luke 23:34; Matthew 27:46). It is likely that the first Christian congregations used selections from the book in their public services. Skip to the fifth century, and we hear the theologian Augustine calling the book the "language of devotion." Jump to the 1500s, and we find Martin Luther calling the Psalms "a Bible in miniature." In the 1990s, poet Kathleen Norris "fell in love" with the Psalms because it became clear to her "that the world they depict is not really so different from our own."

What Are These Things?

The Psalms are universal literature, which means, among other things, that you can simply open your Bible and begin reading and gain something—quite a bit, actually.

> **Prayer Pearls**
>
> I don't know of a single foreign product that enters this country untaxed except the answer to prayer.
>
> —Mark Twain, American author and humorist

If you're like me, that's probably what you'll do at first. I've never been very patient when it comes to background and introductory stuff. If that's your tendency, you may want to spend some time reading, pondering, and praying the Psalms until you've run into enough questions to motivate you to discover more. That's what this chapter is about: getting a little deeper into the Psalms so that they can be read and prayed at even more meaningful levels.

First things first: What exactly are Psalms? Psalms are simply songs, and "The Psalms" is a collection of 150 songs, many of which were used in public worship in ancient Israel. In Hebrew they are called *Tehillim*, meaning "praises" or "songs of praise." This gives some indication of the main theme of the Psalms.

Though many people think of them as all coming from the hand of King David, only about half claim to be written by him. Others were written by temple musicians (with names such as Asaph and Ethan), and a few by David's son (the famous King Solomon); one is attributed to Moses (Psalm 90). In spite of the fact that they were written mostly by the elite, these Psalms speak to people of all stations of life.

They also speak to people in all situations. Some were written during the most glorious era of Israel's history (the reigns of David and Solomon, 1003 B.C.–930 B.C.). But many were written after Israel had been conquered—first by the Assyrians (722 B.C.) and then by the Babylonians (587 B.C.)—deported, and scattered over the Middle East. This event, called the exile, devastated the faith of Israel. Yet, the people continued to pray, and one way they did so was by writing the Psalms.

Getting Around

You'll notice as you begin reading the Psalms that they are divided into five books, and each book ends with a Psalm of praise (also called a "doxology"). As far as we can tell, here is how the books came together:

- Book 1: Psalms 1–41; Compiled during the reign of King David

- Book 2: Psalms 42–72; Compiled and added during the reign of King Solomon

- Book 3: Psalms 73–89; Compiled and added during the exile

- Book 4: Psalms 90–106; Compiled and added during the exile

- Book 5: Psalms 107–150 Compiled and added after the return from exile

This doesn't mean that the themes of the Psalms arise out of the period when they were added. For example, one of the most eloquent expressions of exiled Israel (Psalm 137) is in the after-the-exile section. Likewise, prayers by David (including Psalm 86) are found in the part compiled during the exile.

Yet, knowing when a Psalm was added sometimes can help us see new layers of meaning. For example, after realizing the devastating effects of exile, we can appreciate the sentiments of Psalm 126:

> When the Lord restored his exiles to Jerusalem,
>
> it was like a dream!
>
> We were filled with laughter,
>
> and we sang for joy.

A Psalm like this, then, can be used in prayer to express thanks today to God for delivering us from a crisis, or it can be used as a prayer of hope as we remember that God is a God who rescues.

> **Snapshots of Answered Prayers**
>
> A crowd begged Jesus to heal a deaf and dumb man. He spit on his own fingers, touched the man's tongue, and looking up to heaven he commanded, "Be opened." The man then heard and spoke plainly (Mark 7: 32–36).

Psalms can also be organized thematically:

- *History:* These Psalms (such as 14, 44, and 46–48) rehearse the key moments in Israel's history and recount God's intervention.

- *Appeals:* These Psalms (including 54, 55, 58, and 59) usually ask for vindication against one's own or God's enemies.

- *Hope:* Psalms such as 2, 8, 110, and 132 express hope for a coming deliverer or messiah.

- *Confession:* These Psalms (such as 32 and 51) express sorrow for sin and wish for reconciliation.

- *Praise:* Psalms such as 33, 103, and 139 extol God's goodness.

How to Read a Psalm

If we can understand the nature of Hebrew poetry, we'll get more out of reading and praying the Psalms. The Psalms do not rhyme, and they do not employ the intense metaphors of modern poetry. Instead, they rely on parallelism to express ideas.

Parallelism is merely repeating or furthering the same idea in new form. For example, Psalm 95 begins like this:

> Come, let us sing to the Lord!

> Let us give a joyous shout to the rock of our salvation!

"Sing" is parallel with "give a joyous shout," and "the Lord" is parallel (that is, similar in thought) with "the rock of our salvation." The Psalmist here is merely repeating an idea.

Sometimes the parallelism is a matter of contrast. Again in Psalm 95 we read:

> He [God] owns the depths of the earth,

> and even the mightiest mountains are his.

Here "He owns" and "are his" are parallel, but "depths of the earth" and "the mightiest mountains" are in contrast. The larger point, however, is the same: There ain't nothin' that isn't God's.

Sometimes the parallelism furthers the original thought. In Psalm 103, we read this:

> The Lord is merciful and gracious;

> He is slow to get angry and full of unfailing love.

"He is slow to get angry and full of unfailing love" fills out the meaning of "The Lord is merciful and gracious."

Then there are larger patterns, where entire sections can be parallel or the structure of the Psalm itself might follow an A-B-A-B pattern or an A-B-B-A pattern.

The point here is not to become a literary critic of the Psalms. If you understand parallelism as a poetic tool, though, you won't be tempted to try to find profound meaning in each phrase. Instead, we should let the parallels roll over us like ocean waves, each powerful in its own way; each washing over us the grace of God, but each fundamentally the same.

From the Good Book

And when you pray, do not be like the hypocrites, for they love to pray standing in the synagogues and on the street corners to be seen by men. I tell you the truth, they have received their reward in full. But when you pray, go into your room, close the door, and pray to your Father, who is unseen. Then your Father, who sees what is done in secret, will reward you.

—Jesus, Matthew 6:5–6

Devotional Themes

One way to pray the Psalms is to pick and choose, depending on your mood, needs, and desires. Many topical guides to the Psalms exist, including this one, which I modified from the *Revell Bible Dictionary*:

- Anger: 4, 17, 28, 36, 109
- Anxiety/fear: 3, 11, 27, 46, 49, 91, 121, 139, 146
- Direction: 13, 25, 37, 89, 119, 146
- Disappointment: 16, 92, 102, 130
- Discouragement: 12, 42, 55, 86, 107, 142
- Injustice: 7, 9, 10, 17, 35, 52, 56, 94, 109
- Insignificance: 8, 23, 86, 121, 139
- Joy: 33, 47, 63, 84, 96, 97, 98, 100, 148
- Knowing God: 8, 19, 29, 65, 89, 103, 111, 136, 145, 147
- Loneliness: 3, 13, 17, 25, 27, 69, 91
- Patience: 4, 5, 37, 89, 123
- Reassurance: 1, 15, 18, 23, 26, 112, 121, 128
- Safety, security: 34, 84, 91
- Sickness: 22, 23, 41, 116
- Sorrow, grief: 6, 31, 71, 77, 94, 123
- Thankfulness: 30, 33, 34, 40, 66, 89, 96, 113, 136
- Trouble: 10, 86, 90, 94, 126, 138, 142
- Weakness: 4, 23, 62, 70, 102, 138

The advantage of a topical approach is obvious: We can go directly to a Psalm that can speak to our situation, or one that helps us express to God more closely what we're feeling. On the other hand, we limit the ability of the Psalms to transform us if we pick at them as we would a box of chocolates. The Psalms are a full-course meal, and some of them we have to develop a taste for—and that takes practice.

Week by Week

That brings us to another way to pray the Psalms: reading them through in some orderly fashion, day by day. Many monastic orders do this sort of thing—and have for centuries—reading through all 150 every few weeks or months.

> **Prayer Pearls**
>
> Prayer ... the very highest energy of which the mind is capable.
> —Samuel Taylor Coleridge, English poet

Some people simply read the Psalms all the way through in order, reading maybe five per day (which will get you through the Psalms in a month). Others read by a plan that sorts the Psalms according to the day of the week or season of the church year (see Chapter 35). *The Book of Common Prayer* (which we'll look at in Chapter 29) has suggested Psalm readings that move through the Psalms in seven weeks.

Here is a pattern suggested in the Lutheran *Book of Worship* (1978) for week-by-week reading. (It also offers a different schedule for the church seasons of Advent, Christmas, Lent, and Easter.)

	Sun.	Mon.	Tues.	Wed.	Thurs.	Fri.	Sat.
Week 1							
Morning	150	145	146	147:1–12	147:13–21	148	149
	103	5	42	89:1–18	97	51	104
Evening	117	82	102	1	16	142	138
	139	29	133	33	62	65	98
Week 2							
Morning	150	145	146	147:1–12	147:13–21	148	149
	19	135	123	15	36	130	56
Evening	81	97	30	48	80	32	138
	113	112	86	4	27	139	98

	Sun.	Mon.	Tues.	Wed.	Thurs.	Fri.	Sat.
Week 3							
Morning	150	145	146	147:1–12	147:13–21	148	149
	67	57	54	65	143	88	122
Evening	46	85	28	125	81	6	100
	93	47	99	91	116	20	63
Week 4							
Morning	150	145	146	147:1–12	147:13–21	148	149
	108	62	12	96	116	84	63
Evening	66	73	36	132	26	25	125
	23	9	7	134	130	40	90

Psalms 145–150 are sometimes called the *laudate* ("praise") Psalms, and thus it is appropriate to pray one of them each morning of the week.

Praying the Psalms

There are a number of ways to "pray" the Psalms. Here are three suggestions:

1. **Read and meditate.** You simply read a Psalm a time or two (or three) and reflect on its meaning. For example, I might read Psalm 27, which begins like this:

   The Lord is my light and salvation

   —so why should I be afraid?

   The Lord protects me from danger

   —so why should I tremble?

   I would reflect on the areas of my life in which I am afraid and then ask God to help me trust in his protection.

2. **Adopt the Psalm as your own prayer.** Try to say it as if you are the one praising God, seeking help, or arguing with God.

   This is pretty easy when you happen to be in the mood that the Psalm expresses. When I'm in despair, Psalm 88 is just the ticket: "O Lord, why do you reject me? Why do you turn your face away from me?" Or, when I'm especially thankful for a return of good health, Psalm 30 expresses my feelings well: "O Lord my God, I cried out to you for help, and you restored my health."

And sometimes when I pray the Psalm as if it were *my* prayer, it can help me feel something I'd like to feel. This is especially true of praise. A lot of days, I simply don't feel all that thankful to God, and yet the logical part of me knows that I'm basking in too many blessings to count. Sometimes praying a Psalm of praise can help me feel the way I'm thinking:

Praise the Lord!

Praise the Lord, I tell myself.

I will praise the Lord as long as I live.

I will sing praises to my God even with my dying breath.

—Psalm 146:1–2

3. **Bask in the poetry of the Psalm.** Here the idea is not to understand or use the Psalm for our own ends, but to let it do some work on us. At a minimum, the Psalms are sublime poetry; at their highest, they are the word of God. As such, they have a power to evoke in us thoughts and feelings we were not aware of.

Prayer Hotline

Sometimes I just try to read the Psalm and let its words wash over me. I simply read it aloud over and over, trying to put the analytical part of my mind to rest, trying simply to experience the beauty of the poetry and the wonder of the words.

Whatever method we use, we are wise not to force ourselves into some sublime state of mind, or to beat ourselves up when praying the Psalms "just doesn't work." Some days it will "work" and other days it won't. There will be days when no matter how you prepare yourself, the Psalms will just sit on the page and remain abstract and meaningless. Let it be for that day. The Psalm is still doing its work on you, just as a meal you don't particularly enjoy is still sustaining your body. To be sure, there will be other days when you pray the Psalms and you feel you are in the very presence of heaven.

The Difficult Psalms

This is all well and good when reading the glorious Psalms of praise or the Psalms of deep insight. But what do you do when you run across verses like this?

Let my enemies be destroyed

by the very evil they have planned for me.

> Let burning coals fall down on their heads,
>
> or throw them into the fire,
>
> or into deep pits from which they cannot escape.
>
> —Psalm 140:9–10

Or, worse:

> O Babylon, you will be destroyed.
>
> Happy is the one who pays you back
>
> for what you have done to us.
>
> Happy is the one who takes your babies
>
> and smashes them against the rocks.
>
> —Psalm 137:8–9

These are hardly moods we want aroused in us—and yet it is not difficult to find such angry and vengeful passages in the Psalms. How are we to pray these?

We pray them as honest expressions of the human heart. I may pretend that I never feel such hatred or ever wish violence on others, but the fact is, there are times when I do. If I'm angry at a co-worker, I may not want burning coals to fall upon him, but I have imagined him getting humiliated in front of our publisher or losing his job. And, I have to admit, when I'm really angry, there are moments when flashes of violence pop into my head.

Passages such as these keep the Psalms from becoming one more bit of pious literature. Instead, they are honest prayers of real people experiencing the myriad emotions life arouses in us. If you're interested in merely becoming religious, avoid the Psalms. If you're interested in becoming more deeply human as well as more honestly and vitally connected to God, praying the Psalms will help.

Prayer Hotline

If I'm seriously angry, I may use such a Psalm as a personal expression of how I'm really feeling. If the anger is but a distant memory, I'll use the Psalm as a way of recalling that, yes, sometimes I am like this.

The Least You Need to Know

- The Psalms can be considered poems, prayers, and songs—because they are all three in one.

- The Psalms are divided into five "books," and each book ends with a Psalm of praise.

- The Psalms contain themes that express the major needs, struggles, and joys within human experience.

- There are Psalms to match all our major moods, and we can genuinely express our emotions of the moment to God.

Chapter 19

Praying the Gospels

In This Chapter

- The unique aspects of the four Gospels
- How reading the Gospels can benefit your prayer life
- Prominent themes of the Gospels
- How to use the stories in the Gospels as guides for prayer

It's not much of a leap to read a Psalm, which is already a prayer, and then adapt it and use it to pray today. It's a little harder to imagine using stories as resources for prayer. Yet, biblical stories, especially those found in the four Gospels—Matthew, Mark, Luke, and John—offer some of the richest material for prayer. The key is learning how to use them as material for prayer.

Before we can use these beneficially in prayer, though, we need to understand the nature of the material called "Gospel." Again, if you're not much interested in background material, skip right to the section "Big Themes."

So, What's a "Gospel"?

In older Bible versions, the first verse of the Gospel of Mark reads, "The beginning of the Gospel of Jesus Christ, the Son of God"—as if the word *gospel* was the technical name of the work that was about to follow. Well, it wasn't, but it now is.

Behind the word *gospel* stands a Greek word (the four Gospels were first written in Greek) that means "good news." What Mark was really saying, and what most modern translations say, is "Here begins the good news about Jesus, the messiah, the son of God."

From the Good Book

Keep on asking, and you will be given what you ask for. Keep on looking, and you will find. Keep on knocking, and the door will be open.

—Jesus, in Matthew 7:7

Nonetheless, *Gospel* has stuck and refers not just to Mark's work about Jesus—it also refers to that of Matthew, Luke, and John. These are ancient biographies, all written in the first century, that attempt to inform readers about the life, words, and meaning of Jesus. Though other "gospels" were written, none were considered reliable accounts. Since the earliest days, Christians have used these four to recall the story of Jesus.

I've called these "biographies"—and they are—but you'll run into roadblocks right off if you think they are like modern biographies. If you understand how the Gospels differ from modern biographies, you'll be able to benefit from them more.

Modern biographies are anxious to explore the subject's childhood and youth to discover early influences, decisions, and turning points that determined the course of a person's life. Our age has very much been influenced by Sigmund Freud and others, and we're fascinated with childhood.

Ancient biographies are not. The ancients believed that personality and character were given at birth and merely were manifested in life. If the Gospels focus on an early incident, they do so simply to reveal character. For example, the only childhood story of Jesus recorded in the Bible shows a 12-year-old Jesus instructing religious teachers, who are impressed with the child's wisdom. (Luke 2:41–52)

Modern biographies are also strictly chronological. For the most part, they record the key events in the subject's life in the order in which they happen.

Prayer Pearls

He prays well who is so absorbed with God that he does not know what he is praying.

—Francis de Sales, medieval devotional writer

Ancient biographies are not all that interested in the order of events. Naturally, they have to acknowledge the order of the large events—for Jesus' biographers, that means they recognized that his birth must come before his ministry, and that his ministry must come before his death. But ancient writers were more interested in grouping their material thematically to show the essential character traits of their subject.

When you read the four Gospels, then, you're going to find that each writer orders material differently. This is not because some were good historians and others weren't, but simply because each ordered his material to reveal something unique about Jesus.

For example, the Gospel of Matthew organizes Jesus' teaching into five parts and scatters these five blocks of teaching throughout the Gospel. Matthew is trying to show that Jesus is the new Moses, the new lawgiver. He's imitating the pattern found in the first five books of the Hebrew scriptures, which in Judaism are together called the "Law of Moses."

Each Gospel writer collects his material—incidents, parables, and teachings—in this way. When we read the Gospels, we are wise not to begin with modern assumptions (trying to figure out decisive moments, or seeking to outline a strict order of events), but instead, let each Gospel writer tell the story in his own way.

To Each His Own

So what exactly is the emphasis of each writer? I'd like to look at this briefly not because I want to turn you into a New Testament scholar, but to help you appreciate more deeply each Gospel as you read and pray it. Let's begin by looking at the first three Gospels, which are very similar in style and content. They likely all used a similar source in writing their accounts, and they supplemented that account with their own research.

Tradition says that Matthew was one of the original disciples, and many think he's the same guy as Levi the tax collector (Matthew 10:2–4 and Mark 2:13–14). A second-century writer named Papias said that Matthew "wrote down the oracles [sayings of Jesus] in the Hebrew language." If this tradition is accurate, we're today reading a version edited and passed on by some of Matthew's disciples, because this Gospel seems to have been written about 40 years after Jesus' death and resurrection.

Papias was certainly right about one thing: the Hebrew, or Jewish, nature of the material. Matthew, more than the others, seems to be written for early Jewish Christians and tries to show that Jesus is the Jewish messiah and that he is the fulfillment of Old Testament prophecy.

A typical example occurs early on. When the wise men come to visit the infant Jesus, they quote an Old Testament prophecy:

> O Bethlehem of Judah,
>
> you are not just a lowly village in Judah,

For a ruler will come from you

who will be the shepherd for my people Israel.

—Matthew 2:6

The Gospel of Mark is said to be written by a man named John Mark, who was an early companion of the apostle Paul and, later, of the apostle Peter. Papias calls Mark "the interpreter of Peter," who wrote down Peter's recollections about Jesus.

Mark's audience seems to have been Roman—that is, non-Jewish—and is designed to show that Jesus is the Son of God, a person of swift action and supreme power. He doesn't include nearly the amount of teaching as does Matthew, and his Gospel is fast-paced and takes about a half-hour to read straight through.

Luke was a physician and an early convert who accompanied Paul on some of his journeys. He also painstakingly interviewed many eyewitnesses of Jesus' life in preparing his work ("Having carefully investigated all of these accounts from the beginning …", as he put it).

Like Mark, Luke writes for a non-Jewish, Greco-Roman audience. He's interested in Jesus not just in his divine nature, but especially as humanity in perfection. At the same time, Luke's is the most personal Gospel, in which we get a glimpse into Jesus' intimate relationships, especially with women and children. Luke likes to highlight the miraculous work of the Holy Spirit in the life of Jesus, and he records more of Jesus' teachings on prayer than the other Gospels.

Now for Something Completely Different

The Gospel of John is in a league of its own. You get this sense after reading but a few verses. Where Matthew, Mark, and Luke try to set Jesus into his times as soon as possible, John begins like this:

> In the beginning the Word [Jesus] already existed. He was with God, and he was God. He was in the beginning with God. He created everything there is. Nothing exists that he didn't make. Life itself was in him, and this life gives light to everyone. The light shines in darkness, and the darkness can never extinguish it.

Tradition claims that John was not only one of the 12 disciples, but the "beloved disciple," one with whom Jesus was especially intimate. But his Gospel seems less interested in intimate details than giving a more cosmic view of Christ. Mark begins his work by recording Jesus' baptism, Matthew and Luke begin with Jesus' birth—and John begins at the beginning of the universe: "in the beginning."

John's Gospel was probably written late in the first century, much later than the other Gospels, so it's not likely that we have his original words, but his words transcribed and edited by a group of his disciples.

Jesus is "the Word," the "water of life" (John 4:4–26), the "resurrection and life" (John 5:19–47), the "bread of life" (John 6:26–59), the "light of the world" (John 8:12), and so on. Thus, John is more interested in the spiritual truth of Jesus, not the mere recording of chronological detail (although there are many passages that, in terms of history, are more detailed than the other Gospels). And thus John's Gospel is rich with symbolism and strong contrasts (light and dark, truth and falsehood, love and hate), and belief plays a large role in the book.

Again, this emphasis, as with the other three Gospels, is significant in terms of prayer. If you read through a Gospel prayerfully (more of that in a bit), you'll want to have some idea of the overall theme of the Gospel you're praying through.

Big Themes

No matter which Gospel you pray through, you're going to find certain themes that arise time and again. If these are the type of issues you'd like to explore, praying through the Gospels is a practice to take up. Here are eight of the more prominent themes:

1. **Jesus.** The Gospels are first and foremost about the person of Jesus, as seen most clearly in the opening of the Gospel of Mark: "Here begins the good news about Jesus …." The Gospels are primarily concerned to reveal who he is, what he taught, and his continuing significance for every age.

2. **The kingdom of God.** This is the overarching theme of Jesus' teaching. He begins his ministry with the message, "At last the time has come. The kingdom of God is near! Turn from your sins and believe the good news." (Mark 1:15)

   Jesus is referring to the reign of God, which has a present and a future dimension. In terms of this life, Jesus' teaching about the kingdom highlights the truth that we're in good hands: God is in charge of all that goes on, even when his good purposes remain mysterious. This also implies that a new way of life and a new set of morals must characterize the citizens of the kingdom.

The kingdom also refers to the future reign of God, when history will come to a perfect conclusion, when all sin and death, crying, and pain will be eliminated.

3. **Commitment to Jesus.** Because Jesus is the Lord of this kingdom, the Gospels naturally spend a lot of time emphasizing the need for commitment to his ways and to his person.

4. **Service to others.** It's not a religious life that the Gospels emphasize, but a life lived in the world for the world. So don't start praying through the Gospels unless you're willing to spend time meditating on your need to reach out to others.

5. **Money.** The Gospels spend a lot of words recording Jesus' teachings about money. It appears that Jesus thinks how we spend it says a great deal about our commitments—an uncomfortable but necessary subject of prayer.

6. **Prayer.** If many parts of the Bible help us pray, then the Gospels, more than many others, teach us *how* to pray. Many passages talk about the role of faith and perseverance in prayer.

7. **Love.** If the summary of Jesus' teaching is to love God and to love your neighbor, this is also the summary of the Gospels. If you want to grow in love, then the Gospels are the place where you'll see how better to do this.

8. **Atonement.** Naturally, the theme toward which all the Gospels move is the death of Christ, which makes possible reconciliation with God. In one sense, each of them is a mere retelling of the suffering and death of Christ (called "the passion"), with an extended prologue of Christ's ministry. The passion narratives actually take up close to one-half of each Gospel.

Each of these themes can help us have breakthroughs in prayer, but the atonement does this more than most since it deals with a core issue: our relationship with God.

The famous nineteenth-century evangelist D. L. Moody talks about a judge for whom Jesus' death was the thing that allowed him to find release from his sins. One night, when his wife was at prayer meeting, he began to grow uneasy and miserable. He was not a Christian at the time, and he did not know what the matter was. Finally, he went to bed before his wife returned home.

But he could not sleep all night. He got up early, told his wife that he was going to skip breakfast, and went to his office. He told his clerks to take the day off, and he shut himself in his office. "I kept growing more and more miserable," he said, "and finally I got down and asked God to forgive my sins."

He had heard that prayer, especially this sort of prayer, should be said 'for Jesus' sake'—not as a magic incantation, but as a sign of humble dependence on the one who came and died for our sins. But he balked at saying, "for Jesus' sake." He had been a Unitarian and he did not believe in the atonement. But he did start praying. "God forgive my sins." Still no answer came. At last in desperation, he cried, "Oh God, for Christ's sake forgive my sins." It was then, he said, that he "found peace at once."

Reading the Gospels Prayerfully

There are two ways to use the Gospels to enrich your prayer life. In the first, the left side of the brain (the rational part) plays a larger role. This method I've called meditation. It's a matter of trying to understand a passage as a literary work in which the author is trying to make a point. To read meditatively is simply to try to discern the author's point and then to ask appropriate questions about one's own life in self-examination. (See Chapter 11 for more on this.)

Let's say I'm reading Mark 4:35–41: Jesus and his disciples are in a boat when a "fierce storm" arises, in which "high waves began to break into the boat." All the while, Mark notes, Jesus was sleeping in the back of the boat—until the frantic disciples wake him: "Teacher, don't you even care that we are going to drown?"

Mark continues, "When he woke up, he rebuked the wind and said to the water, 'Quiet down!' Suddenly the wind stopped, and there was a great calm. And he asked them, 'Why are you so afraid? Do you still not have faith in me?' And they were filled with awe and said among themselves, 'Who is this man, that even the wind and waters obey him?'"

I would begin by analyzing the various purposes of the passage: to show the power of Christ, and to teach the importance of trust in the midst of fear. I would pick one of the themes—let's say, trust—and ask myself in what areas of my life I remain afraid, and in what ways I find it difficult to trust Christ. Let's say that I was worried about my finances, that they were in a mess and that I simply found it hard to trust that Christ was present and caring about this situation. I would then pray for Christ's help: to be aware of his presence, to trust him to watch over me even when a financial storm was pelting me.

There is another way to deal with stories. Rather than stand apart from the passage—analyzing it, dissecting it, figuring it out—I could enter into the passage and experience it, and let it figure me out.

Prayer Hotline _____

One key to reading a Bible passage prayerfully is to look for repeated words and phrases, or parallel ideas of synonyms. The biblical writers were deliberate in what they were trying to communicate, and if an idea is emphasized in this way, it's probably worth paying attention to.

Taking the same passage used previously, I might imagine myself as one of the disciples. I would try to put myself in the boat, to watch the storm clouds approaching, feel the wind whip over the surface of the lake, watch whitecaps form, feel the spray and then a full wave, feel the boat rock. I'd try to feel the fear, and then I'd try to imagine what I'd most fear losing in life.

Then I'd hear the strong words of Christ, feel the wind die suddenly, note the waves calm—and feel the wonder and peace of God's power.

I can't say what exactly I'd "learn" from this because the associations would move freely back and forth from the present to the past and back to the present. The image of losing my job might rise in my mind while I'm on the boat, or maybe the feeling I had when I lost a friend to drowning. In any case, this method has a way of bringing up all sorts of odd and wonderful connections that can then become a part of more rational prayer.

I might, for example, become aware of how much I still am affected by my friend's drowning, along with residual guilt that I never paid him proper respects. I'd include whatever thoughts and emotions and recollections that arose in my prayer.

There are many more ways to pray the Gospels (see Chapter 11, and that chapter's last section on "*Lectio Divina*" for another suggestion). Nor will every passage elicit equally "useful" prayer material. But the Gospels have endured as prayer resources precisely because they are able to speak to the human soul at a depth that transcends every age and culture.

The Least You Need to Know

- The Gospels are the four stories of the life of Christ and represent "the good news" of what he has done for us.

- As you pray through the Gospels, you need to know that the good news of the kingdom will also make some demands on you.

- Don't be surprised if you find a lot of references to themes like money, prayer, love, and Jesus in the Gospels.

- As we pray, we begin by analyzing its purposes and personally entering into the reality of the stories.

Chapter 20

Shaping the Future

In This Chapter

- One of the most instructive and humorous stories—and a great example of prayer—in the Bible
- God's subtle appearances
- How in prayer we can become co-creators of history
- The limits of "Thy will be done"

It's time to get more specific now. Instead of looking at entire sections of the Bible to see how they can enhance prayer, for the next few chapters, we'll focus on some of the most well-known prayers of the Bible. This will help us see how dynamic and varied prayer can be, and it will teach us better how to pray through a variety of issues that most concern us.

We begin with one of the most common human concerns and one of the earliest biblical prayers. This concern has to do with the shape of the future: Is God's will set in stone? What role do we play in shaping our future? Do we simply submit to God's plan, or do we help shape it? This is something that a man named Abraham had to figure out. His encounter with God as recorded in Genesis 18 is one of the most humorous and instructive encounters in the Bible.

Subtle Arrival

The story begins innocently enough: "One day about noon, as Abraham was sitting at the entrance to his tent, he suddenly noticed three men standing nearby."

Abraham greeted his visitors and, with impeccable Middle Eastern manners, offered them hospitality: "Rest in the shade of this tree while my servants get some water to wash your feet," he said. "Let me prepare some food to refresh you. Please stay a while before continuing on your journey."

What Abraham didn't know at that moment was that he was entertaining the Lord. We readers are let in on the secret right away, though. The writer helps us understand right off that "the Lord appeared again to Abraham while he was camped near the oak grove belonging to Mamre" (about 17 miles south of Jerusalem). As the story unfolds, though, it becomes clearer to Abraham: "The men said" and "the Lord said" are used interchangeably, and we are given to understand that in some mysterious way, God appeared to Abraham through these Bedouin visitors.

This is a key point in prayer. Prayer is an encounter with God, and as such, it is not confined to those private moments when we are bowed in prayer. God will come to meet us at the oddest times—in the middle of the day while we're daydreaming outside our tents—and in the most mundane forms, such as through other people.

Early in college, I believed I had received a "call" to become a minister, so to get myself ready for ministry, I volunteered to help lead a variety of activities in my church—becoming a sponsor for the junior high program, helping lead the college group, and so on. As the demands of the activities increased, and as my personal resources became depleted, I sank into discouragement. In anger and despair one day, I resigned all my church responsibilities and determined to do nothing more until I had clear direction from God.

A few months later, I was approached by some Christian friends at college, and out of the blue they asked if I would lead a Bible study held on campus. This came as a shock because I had only begun attending this Bible study and had made it a point to not get more involved than that. The timing, the request, and some inner sense convinced me then—as it does today—that God came to me in these friends and spoke to me.

The encounter, naturally, was ambiguous. No halos floated above my friends' heads, and their voices didn't boom majestically. But it was clear to me as I reflected—and prayed—about their request that this was nothing less than the voice of God to me. I tell this story not to say that I'm special, but only because it is so typical of many people's encounters with God. God does meet us outside of our prayer time, so all of life becomes material for prayer.

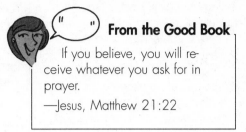

From the Good Book

If you believe, you will receive whatever you ask for in prayer.

—Jesus, Matthew 21:22

God's Chosen = Us!

Let's take up our story of Abraham again.

Then the men got up from their meal and started on toward Sodom. Abraham went with them part of the way. "Should I hide my plan from Abraham?" the Lord asked. "For Abraham will become a great and mighty nation, and all the nations of the earth will be blessed through him. I have singled him out so that he will direct his sons and their families to keep the way of the Lord and do what is right and just." The meaning is that Abraham will be the father of, or the beginning of, the people of Israel.

First, note again the identification of these men with "the Lord." Second, note the special relationship of Abraham and God: Abraham is specially chosen by God to be a "blessing" to others, to be an instrument of God's love and grace.

"Why Abraham?" is the question that naturally arises, and a host of others soon follow. Rather than step into that theological minefield, let's take the long view: God's choosing Abraham was only the first step in his choosing all humankind, which according to Christian teachings is what happened when Christ lived and died for us. For us today, the issue is not why Abraham was chosen, but why we are chosen to carry God's blessing to others.

Actually, even that is not the question: We're chosen because God is gracious. We certainly haven't done anything to deserve such a role in history. And yet, here we are.

This is, to say the least, a helpful perspective to enter into prayer with. We are not outsiders who must plead for an audience, but people who already have a special place in God's heart. We are sons and daughters, not strangers.

From time to time, children come knocking at my door, selling things such as peanut brittle or tickets to a pancake breakfast to raise money for Boy Scouts, Little League, or whatever. They usually make their pitch hesitantly, cautiously, without a lot of confidence that I'll buy from them.

When my youngest daughter approaches me about buying Girl Scout cookies, however, she's not only confident, but she almost demands that I buy them. The difference, of course, is that she is my daughter and has a special relationship with me. She feels free, therefore, to be more bold with me. This is not unlike our relationship with God. We come as his children, and so we can be bold.

When God debated whether to let Abraham in on his divine plans, this isn't just telling of his particular relationship with Abraham. This is a literary device to show that God had the option of not letting Abraham—or us—in on the deal. But biblical history shows that time and again he *has* let us in.

This is an illustration of the biblical belief that we can shape the future through our prayers—which is what we come to next.

At a Board Meeting with God

The story continues:

So the Lord told Abraham, "I have heard that the people of Sodom and Gomorrah are extremely evil, and that everything they do is wicked. I am going down to see whether or not these reports are true."

The upshot, the writer suggests, is that God planned to destroy Sodom and Gomorrah—and every last person in them. Abraham was horrified, and the ensuing dialogue has always struck me as one of the more humorous passages of the Bible.

Abraham reproached him and said, "Will you destroy both innocent and guilty alike? Suppose you find 50 innocent people there within the city—will you still destroy it, and not spare it for their sakes? Surely you wouldn't do such a thing, destroying the innocent with the guilty exactly the same. Surely you wouldn't do that! Should the judge of all the earth do what is right?"

And the Lord replied, "If I find 50 innocent people in Sodom, I will spare the entire city for their sake."

Then Abraham spoke again. "Since I have begun, let me go on and speak further to my Lord, even though I am but dust and ashes. Suppose there are only 45? Will you destroy the city for lack of five?"

And the Lord said, "I will not destroy it if I find 45."

Then Abraham pressed his request further. "Suppose there are only 40?"

And the Lord replied, "I will not destroy it if there are 40."

"Please don't be angry, my Lord," Abraham pleaded. "Let me speak—suppose only 30 are found?"

And the Lord replied, "I will not destroy it if there are 30."

Then Abraham said, "Since I have dared to speak to the Lord, let me continue— suppose there are only 20?"

And the Lord said, "Then I will not destroy it for the sake of the 20."

Finally, Abraham said, "Lord, please do not get angry; I will speak but once more! Suppose only 10 are found there?"

And the Lord said, "For the sake of the 10, I will not destroy it."

Then the Lord went on his way when he had finished his conversation with Abraham, and Abraham returned to his tent.

This story illustrates God's "flexibility" regarding his will for the planet. (In fact, according to Genesis, God could not even find 10 faithful, so Sodom and Gomorrah were destroyed.) Maybe we cannot alter God's plans completely, but like Abraham, we can influence them in significant ways. This means our own future—what happens at our jobs, in our families, in our neighborhood, and even what happens in our nation.

> **Prayer Pearls**
>
> Beware in your prayer, above everything, of limiting God, not only by unbelief, but by fancying that you know what he can do.
> —Andrew Murray, South African devotional writer

One big difference between Abraham's story and ours is this: We often don't have a vivid conversation in which we see the future and its paths before us. Nor can we easily tell what exact difference our prayers make. It's like asking what would have happened if Ronald Reagan had not been elected president. We know what history was like with him as president, but we can only guess what it would have been like if Walter Mondale had been elected. At one level, we know that our one little vote didn't make a difference. At another level, every little vote for Ronald Reagan did.

At an even more profound level, my little prayer doesn't seem to make a difference, and yet it does. The biblical teaching is that it alters the future, though we cannot say exactly how the future would have been without our prayers. This is a rather sobering idea: God is not merely in the business of running the planet, but he invites us to help him run it. As such, he lets us in on his larger plan and then—as we'll see in a moment—allows us to help shape that plan.

This naturally changes the setting of prayer. Honest prayer will always be about my world and my personal concerns. But here we see that it is much larger than that. We are not only coming before a loving father with our personal needs in prayer, but we are also sitting in a board meeting in which our future—and even the future of the planet—is being discussed.

Jim Bell, co-author of this book, tells a delightful story of how this worked out in his own life:

> I spent my undergraduate junior year abroad in Dublin, Ireland. I lived in a Christian community with some other Irish students. Some Irish girls would come over from time to time to pray and have Christian fellowship with us. One weekend one of the girls who was a good friend was praying with me and told me she felt the Lord wanted me to ask Him about the deepest desire in my heart. I wasn't sure but after a while I realized that it was the need for a wife, but after I graduated. I asked God, while He was at it, to give me a wife from Ireland.
>
> A year and a half later, right after I graduated, I met my beautiful wife Margaret in the States the day after she had left her old boyfriend to follow Christ. She had come over from Ireland the year before. Her first prayer was, "I need a husband and I need him now." In I walked to the church service she was attending the next day. When I asked her where she was from in Ireland she told of a little village named Roundwood. I was astounded. The girl in Ireland who had asked me to name my desire for a wife during my stay there was my wife's childhood friend!

Thy Will Be Done—My Way

This dialogue also illustrates another point: "Thy will be done" is the last prayer we pray, not the first. Ultimately, we're concerned about aligning our wills with God's, and when God seems intent on letting things take a certain course, we should submit as gracefully as we can. But in the meantime, we're free to argue, gripe, complain, wrestle, and fight with God. That is prayer at its most dynamic.

Pastor Randy Frazee talks about the time his mother was dying. He asked God specifically to give his mother 18 more years of life. He prayed the prayer 50 times, he says. "I counted. Fifty times I asked God to grant my request. I did this because

I had studied the teaching of Jesus on prayer; he admires someone who knocks at the door continuously. This gave me the notion that if I knocked continuously, eventually God would arise from his seat and fix my problem."

Frazee asked for 18 more years because, first, this would allow his mother to live to be 80, and second, that would allow her to see her new grandchild graduate from high school.

This request did not just come out of thin air. He had been reading about King Hezekiah's desperate prayer in 2 Kings 20, especially the part where the Lord tells his prophet Isaiah to tell Hezekiah, "I have heard your prayer and seen your tears. I will heal you. On the third day from now you will go up to the temple of the Lord, and I will add 15 years to your life. And I will deliver you and this city from the hand of the king of Assyria. I will defend this city for my sake and for the sake of my servant David." God heard Hezekiah's prayer, saw his tears, and gave him 15 more years. So Frazee thought his own request for 18 years not out of line. But God didn't give Randy's mother 18 more years, not even 18 months, not even 18 days. Within 18 hours his mother passed away.

Randy was stunned, and he let his shock be known to God: "What's that all about? Does God not love me? Have I not served him like Hezekiah did? Did he not see my tears when I turned my face to the wall and wept bitterly? Why did God come through for Hezekiah and not for Randy Frazee?"

Randy was having a genuine encounter with God—and those don't always get wrapped up neatly as in fairy tales. As we have noted again and again, prayer is conversation with God, the means of conducting a dynamic relationship—and an honest relationship. Abraham likewise questions the great Judge's very sense of justice and keeps pursuing him until he gets a satisfactory answer.

In his book *Daring to Draw Near: People in Prayer*, John White writes: "You cannot have a relationship with God without standing, at one time or another, precisely where Abraham stood." He goes on to explain his own dismay at various biblical incidents: one where God is said to have killed a man for simply touching the chest that held the Ten Commandments (2 Samuel 6:6):

> I remember kneeling on the boards of an old church hall, begging God to show me that he was not the God of 2 Samuel 6. How could I preach his saving mercy if he were in fact a petulant tyrant?

> I was frightened both by what I seemed to be seeing and by my own temerity in daring to judge the judge of the universe. Lord, how could you *be* like that?

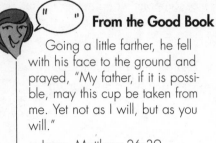

From the Good Book

Going a little farther, he fell with his face to the ground and prayed, "My father, if it is possible, may this cup be taken from me. Yet not as I will, but as you will."

—Jesus, Matthew 26:39

And his answer has always been to show me more of himself than I had seen before, so that my tears and perplexity gave way to awe and to worship.

True submission to God comes not by blindly and naively accepting whatever happens, but by working through your thoughts and emotions honestly and persistently with the one you both question and want to submit to.

At any rate, these are but some of the riches this dynamic prayer yields. It is well worth many a morning's meditation.

The Least You Need to Know

- ◆ The story of Abraham can be returned to again and again for insights into prayer.

- ◆ If we are God's children, we play a role of helping to shape the future through our prayers.

- ◆ We cannot know how the future would be affected if we didn't pray, but we do know that our prayer has an effect on the outcome.

- ◆ We are free to wrestle with God and express our disagreement and displeasure with the way things are.

Chapter 21

Handling Fear

In This Chapter

- ◆ One of Moses' most well-known prayers
- ◆ How God deals with our fears
- ◆ How fear can be handled through prayer
- ◆ We don't have to be paralyzed by fear

Fear is a constant. We fear losing our jobs. We fear failing. We fear losing loved ones. We fear not having enough money in retirement. We fear dying. And on it goes. For some of us, these fears lie beneath the surface of our lives and erupt, volcano-like, only periodically—but when they do erupt, they can paralyze us.

For others of us, every morning we wake with a sense of dread of what might go wrong. This is why fear is such a big theme in the Bible and why it is such a common topic of prayer. Moses is known for heroically leading the people of Israel out of Egyptian bondage. What is less known is his encounter with God early in his life (in Exodus 3 and 4). This has much to teach us about how to pray through our fears.

Holy Ground

Before Moses became a powerful political and military leader, he was a shepherd. One day as he was tending his sheep near the wilderness of Sinai, he saw something strange: a bush that was engulfed in flames and yet was not consumed. This naturally aroused his curiosity, so he drew nearer. When he did, he heard a voice: "Moses! Moses!"

Stunned, no doubt, he replied, "Here I am."

"Do not come any closer," the voice said. "Take off your sandals, for you are standing on holy ground."

> ### Prayer Pearls
>
> Prayer makes visible the right and reveals what is hampering and false. In its radiance, we behold the worth of our efforts, the range of our hopes, and the meaning of our deeds. Envy and fear, despair and resentment, anguish and grief, which lie heavily upon the heart, are dispelled like shadows by its light.
>
> —Abraham Joshua Heschel, American Jewish theologian

The reader, of course, is tipped off at the beginning about what is going on. It is "an angel of the Lord" who is appearing to Moses in the burning bush, and the voice is that of the Lord. For our purposes, the story illustrates again the varied ways in which God chooses to meet us.

With Abraham, God came to him through a chance encounter with passing travelers. With Moses, he came through creation. Again, we need to be ready to pray, to dialogue with God, at any moment—not just in our living rooms, not just in church, not just with people—but also when no one's around and we're in the middle of nowhere. Wherever we meet God, it is "holy ground"—a special place where extraordinary things may happen.

There is usually something appropriate about the way God chooses to meet us. Abraham was approached through human agents, as if to accent that it was flesh-and-blood humanity who lived in Sodom and Gomorrah and that real people were under the threat of punishment. We might wonder if Abraham's concern for those cities was heightened by the fact that he had encountered God in human form.

Moses met God in nature, where God's incomparable power and beauty are found. It's as if God was trying to accent his ability to conquer Moses' fears.

God's Family History

The voice finally identified itself to Moses: "I am the God of your ancestors—the God of Abraham, the God of Isaac, and the God of Jacob."

In other words, "I have a history with you and your family." God had met, comforted, guided, inspired, and sustained Moses' extended "family," the Israelites. Thus, Moses stood in a tradition that had a special relationship with God.

So it wasn't as if Moses was encountering a stranger. Because he knew his people's history, he knew something about the history of this God. He knew that God was just, gracious, and powerful. He knew that God was *God*, which is why the Exodus writer notes, "When Moses heard this, he hid his face in his hands because he was afraid to look at God."

This is a key aspect of prayer that we've touched on only briefly. Our history-impaired age is fascinated with the latest craze, and most things—like fashions or computers—a year old are considered ancient and not worth bothering about. This is a disastrous attitude to take into prayer, in which we would hanker after novel spiritual experiences or practices; this addiction to the new and different robs us of much wisdom and strength that prayer can impart.

Instead, we can pray to a God who has met, comforted, guided, inspired, and sustained people for centuries. We can read their stories and pray their prayers and find rich resources for our lives today. We aren't the first generation that is attacked by fears that threaten to overwhelm us. And the God who helped our forefathers is the same God who meets us today.

> **Snapshots of Answered Prayers**
>
> Zechariah, the father of John the Baptist, prayed a prophetic prayer about his son's ministry and that of Jesus. But he was earlier struck dumb because he disbelieved an angel's message. Nonetheless, John and Jesus fulfilled this prophecy in that very generation. (Luke 1:67–90)

God Knows Our Suffering

The story continues: "Then the Lord told him, 'You can be sure I have seen the misery of my people in Egypt. I have heard their cries for deliverance from their harsh slave drivers. Yes, I am aware of their suffering."

This is one of the most profound truths of prayer, and yet it is one of the hardest to believe sometimes. God does indeed care about our suffering, but when we are forced to endure pain for months or years without relief, we doubt that God cares. We even doubt that God exists.

A cute story about a girl named Susan is told, and whether true or apocryphal, her actions in it illustrate God's empathy with our suffering. A 9-year-old boy named Ted sat at his desk in school when all of a sudden a puddle formed between his feet, and the front of his pants were wet. He froze, feeling panicky, because he knew when the other boys found out he had wet his pants, he would never hear the end of it.

A girl in the class, Susan, had just refilled the class's goldfish bowl, and was carrying it back to its place. She noticed the puddle under the chair, and also that the teacher was about to walk up the aisle and would no doubt see it. Immediately, she stumbled and dumped the goldfish bowl in Ted's lap.

Now, rather than being the object of ridicule, this boy became the object of sympathy. The teacher rushed him downstairs and gave him gym shorts to put on while his pants dried out. When he came back to class, all the kids were on their hands and knees cleaning up around his desk. The sympathy he received was wonderful! And the ridicule that would have been his was transferred to Susan. When she tried to help, they told her to get out of the way: "You've done enough, you klutz!"

At the end of the day, Ted and Susan were waiting together at the bus stop. Ted walked over to Susan and whispered, "Susan, you did that on purpose, didn't you?" Susan whispered back, "I wet my pants once too." This is why the Bible never tires of reminding of this—the "good news about Jesus Christ" is that he is the definitive expression of God's care for us. The New Testament author of the Book of Hebrews put it this way:

> We have a great High Priest who has gone to heaven, Jesus, the Son of God. Let us cling to him and never stop trusting him. This High Priest of ours understands our weaknesses, for he faced all of the same temptations we do, yet he did not sin. So, let us come boldly to the throne of our gracious God. There we will receive mercy, and we will find grace to help us when we need it.

Though this might be clearer to us today, it was not all that clear to Moses.

Telling God Like It Is

After the Lord told Moses of his concern for his people, he added this: "I have come to rescue them from the hand of the Egyptians and lead them out of Egypt to their own good and spacious land."

All well and good, thought Moses, until the Lord continued: "Now go, for I am sending you to Pharaoh. You will lead my people the Israelites out of Egypt."

At this, Moses panicked. "But who am I to appear before Pharaoh? How can you expect me to lead the Israelites out of Egypt?"

A natural enough reaction, we might think, except for a few facts. Moses had been raised in the house of Pharaoh, so he knew something about the halls of power and how to manage himself in that world. He had already committed murder in defending an Israelite who was being brutalized, so he obviously had courage to act boldly. And he clearly had some innate leadership gifts because, in fact, he did become Israel's greatest leader.

At this point, though, Moses was not aware of those experiences and gifts. He was instead overwhelmed with fear. He was acting very much as we do when faced with a new situation.

What exactly was he afraid of? It's hard to say, but four things come to mind immediately:

1. **Responsibility.** Responsibility is a burden. It's the thing that gets you in the office early and makes you stay late. It keeps you up at night with worry. It makes you cautious because the success—and possible failure—of others depends on you. And when you're responsible for others, it makes you care—and hurt—more than is comfortable. Tending a few sheep in a wilderness far removed from the politics of Egypt is about all the responsibility Moses wanted.

2. **Failure.** Closely related is the fear of failure. We like to think of ourselves as competent individuals, people who can do what's asked of us and do it well. When given an opportunity to do something grand, most of us panic because we're afraid we'll fail. This is Moses.

3. **Making a fool of yourself.** This covers a lot of ground; we spend lots of time and money making sure we won't appear foolish. We buy the right clothes and drive the right car and learn to say the right things so that we will fit in. This is why the fear of public speaking (which we'll soon see is one theme in this story) is the greatest fear, rated higher by Americans than even death. If we die, we don't have to face the scrutiny of others. If we goof up speaking in front of others, we still have to step down from the podium and walk among those who may be snickering at us.

4. **Fear of the unknown.** Bill White of Paramount, California, tells about a night he was driving to a quiet beach. On a dark stretch of Interstate 5, he spotted a solitary man beside the road waving a white flag. Two thoughts immediately rushed into his mind. First, *You need to stop for this man.* White felt this was from God. Second, *Are you crazy? It's probably a setup for a gang attack.*

   But he nonetheless pulled over, and discovered that the man had crawled up the shallow ravine beside the road, having escaped from a truck that had rolled over. His friend was still trapped in the truck. White realized that more help was needed, so he crawled back up to the Interstate and tried to wave down another driver, but many passed White before anyone pulled over. These drivers, too,

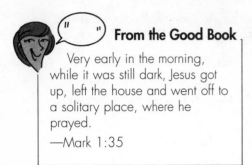

From the Good Book

Very early in the morning, while it was still dark, Jesus got up, left the house and went off to a solitary place, where he prayed.

—Mark 1:35

were rightfully concerned about risking themselves to enter an unknown and potentially dangerous situation!

The point is this: Fear comes in many forms and plagues us in a variety of ways. Moses could hardly know what God was getting him into, and he was naturally afraid. Moses refused to put on a pious act ("Yes, Lord, if you want me to lead the people, I will") but instead blurted out exactly how he was feeling: "How can you expect me to lead the Israelites out of Egypt?"

Meeting God at Every Excuse

Here's where the prayer—Moses' dialogue with God—gets interesting, because Moses refused to be comforted. He was so overwhelmed with fear that he simply would not let God help him deal with his fears.

To Moses' initial objection, God replied, "I will be with you." To this Moses said, "If I go to the people of Israel and tell them, 'The God of your ancestors has sent me to you,' they won't believe me. They will ask, 'Which god are you talking about? What is his name?' Then what should I tell them?" To which God replied, "I Am the One Who Always Is. Just tell them 'I Am has sent me to you.'" Moses protested again: "Look, they won't believe me! They won't do what I tell them. They'll just say, 'The Lord never appeared to you.'"

Seeing that Moses doubted his own abilities, God decided to do something miraculous—as if speaking out of a burning bush wasn't enough. But God had to do more, so he helped Moses himself perform a couple of miracles.

First he ordered Moses to throw his shepherd's staff to the ground. The writer of Exodus records, "So Moses threw it to the ground, and it became a snake!" Moses' reaction? "Moses was terrified, so he turned and ran away." God brought Moses back and convinced him to grab the snake, whereupon he found himself holding his staff again.

Knowing that selling Moses on leadership would be tough, the Lord got Moses to perform another miracle still: Moses was able to make his hand become leprous and then clean. And as if this were not enough, God told Moses that if he took water from the Nile River and poured it on the ground, the water would turn into blood.

Prayer Pearls

When you pray, you open yourself to the influence of the power which has revealed itself as love. The power gives you freedom and independence. Once touched by this power, you are no longer swayed back and forth by the countless opinions, ideas, and feelings which flow through you. You have found a center for your life that gives you a creative distance so that everything you see, hear, and feel can be tested against the source.

—Henri J. M. Nouwen, Roman Catholic priest and writer

At this point, Moses was nearly checkmated. He knew that if he were to do these sorts of things in front of the Israelites or Pharaoh, they'd be inclined to believe his claims. But fear still ruled the heart of Moses, and he made one last desperate attempt to squirm out of his new job: "O Lord, I'm just not a good speaker. I never have been and I'm not now, even after you have spoken to me. I'm clumsy with words."

The writer of Exodus suggests that at this point, God becomes a bit impatient: "Who makes mouths? Who makes people so they can speak or not speak, hear or not hear, see or not see? Is it not I, the Lord? Now go, and do as I have told you. I will help you speak well, and I will tell you what to say."

That should have settled it. God does seem capable of doing that sort of thing. But a frightened Moses would have none of it: "Lord, please! Send someone else."

The story concludes, "Then the Lord became angry with Moses. 'All right,' he said. 'What about your brother Aaron, the Levite? He is a good speaker …. You talk to him, giving him the words to say. I will help both of you to speak clearly, and I will tell you what to do.'"

Checkmate. Moses could think of nothing more to say.

God's Failure

Moses failed the interview with flying colors. He had the opportunity to become a pious man of great faith. Instead, he was forced to slink away a defeated and reluctant leader.

If Moses failed his test, so did God. He brought to bear as much power and wonder as would seem necessary to convince a mortal, but Moses refused to be convinced. It is fear that wins the day, not God.

Then again …. God has a funny way of appearing defeated only to come out the victor in the end—Jesus on the cross is but the supreme instance. In this case, when we take the long view, we see something different than the failure of Moses. What we read as we continue is a story of Moses' remarkable leadership, his great courage, his keen insight, and his heroic sacrifice. He becomes, in short, an extraordinary leader of the people of Israel, leading them out of Egyptian slavery, and thus one of the greatest men in human history.

Prayer Hotline

We must rid ourselves of the idea that we need to feel good after we're done praying. Prayer is not a magic potion to feel good. Sometimes the answer to prayer is that we are to live a little longer with our uncertainty, doubt, and fear. It is God's way of teaching us faith and patience, of helping us grow and mature.

The lesson in prayer is simple: Our fears are not to be shoved down in the name of faith or piety. Our fears should be expressed frankly, persistently, and honestly to God. He is so gracious that he will respond to each and every objection, changing his very will to accommodate our petty concerns. In the end, you see, he is working with us to develop us, to help us blossom into the people he has created us to be, fulfilling the life purposes he wants us to fulfill.

The path to those ends, though, is through honest—and, yes, fearless—prayer before God. If he can transform a coward like Moses, surely he can work with us.

The Least You Need to Know

- ◆ We can learn a great deal about prayer from the early story of Moses.

- ◆ God sees and cares about our suffering.

- ◆ Like Moses, we may become fearful and may make excuses when we realize what God expects of us.

- ◆ God is capable of using our fears and failures to work on his own behalf in achieving his will.

Chapter 22

Mending Relationships

In This Chapter

- ◆ Jesus' most personal prayer
- ◆ The importance of praying for those close to us
- ◆ Praying for others without feeling the need to control the outcome
- ◆ How to pray for relationships that are broken

We joke about relationship movies being "chick flicks," but they are really "people pictures" because all of us are deeply concerned about relationships. We want to be close to others, but that is a difficult thing to achieve. Relationships, we soon discover, are fragile things; they tear apart with the slightest tug—and sometimes they tear in such a way that we cannot imagine ever putting them back together.

When relationships are torn, so are our hearts. The joy we experience in whole relationships is matched by the pain we feel when they are broken. It is no wonder that relationships—not only our own relationships, but other people's relationships with one another—occupy so much of our minds and hearts. As such, it is an appropriate topic of prayer.

A Last Prayer for Friends

Jesus spent three intense years developing relationships with 12 men. He was training them to follow in his footsteps, which is why we call these men "disciples." He was teaching them to go out and spread his message as well, which is why they are also called "apostles." But besides these purposes, Jesus gathered them so that they might become his friends.

> ### Prayer Pearls
>
> When you are sad, tired, lonely, and full of suffering, take refuge in the sanctuary of your soul and there you will find your brother, your friend, Jesus, who will console you, support you, and strengthen you.
>
> —Charles de Foucauld, French soldier and missionary

It is interesting to look back on the moment when Jesus first gathered these 12 men. In the Gospel of Mark we read, "He appointed 12, whom he also named apostles, to be with him ...." (3:14, New Revised Standard Version) Mark adds a number of jobs Jesus intended the 12 to fulfill, but he lists being with Jesus and with one another first. He knew that this, as much as what he taught, is what would shape them.

On the advice of Alexander Graham Bell, the parents of Helen Keller sent for a teacher for their 6-year-old daughter, who was blind, deaf, and mute. After an initial period of frustration, 19-year-old Anne Sullivan managed to teach Helen a manual alphabet, and then eventually Braille. Eventually, Helen was accepted at Radcliffe College, where Anne spelled out the lectures on Helen's hand. Anne was Helen's constant companion when Helen wrote or traveled the world making speeches.

Nearly 50 years of companionship ended when Anne died in 1936. Helen wrote, "My teacher is so near to me that I scarcely think of myself apart from her. I feel that her being is inseparable from my own, and that the footsteps of my life are in hers. All the best of me belongs to her—there is not a talent or an inspiration or a joy in me that has not been awakened by her loving touch."

Such is the power of close friendship, even between teacher and pupil. This helps us appreciate something Jesus did at the end of his life. When he kneels to pray his final prayer (recorded in John 17) the night before he is to die, his main concern is these 12 friends. Let us now turn to that prayer to discover how to better pray about relationships.

Those Given to Us

Toward the beginning of this prayer (John 17:9), Jesus says, "My prayer is not for the world, but for those you have given me ...." This comes as somewhat of a surprise for those raised on the notion that Jesus died "for the world." He did, indeed, but Jesus was not abstract in his love. It was directed to real people, not to generalizations such as "the world" or "humanity."

The old joke goes, "I love humanity; it's people I can't stand." Well, Jesus wasn't as interested in humanity as he was in people, especially those closest to him. In fact, he had a special understanding of these people: He said these were people God had given him, people God wanted him to be especially concerned about, and individuals with whom he was to play a unique and indispensable role.

This is the context in which we are to pray for our own relationships. It is good and right to pray for the world—for hunger, injustice, oppression. If such topics are not a part of our prayers, we have some serious restructuring of our prayer life to do. But the relationships we have—with *our* family, *our* friends, and *our* neighbors—are given to us by God. In them we play a unique and indispensable role, and it is right that they are a high priority in our prayers.

Prayer Hotline

As we pray for others, we might pray for ourselves, especially to understand the role we are to play in these people's lives and to be faithful in doing what we're called to do with them.

If a new couple moves in next door, this is not an accident. In God's providence, they have now entered my life—and I have entered theirs. Therefore, they are people I can be praying for—for their marriage, for their infant, that they might settle into the community. But I'm also supposed to play some special role in their life. It may be as simple as inviting them to my church, or having them over for dessert to help them feel more welcomed. It may mean putting up a fence together. It may mean becoming lifelong friends. Who knows? But this much I do know: These people have entered my life for some purpose, however small, and I have a role to play in their lives, however small.

Letting Go

Jesus finishes that thought with this: "My prayer is not for the world, but for those you have given me, *because they belong to you*." (John 17:9) This is the second context in which prayer for others takes place. It's mighty easy to forget this and to begin praying and living as if our loved ones belong to us.

Almost any relationship will do as an example, but take that of husband and wife. Let me speak for myself: In 30-some years of marriage, there have been a few times when

I have tried to fashion my wife in my own image. I've wanted her to be more interested in theology. I've wanted her to be more interested in sex. I've wanted her to be more organized. I've wanted her to be, well, more like me (let's not go too far with that thought—I recognize the absurdity). And there have been a few times when I've nagged, cajoled, bribed, and manipulated her to be different.

All this is to no avail, of course. It only makes things worse—more tension, more arguments, more dissatisfaction. Only when I can let go of her can I have a healthy relationship with her again. That means I need to recognize that Barbara does not belong to me but to God, that God has made her unique and special, for unique and special ends that may or may not coincide with my plans.

The temptation in prayer is to try to "fix" people; we're pretty good at seeing how people need to be fixed. But we are wiser to let God figure out what ought to be fixed and how the fixing ought to be done—if it needs to be done at all. When we begin praying for others, we should recognize right off that they belong to God and that he has a wonderful plan for their lives—much better than ours.

In a sermon, "Year of the Jubilee," author and speaker Tony Campolo tells of the time, when on a weekend speaking trip to Oregon, he prayed for a man who had cancer. Later in the week he received a phone call from the man's wife.

She said, "You prayed for my husband. He had cancer."

Campolo replied, "Had?" He thought, *Whoa*, and was sure that the man had been cured.

The wife said, "He died."

Campolo expressed how terrible he felt for her.

"Don't feel bad," she replied. "When he came into that church that Sunday, he was filled with anger. He knew he was going to be dead in a short period of time, and he hated God. He was 58 years old, and he wanted to see his children and grandchildren grow up. He was angry that this all-powerful God didn't take away his sickness and heal him. He would lie in bed and curse God. The more his anger grew towards God, the more miserable he was to everybody around him. It was an awful thing to be in his presence. After you prayed for him, a peace had come over him and a joy had come into him. Tony, the last three days have been the best days of our lives. We've sung. We've laughed. We've read Scripture. We prayed. Oh,

> **Snapshots of Answered Prayers**
>
> A Roman centurion asked Jesus to heal his servant, but said he wasn't worthy for Jesus to even enter his house. Jesus marveled that he believed that only a word from a distance could heal his servant. Jesus had not seen such faith among his own people. (Matthew 8:5–13)

they've been wonderful days. And I called to thank you for laying your hands on him and praying for healing."

She concluded, "He wasn't cured, but he was healed."

This doesn't mean that we shouldn't pray specifically for others, especially when the need is obvious: "Lord, heal Frank of alcoholism." "God, help Ruth to not be so bitter." But it also means to say all such prayers while trusting in God to answer the prayer in the time and in the way he will.

The Mother of All Requests

Now we'll jump to the heart of Jesus' last prayer: "I am praying not only for these disciples, but also for all who will ever believe in me .... My prayer for all of them is that they will be one, just as you and I are one." (John 17:20, 21)

Jesus is praying for all his later followers (that is, the people we now call "Christians"), and his request is pretty simple: that there will be no divisions among them.

Uh, what happened? Christians have become one of the most divided people on earth. As of last count, there were more than 20,000 denominations worldwide.

A number of things need to be said about Jesus' request and its dubious result—first, two things that have nothing to do with the theme of this chapter but that reinforce things said elsewhere in the book:

♦ This goes to show that the lack of an answer to prayer has nothing to do with the pray-er's lack of faith (as some suggest). No one has had more faith than Jesus, and yet his prayer has not been answered—yet.

♦ This also suggests that it is appropriate to pray for some things that won't see fruition for some time. I have no doubt that Christians—in fact, the whole world—will someday be one. God's kingdom *will* come. And if Jesus thought it was worth his time praying for such "long-distance requests," it's probably worth my time as well. If nothing else, it keeps the hope alive that God's rule will, in fact, eventually prevail.

Then let's look at a couple of things related to the business of relationships:

♦ Jesus knew that the greatest problem his followers would face would be division. After all, broken relationships are *the* problem of humanity. This is the problem that most concerns Jesus, and it's not surprising that it is the problem that most concerns us.

◆ Though Jesus prays specifically for the Christian church ("all who will ever believe in me"), it doesn't take a German theologian to see that the prayer for unity is the fundamental prayer for all people, for all relationships. Jesus did, in fact, die for the whole world, that each person could be reconciled to God and to others.

To put it simply, there is no more important prayer we can pray than that broken relationships be healed—the relationship of God and the individual, and the relationships of people with one another. To say such prayers is to participate with Christ in his mission of reconciling the world to himself and people to one another.

Practically speaking, this means a couple of things:

◆ **We can't simply pray for people as isolated individuals.** People are already in relationships, and everything an individual does affects those relationships. When we pray for Frank's alcoholism, we are wise to pray for all those affected by Frank's alcoholism. When we pray for Susan to do well on an exam, we are wise to pray for friends and family to be supportive. When we pray for Tom's bitterness toward Mary, we are wise to pray for Mary as well, that she might not become bitter in return. You get the picture.

◆ **We must mend our own relationships—even when the break is not our fault.** It goes without saying that if we have done something to cause a tear in a relationship, we should seek forgiveness and reconciliation. But healed relationships are so important to Jesus, he asks us to go a step further. Note what he says in a passage from his "Sermon on the Mount": "So if you are standing before the altar in the temple, offering sacrifice to God, and you suddenly remember that someone has something against you, leave your sacrifice there beside the altar. Go and be reconciled to that person. Then come and offer your sacrifice to God." (Matthew 5:23–24) Note that it is not the worshipper who has something against the other, but the other who has something against the worshipper.

In the real world, of course, it is not always possible to seek reconciliation with people angry with us. We often don't know when someone has a grudge against us. Sometimes people die while still angry with us. Sometimes they live too far away for us to attempt to heal the break. But this is not a new legalism that Jesus is weighing us down with; it is a recognition that relationships are so important that, as people of prayer (and as people who seek a closer relationship with God), we should do everything possible to heal our broken relationships with others.

Perhaps you can see why, from another perspective, Jesus tells us to pray, "Forgive us our debts, *as* we forgive our debtors." Prayer ultimately is about one thing: unity. That means oneness—and healed relationships. We can't compartmentalize, hoping to get right with God and not try to get right with others. It's not so much that it is wrong—it just doesn't make sense.

God by the Back Door

There is one more practical result from praying for and seeking reconciliation. Jesus notes it toward the end of his prayer. Speaking of his disciples, he says, "I have given them the glory [that is, the power and honor] you gave me, so that they may be one, as we are—I in them and you in me, all being perfected into one. Then the world will know that you sent me and will understand that you love them as much as you love me." (John 17:22, 23)

One thing that people of prayer begin to enjoy more and more is a loving relationship with God. They experience love as they've never known it. Naturally, they want others to enjoy this experience, but just telling others about it often makes little impact. Outsiders tend to think of Christians as people who just happen to be "into religion"; they have no clue that what we experience is something they can experience as well.

Jesus assumes that the godly love we experience in prayer is the same love that reconciled people experience. If people become one—and especially if people become one with God as they become one with one another—this is what will impress others. This is what will help others glimpse the larger reality of the love that surrounds them.

A treasurer in a church in northern Illinois recently embezzled over $100,000 from the church's building fund. When the church board discovered it, many members were furious. But taking the Bible as his cue, the pastor tried to combine justice with mercy, insisting that the man pay the church back while encouraging reconciliation between him and angry members. A few weeks after the discovery, after a plan of repayment had begun, the pastor held a service in which the man publicly asked for forgiveness. Afterward, many of the people who had been angry with him came up and embraced him. Tears flowed freely. For members and visitors alike, it was a very moving service, demonstrating the healing power of the gospel of love.

> **From the Good Book**
>
> In that day you will no longer ask me anything. I tell you the truth, my father will give you whatever you ask in my name. Until now you have not asked for anything in my name. Ask and you will receive, and your joy will be complete.
>
> —Jesus, John 16:23, 24

Mending relationships—it's hard to imagine that there's anything more vital to pray about.

The Least You Need to Know

- ◆ Jesus taught that praying for those close to us—family, friends, neighbors—is one of the most important purposes of prayer.

- ◆ We need to avoid trying to "fix" people when we pray, to try to make them in our image rather than God's.

- ◆ Because Jesus prayed for unity in the church, we must pray for reconciliation with others, even if the reason for arguing was not our fault.

- ◆ If we experience a growing love relationship with God in prayer, we will want to have stronger relationships with others.

Chapter 23

Suffering: Three Approaches

In This Chapter

- ◆ Three prayers of biblical sufferers: Jonah, Job, and Jesus

- ◆ Praying when suffering makes you feel God has left you

- ◆ Learning to pray through your anguish

- ◆ Examples of how to pray while suffering

To live is to suffer, and to suffer is to pray. It is almost a reflex action when we're facing one of life's storms. My wife announces that she's going into the doctor the next day to have him look at what she thinks is a lump on her breast. My first thought is "Oh God, no!"

But aside from the sudden and desperate cry, how should we pray? What exactly should we pray for? For immediate delivery? For patience to bear the trial? Or should we complain about the injustice of it all?

If suffering is one of life's mysteries, how exactly to respond to it—more specifically, how exactly to pray through it—can also be a puzzle.

Prayer from the Belly of a (Big) Fish

The Bible has its share of prayers that were said in the midst of suffering, but three prayers stand out. Every serious pray-er should know the prayers and the context in which they were said, for they have a lot to teach us. We begin with a prayer found in the well-known parable of Jonah.

Though some take the story as history, I do not. But whether history or parable, the story is divinely inspired to teach us about many things, including prayer.

The plot is well known: Jonah is asked by God to go to the city of Ninevah and preach God's coming judgment. Jonah wants none of it and boards the first ship heading in the opposite direction, thinking he can escape God.

Soon a storm arises, and even the seasoned sailors fear for their lives. They learn of Jonah's story and figure out that his disobedience to God has caused the storm. Jonah volunteers to be thrown overboard to save the ship, and after trying to manage the ship a bit longer, the crew finally obliges. This part of the story concludes, "Now the Lord had arranged for a great fish to swallow Jonah. And Jonah was inside the fish for three days and three nights." (Jonah 1:17)

We do not need vivid imaginations to figure out that life in the belly of a big fish is no pleasure cruise. Any consciousness one might experience would be completely dominated by despair: It's only a matter of minutes before death. Time to get the soul in order, if nothing else.

Jonah, however, takes a surprising approach. We best hear his "last" prayer in his own words, in full:

> I cried out to the Lord in my great trouble, and he answered me. I called to you from the world of the dead, and Lord, you heard me! You threw me into the ocean depths, and I sank down to the heart of the sea. I was buried beneath your wild and stormy waves. Then I said, "O Lord you have driven me from your presence. How will I ever again see your holy temple?"

> I sank beneath the waves, and death was very near. The waters closed in around me, and seaweed wrapped itself around my head. I sank down to the very roots of the mountains. I was locked out of life and imprisoned in the land of the dead. But you, O Lord my God, have snatched me from the yawning jaws of death!

> When I had lost all hope, I turned my thoughts once more to the Lord. And my earnest prayer went out to you in your holy temple. Those who worship false

gods turn their backs on all God's mercies. But I will offer sacrifices to you with songs of praise, and I will fulfill all my vows. For my salvation comes from the Lord. (Jonah 2:2–9)

Faith at the Bottom

The prayer shows signs of having been composed in a completely different setting than in the belly of a big fish. Though it makes use of imagery of the sea, it was more likely written on dry land and to be said in the Jerusalem Temple. But it was a nice literary move to place it in the mouth of Jonah at this point in the story. It was done to make a number of points, one of which is about prayer.

We're not completely aware of the full context of this prayer until we read the first sentence that follows the prayer: "Then the Lord ordered the fish to spit up Jonah on the beach, and it did." (Jonah 2:10)

What's remarkable about the prayer is this: Jonah thanks God, praising him for his deliverance *before* it happens.

While in the belly of the fish, Jonah prays, "I cried out to the Lord in my great trouble, and he answered me. I called to you from the world of the dead, and Lord, you heard me!"

While sinking deeper and deeper into the ocean depths, Jonah cries out, "I was locked out of life and imprisoned in the land of the dead. But you, O Lord my God, have snatched me from the yawning jaws of death!"

When only seconds of life could possibly remain, Jonah says, "But I will offer sacrifices to you with songs of praise, and I will fulfill all my vows. For my salvation comes from the Lord."

Jonah shows a type of faith in the midst of suffering that is rare but real. This may be a parable, but the reaction to suffering is genuine. Some people, when they see death staring at them in the face, simply smile and say, "Praise the Lord." They are confident that God will rescue them—and if not, what does it matter? They'll be with the Lord in a few minutes anyway.

This remarkable sort of faith doesn't seem to be given to everyone. It is not something to aspire to—it is a gift. If you are suddenly given such hope in the midst of suffering, don't necessarily chalk it up as a "psychological defense mechanism" or "denial." It could very well be a gift of the Holy Spirit, and you should pray just as your soul soars.

But even when one doesn't *feel* confident, one can nonetheless trust that, even in dire circumstances, God can rescue. A 1997 *People* magazine article tells the story of 5-year-old Hilary Russell and her parents, Susan and Richard. They were visiting a deserted stretch of a Miami beach in 1978. As Richard, a poet and English professor, and Susan, a photographer and onetime lifeguard, spread out a blanket, Hilary dashed into the water. She quickly waded into trouble, and when her parents yelled for her to come in, it was too late. She was caught in the riptide.

Susan plunged into the water but made little headway towards her daughter. She felt for sure that her daughter was going to drown. Richard suddenly noticed a dark-haired man standing in the water about eight feet beyond Hilary. He says he "just plucked her out of the water and held her in his arms." Susan was astonished at how effortlessly the man strode through the water toward the shore. Twenty years later, Hilary remembers the man: "He was tan and the hair on his arms was dark and it glistened even though it was cloudy out."

The man placed Hilary back in Susan's arms. The Russells embraced their daughter, but when they turned around to thank the man, he was gone. Today Susan says, "I'm not real sure if there are higher powers." But her husband says, "It occurred to me that maybe he really was an angel."

Tragic Job

Though we might be tempted to think that this is *the* right way to pray, it apparently is not. The Bible records other instances of saintly people praying in utterly different ways. At the other end of the spectrum from Jonah stands the tragic figure of Job. Again, we're dealing with a parable, but this is one of the most profound that has ever been told.

The plot line unfolds pretty quickly in the first two chapters. Job is described as a "blameless man, a man of complete integrity. He feared God and stayed away from evil." (Job 1:1) Furthermore, Job was a pious man who never neglected his religious duties.

Job was also a blessed man: He had seven sons and three daughters. He owned thousands of sheep and camels, and hundreds of oxen and donkeys, and he employed many servants. "He was, in fact," the story says, "the richest man in the entire area." (Job 1:3)

At this point, Satan, God's great adversary, asked permission to test Job. Satan believed that Job was devout and righteous simply because he had been so richly blessed. "Take away everything he has," Satan concluded, "and he will surely curse you to your face." (Job 1:11)

God granted the permission, and the game was on. In short order, Job lost his herds to marauding bands and to fire; his home collapsed in a storm that killed all of his children, who were inside at the time. Finally, he was struck down with a case of boils that completely covered his body. The writer sadly concludes, "Then Job scraped his skin with a piece of broken pottery as he sat among the ashes." (Job 2:8)

At the end of this string of tragedy, his wife came up to him and told him, "Curse God and die." (Job 2:9)

But Job replied, "You talk like a godless woman. Should we accept only good things from the hand of God and never anything bad?" (Job 2:10)

The writer notes, "So in all this, Job said nothing wrong." (Job 2:10)

> **Snapshots of Answered Prayers**
>
> In 2 Kings 20:1–11 King Hezekiah of Israel was deathly ill and prayed for healing. The prophet Isaiah then told him that God would add 15 years to his life, and as a sign moved the sun 10 steps backward on his sundial!

God's Critic

Job may not have cursed God, and he may not have said anything wrong, but that didn't keep him from speaking his mind honestly. After sitting with three friends for seven days in silence, he finally blurted out:

> Cursed be the day of my birth, and cursed be the night when I was conceived. Let that day be turned to darkness. Let it be lost even to God on high, and let it be shrouded in darkness …. Curse it for its failure to shut my mother's womb, for letting me be born to all this trouble.
>
> Why didn't I die at birth as I came from the womb? Why did my mother let me live? Why did she nurse me at her breasts? For if I had died at birth, I would be at peace now, asleep and at rest. (Job 3:3, 4, 11–13)

He may not curse God, but Job does complain:

> If my sadness could be weighed and my troubles be put on the scales, they would be heavier than all the sands of the sea …. For the Almighty has struck me down with his arrows. He has sent his poisoned arrows deep within my spirit. All God's terrors are arrayed against me. Don't I have a right to complain? (Job 6:2–5)

And the more Job thinks about it, the more anguished become his prayers:

> I cannot keep from speaking. I must express my anguish. I must complain in my bitterness. Am I a sea monster that you place a guard on me?

> What are mere mortals, that you should make so much of us? For you examine
> us every morning and test us every moment. Why won't you leave me alone—
> even for a moment? Have I sinned? What have I done to you, O watcher of
> all humanity? Why have you made me your target? Am I a burden to you?
> (Job 7:11, 17–20)

Here we have not only some of the most moving poetry ever written, but an eloquent
example of prayer in the midst of suffering. It is difficult to believe that God would
honor this sort of thing, but at the end of the story of Job, God does exactly that.

God came in a whirlwind and, yes, chastised Job for becoming "God's critic." Job,
in turn, humbly submitted himself to God's power and wisdom: "I was talking about
things I did not understand, things far too wonderful for me …. I take back everything I said, and I sit in dust and ashes to show my repentance." (Job 42:2, 5)

In the end, though, God rewarded Job by returning his lost fortunes, giving him
twice as much as before. Job may have spoken ignorantly and arrogantly when he
questioned God and complained against him, but it was not an unforgivable sin.
The unforgivable sin is to reject God in such circumstances, to harden our hearts
and have nothing to do with him again. That is unforgivable because we put ourselves
in a stance toward God that will not allow him to forgive, let alone allow ourselves to
repent.

Job was angry, and for good reason. But he never forsook God. He simply wanted to
have an argument with him. He lost the argument, yes, but he did not lose his God.

Looking for a Way Out

A third approach to prayer in suffering is modeled by Jesus, and it looks at suffering
in a completely different way—probably the way most of us pray in painful circumstances.

Jesus had known his fate for weeks, if not months, and it came crashing down on him
the night before he was to die. Jesus had just finished eating his last meal with his disciples, his friends. Weighed down with grief, he decided to go off with his closest
friends and pray. Gospel writer Mark is sparse with the words he uses to describe the
scene, but the effect is potent:

> And they came to an olive grove called Gethsemane, and Jesus said, "Sit here
> while I go and pray." He took Peter, James, and John with him, and he began to
> be filled with horror and deep distress. He told them, "My soul is crushed with
> grief to the point of death. Stay here and watch with me."

He went on a little farther and fell face down on the ground. He prayed that, if it were possible, the awful hour awaiting him might pass him by. "Abba, Father," he said, "everything is possible for you. Please take this cup of suffering away from me. Yet I want your will, not mine." (Mark 14:32–36)

The prayer has two dimensions. The first is an honest expression of what Jesus feels he wants: He wants to live. He tells God so, and he pleads that he might be spared the cruel death of being nailed to a cross.

We don't know how long Jesus prayed this way, for Mark has greatly shortened the scene. It may have been an hour; it may have been all night. He may have been praying this prayer every night for months. But this night it is said with such anguish that we sense the pain even 2,000 years removed.

This is the prayer most of us pray when facing pain and distress. We don't want our loved ones to have cancer. We want to be spared bankruptcy. We don't want to live with unrelenting back pain for decades. Sometimes, as we noted in early chapters, God honors the request. The cancer is healed, the business comes in, the vertebrae is restored. And like Jonah, we exult in God's goodness—though *after* the fact. And sometimes, for reasons known only to God, we hear silence in return. This is what Jesus heard, so much silence over the next few hours that as he hung on the cross, he shouted, "My God, my God, why have you forsaken me?"

Yet Jesus had the courage to go through the mockery of a trial and the brutality of a whipping and the cruelty of crucifixion because of something he said that night: "Yet I want your will, not mine." (Mark 14:36)

The very words that sound as if we're giving up are, in fact, the most powerful words we can utter in our despair. For to say, "Thy will be done" is to put ourselves completely into the hands of God, whose love, strength, and grace can sustain us through any storm or as we hang upon the cruelest of crosses.

Prayer Hotline

Emotions have a way of getting in the way of prayer—either discouraging us from praying, or distracting us while we pray. Sometimes there is nothing to be done but to follow the words of the Egyptian monk Evagrius Ponticus: "Keep trying. If we knock on the door hard enough it will be opened."

The Key to Prayer in Suffering

How *should* we pray in suffering? I have no idea. I do know there is hardly a wrong way. The point is to do whatever needs to be done to stay connected with

God—whether that means trusting God to save, like Jonah, or fighting for understanding, like Job, or submitting to God's will, like Jesus.

So what is the key? Just do it.

The Least You Need to Know

◆ A prayer of faith is to thank God for his deliverance, as Jonah did, even in the midst of our suffering.

◆ Sometimes we are angry for good reason, and, like Job, we can express it to God with the hope of an answer in the end.

◆ Jesus is our model for prayer in suffering: making an honest request but also saying, "Thy will be done."

◆ We should not forsake God when we're suffering, for he certainly doesn't forsake us.

Chapter 24

Cleansing Prayer

In This Chapter

◆ How to approach God in prayer when you feel you've done something terrible—or when you feel as if you don't deserve his love

◆ Why confession is so important

◆ One of the most meaningful prayers of confession ever recorded

◆ How prayer can cleanse your whole being

Compared with King David, President Bill Clinton was a minor-league sinner. I don't mean to minimize his affair and perjury, but it just doesn't stand up to the biblical David's full-blown adultery with Bathsheba, followed by the premeditated "murder" of her husband, Uriah. (David ordered Uriah to the front lines and instructed his commander not to support Uriah's division in battle.)

If David's sin was great, so was his confession—in fact, it is one of the most moving and meaningful prayers ever written. From it we can learn a great deal about how to approach God when we are weighed down with guilt—a not uncommon experience for any of us. The one thing we want more than anything else is forgiveness, an understanding that we really are cleansed and that we can enjoy a new start. And there have been few prayers written in history that have the power to do that as well as the one recorded in Psalm 51.

Lasting Confession

You can read all the tantalizing details of David's escapades in 2 Samuel 11 and 12. This is a study rich in psychological insight and will pay dividends as an object of devotional study.

Even if we don't commit such "big" sins, though, we each know moments when we realize that we've done something despicable. It may be the betrayal of a confidence, a racist remark, or the neglect of a beggar.

In the fall of 2002 in Mishawaka, Indiana, a department store parking lot surveillance camera caught Madelyne Toogood repeatedly hitting her 4-year-old child. The video was turned over to the police, who immediately tried to arrest the woman. The woman, in turn, when she realized the police were chasing her, took off, heading east, and managed to elude police for a week.

> ### Prayer Pearls
>
> Every Christian needs a half-hour of prayer each day, except when he is busy—then he needs an hour.
>
> —Francis de Sales, Roman Catholic devotional writer

The video fell into the hands of the media, and it wasn't long before the clip was shown on television all over the country. During her escape, Toogood stopped at a hotel in New Jersey and saw the clip on the news. She was shocked. "I was sick to my stomach," she said. "I was mortified. I wasn't raised to do that. I was thinking I looked like a monster. I couldn't believe I did that to my beautiful 4-year-old daughter."

Whether or not they're caught on camera, our sins are often played over and over in our minds. Whatever the cause, we feel guilty, lonely, disgusted, and frightened. We want to say something to God, but no words we manufacture can express our tangled emotions.

Psalm 51 has remained a perennial resource for praying about such matters, for confessing both the petty sins of daily life and especially the extraordinary sins that weigh us down (which we'll focus on in this chapter). This Psalm is so rich and holds together so well that we should take it in fully before looking at some of its parts:

> Have mercy on me, O God,
>
> because of your unfailing love.

Because of your compassion,

blot out the stain of my sins.

Wash me clean from my guilt.

Purify me from my sin. For I recognize my shameful deeds—

they haunt me day and night.

Against you, and you alone, have I sinned;

I have done what is evil in your sight.

You will be proved right in what you say,

and your judgment against me is just. For I was born a sinner—

yes, from the moment my mother conceived me.

But you desire honesty from the heart,

so you can teach me to be wise in my inmost being. Purify me from my sins, and I will be clean;

wash me, and I will be whiter than snow.

Oh, give me back my joy again;

you have broken me—

now let me rejoice.

Don't keep looking at my sins.

Remove the stain of my guilt.

Create in me a clean heart, O God.

Renew a right spirit within me.

Do not banish me from your presence,

and don't take your Holy Spirit from me.

Restore to me again the joy of your salvation,

and make me willing to obey you. Then I will teach your ways to sinners,

and they will return to you.

Forgive me for shedding blood, O God who saves;

then I will joyfully sing of your forgiveness.

Unseal my lips, O Lord,

that I may praise you. You would not be pleased with sacrifices,

or I would bring them.

If I brought you a burnt offering,

you would not accept it.

The sacrifice you want is a broken spirit,

A broken and repentant heart, O God,

you will not despise.

Key Assumptions

There is no way even to begin to exhaust the lessons for cleansing prayer from this particular prayer, so I'll limit myself to a few highlights.

To begin, we should note the assumption that David makes entering into prayer: God is a God of "unfailing love" and "great compassion." This is not an easy assumption to make, because after a grave sin, we feel as if God will not listen to us—as if he has, in fact, already rejected us.

That's because that's how we tend to act when someone has seriously betrayed us. I know if my son were to become a pimp and a drug-pusher, let's say, I would be horrified, angry, and confused. I would have a difficult time speaking with him, let alone inviting him into my home. If he took up such a life, he would be rejecting all I had taught him and all that I stood for.

Snapshots of Answered Prayers

King Solomon was asked by God to name his heart's desire. Solomon prayed for wisdom and God said that because he didn't pray for riches or a long life, he would give him riches as well as wisdom. Read 1 Kings 3:16–28 to see how Solomon applied this wisdom.

David's prayer, however, will have none of this and starts off with a surprising assumption. God is just, yes. God abhors sin, yes. God has the perfect right to punish sin, yes. But this is not God's essence. Love and mercy are. We approach him with sorrow, yes, but not in fear—that is, not the type of fear that wonders what our relationship is with him. We don't have to wonder. We can begin with the assumption that God is there to receive us in all our messiness.

David makes another assumption: He can be purified from his wrongdoing. This is also startling, considering the gravity of his sins. You'd think he could never be "purified" from them.

To be purified, or cleansed, of sin doesn't mean that we don't continue to suffer regret, though. I still shake my head at sins I committed in adolescence! What David rightly assumes is that God has the power and grace to not let our sin stand in the way of a deep relationship with him.

Again, even this is difficult for us to imagine. If my friend betrays me—let's say, lies to a vice president in the company so that he can advance at my expense—it's difficult to imagine how that could *not* stand in the way of our relationship. Even if I formally forgave him, I would have a tough time trusting him for the rest of my life.

But this is precisely why biblical literature is called a "revelation." This business of mercy and spiritual purity is not something we would think up on our own. It is a truth about God that had to be revealed by God—and in this Psalm, it is revealed as clearly as anywhere in the Bible.

A Spade Is a Spade Is a ...

David's clear view of God's compassion is matched by the crystal clear view of his own sin. In this, he models the three key elements of a confessional prayer:

1. **He takes ownership of his actions.** "I recognize my shameful deeds." No excuses. No rationalizations. Human beings are natural rationalizers, and we can manufacture excuses in less time than it takes to say, "I'm sorry."

> **Prayer Pearls**
>
> He who prays as he ought will endeavor to live as he prays.
> —John Owen, Puritan theologian

Took too much time for lunch and still left the office early? "Well, I've put in plenty of overtime in my days here—and besides, I do more work in six hours than most people do in eight."

Spent a little too much time fantasizing about that woman (or man) at the video store? "Aw, they're harmless thoughts. Besides, I don't do it all that often."

Yelled at your daughter for not cleaning up the living room even though it wasn't her job? "I'd had a tough day—and besides, she doesn't do enough work around here."

But David doesn't fall for this human failing (as in, "The pressures of government were overwhelming; my wife and concubines weren't satisfying me; and besides, her husband died in battle—what more glorious end would a soldier want?"). David doesn't need to make excuses, of course, because he knows that he's in the presence of "unfailing love" and "compassion." There's no need to cover his you-know-what.

2. **He recognizes who he has wronged, really.** "Against you, and you alone, have I sinned." It looks as if David has committed a sin against Bathsheba, Uriah, his own wives, and himself—and he has. After all, these are the people most directly hurt by the whole affair. But David also knows the ultimate source of his remorse, the ultimate being to whom he is responsible for his actions.

   David knows what we usually learn only from experience: We can apologize to others and try to make it up to them for the rest of our lives, but unless we also deal with God, we'll find no satisfactory cleansing. He's the one who created the moral universe in which we live. He's the one with whom we've ultimately broken faith.

3. **He admits that his behavior is part of a pattern.** "For I was born a sinner—yes, from the moment my mother conceived me." This may strike us as unhealthy self-abasement, but it's really an honest admission of the way things are.

   To say, "I'm a sinner and have been so since my birth" is not a statement about who I am at my core. No, I'm a child of God, created in his image. But let's face it, since childhood I have sinned—I've done and said things that get in the way of my relationship with God and that spoil my relationships with others.

   David is simply saying that his adultery and murder are part of a larger pattern. He's not going to blather on about how this was so uncharacteristic of him, that he must have been temporarily insane, or that he ate too many Twinkies, or whatever. No, he admits that he's the type of person who could commit adultery—and who could commit adultery again.

From the Good Book

For you did not receive a spirit that makes you a slave again to fear, but you received the spirit of sonship. And by him we cry, "Abba, Father."

—Paul, Romans 8:15

This is probably the crux of the whole prayer. The sin we confess needs to be confessed, but it is simply a symptom of a larger problem. Unless we own up to the larger problem, we're not going to be cleansed and we're not going to make any progress in the spiritual life.

That's the great paradox of confession: If we admit we're stuck with our sinful tendencies, we have a much better chance of getting unstuck. But the moment we think we can get ourselves unstuck by trying just a tad harder, we're doomed to getting stuck.

Cleanliness Is Next to Joyfulness

Along the same lines, that's the point of the next section of this prayer: Only God has the power to heal and cleanse our hearts. "Create in me a clean heart, O God. Renew a right spirit within me." (Psalm 51:10)

The temptation, of course, is to apologize, to vow to do better, and then to reach down to those proverbial bootstraps and start tugging. We'll never experience cleansing under these circumstances, though: first, because we can't improve ourselves by our own strength; and second, because we'll fall into self-defeating behavior.

If my wife has "sinned" against me—let's say she makes fun of me at a party and hurts my feelings—she apologizes and says, "I'll make it up to you." She makes me a special dinner. She gives me a massage. She buys me tickets to a Chicago Bulls game. She compliments me in front of friends at the next party.

But whatever she does has nothing to do with what she has already done. It doesn't "settle the score." It doesn't erase what has been done. It can't take away the experience of embarrassment and shame—and she knows it. She'll never feel comfortable in our relationship, no matter what she does, until I forgive her. And for that forgiveness to be healing forgiveness, it cannot hinge on her future good behavior. It's a gift, or it's nothing.

Sometimes it's difficult to simply accept this gift. Latin American evangelist Luis Palau tells about a time in Guatemala when a man who had seriously sinned came up to him. The man had repented, but he was still without joy. Palau says he did something that day he had never done before: He put his arm around the man and said, "Brother, you've repented; your sins are forgiven. Let me pray with you." Afterwards the man said, "Oh, thank you, thank you. Now I'm free!"

Sometimes God has to speak to us through another before we're assured that we are forgiven. Whatever it takes, we must allow God to heal and cleanse us. Instead of a flurry of vows and promises about how we'll never do that again, we are wiser simply to say, "You, Lord, create in me a clean heart. You, Lord, renew a right spirit in me. And help me not get in the way."

Of course, you'll want to change the behavior or situations that brought about the sin in the first place, but not as a way to make it up to God. Do this simply because you don't want to make the same mistake twice. In the meantime, we pray for God to change us from the inside so that we won't even be tempted the next time.

Prayer Pearls
Don't pray when you feel like it. Have an appointment with the Lord and keep it.
—Corrie Ten Boom, Christian writer

Getting the Word Out

This is probably the most unnerving part of the confessional process, but if experience is any guide, it is an essential step in the process of cleansing. We need to tell our story, from sinful beginning to confessional end, to someone else: "Restore to me again the joy of your salvation, and make me willing to obey you. Then I will teach your ways to sinners." (Psalm 51:12, 13)

By "sinners" David just means "other sinners like me"—or, more simply, other people. And by "teaching your ways," he means he wants others to understand how God has dealt with him and his sin. If this seems a stretch of an interpretation, simply look at the Psalm itself: It is David announcing his story to others.

We needn't be as public as David. Sharing our story with one or two close friends, a pastor, or a spiritual adviser is sufficient. But as many recovery groups, including Alcoholics Anonymous, have discovered, there is no complete healing until we tell our story. Why this is so, it's hard to say. That it *is* so is the experience of thousands upon thousands of people. God completes his cleansing process in and through other people—as we talk, as they listen, as we share intimately with another human being.

Humility, not Piety

At the end of his prayer, David says one more thing that seems troubling but is crucial: "If I brought you a burnt offering, you would not accept it. The sacrifice you want is a broken spirit, a broken and repentant heart, O God, you will not despise." (Psalm 51:16, 17)

When we hear that someone's "spirit has been broken," we think of someone having lost all hope and self-respect. This is *not* what David has in mind, though. A spirit of haughtiness, pride, stubbornness—this is the sort of thing that needs to be broken.

But here's the interesting thing: If you start to get religious about this whole business, you may end up with even more haughtiness and pride than ever. And this is why David puts these two ideas—religiosity and humility—side by side. Let me explain.

To begin, I'm not against religion as such. As you see in Part 6, I encourage you to become part of a worshipping community if you want to really develop your prayer life.

But church is no nirvana. For all its strengths, it has the odd tendency to nurture pride and arrogance. The inner dialogue, which is usually very subtle and which takes months to develop, goes something like this:

"I've sinned indeed. I need to get some help in this. I think I'll start attending worship …." Then a few months go by. "This is really making a difference. I'm much more in control of myself these days. I wish I knew about this sooner. My friends at work could sure use this stuff …." A few more months go by. "If my friends would just get their acts together, like I did, and start coming to church, they wouldn't be in such a mess. I'm a much better person than I've ever been."

Prayer Hotline

While God doesn't care if we're "religious," he has chosen to reveal himself week by week in public worship, and to reveal to us our hidden sins. Most churches include some form of confession as part of the service. Thus, attending weekly worship is one way to keep cleansing your soul.

You get the idea: a slow and steady accumulation of spiritual pride. In some churches, the pastor will periodically remind people of this temptation, but the temptation is a constant one for the religious.

David wants to clarify at the end of his prayer that, as important as religion is (he himself was an extremely devout Jew), it's not at the heart of cleansing prayer. Humility is. At the heart of humility is a realistic appraisal of who God is (unfailing love), who we are (habitual sinners), and where our help lies (in God). Needless to say, this prayer deserves repeated visits for meditation and prayer.

The Least You Need to Know

- To be cleansed of our guilt in prayer, we need to take ownership of our actions and recognize who we have wronged: God.

- Confessing our sins to others and God is a necessary part of taking responsibility for them.

- Only God, through his power, can accomplish lasting cleansing and healing of our soul.

- The outcome of cleansing prayer is humility: recognizing who we are and how much we need God.

Seeking the Best for Others

In This Chapter

- ◆ How to best pray for others
- ◆ One of the prayers of the apostle Paul
- ◆ The importance of moving beyond mere material, physical requests for others
- ◆ How to incorporate key biblical phrases into your prayers for others

One thing I discovered early on in prayer is how quickly I become bored praying for others. I mean, after I've said, "Bless my brother-in-law," for two weeks running, what then? This gets pretty monotonous pretty quickly. How exactly should I pray for him? How do I determine what he most needs without butting into his personal life?

Well, I find a classic prayer and use it as a guide, like those found in the letters of the apostle Paul. When I figured out how to use such a prayer, it recharged my interest in praying for others. Perhaps it will do the same for you.

Beyond Daily Bread

Paul was the most influential Christian in the early years of the church. He founded churches throughout Asia Minor (what today we call Turkey) and in Greece, and he had relationships all over the Mediterranean world.

In his letters to his friends, Paul usually told them how exactly he was praying for them—and in some letters he actually prayed for them. These prayers can teach us a lot about how to pray for others more fully.

Our natural tendency is to begin with the concrete, such as praying for health and for success in endeavors: "Lord, help John get over his flu rapidly, and help him do a good job at his presentation tomorrow." That sort of thing. We might add requests for peace or freedom from worry.

Paul's prayers take us to a new level: He is concerned mostly for the spiritual welfare of his friends, and all his prayers are directed to that end. You'll never hear Paul tell his friends that he's praying for their health.

This isn't because Paul despised such prayers. Having been raised in a Jewish environment, there's little doubt that very concrete prayers for concrete blessings were a normal element of his prayers. But in his letters, he wants his readers to realize that he is also praying for them on a different level: for their spiritual needs.

That's all well and good for a spiritual giant like Paul, but can we do the same? To some people, this is presumptuous: "What gives us the right to tell someone else how to run their spiritual lives? That's an individual decision and a matter of privacy."

I won't get into that here other than to say: No, we shouldn't try to tell people how to run their spiritual lives—though I think it's okay to ask God to do that. Furthermore, a person's spiritual life may be private, but that doesn't mean that it's not our business. My brother-in-law's finances, for example, are none of my business, but I still want him to use his money wisely and to stay solvent.

Such is the nature of praying for others' spiritual lives: We're not trying to make them become like us, or whomever. We just want what's best for them in God's mind—which is why we're asking him in the first place.

In particular, let's look at one of Paul's prayers for the people of Ephesus (on the west coast of modern Turkey), a group he lived with for a time. In this prayer (Ephesians 1:15–23), we see four key themes that can become a part of our prayer for others.

Thankfulness

Paul starts on a characteristic note: "I have never stopped thanking God for you …." Paul was one thankful person, and one of the things he is most thankful for is his friends.

To friends in Philippi, he wrote, "Every time I think of you, I give thanks to my God." (Philippians 1:3) To friends in Colosse, he says, "We always pray for you, and we give thanks to God …." (Colossians 1:3) Even to new acquaintances in Thessalonica (whom he had known for only two weeks), he says, "We always thank God for all of you and pray for you constantly." (1 Thessalonians 1:2)

> **Prayer Pearls**
>
> God will either give you what you ask, or something far better.
> —Robert Murray McCheyne, Scottish evangelical pastor

This is not how we usually think of our friends. Friends are people to worry about, or to fix, or to use, or to help. But here we see a whole new approach: We can thank God for friends—and not just at Thanksgiving.

For me, probably the biggest temptation in prayer is to try to "fix" my loved ones. I see a problem—she worries too much; he needs more patience; she needs to be more sensitive; whatever—and I pray for that, hoping that God will fix the person in that way.

A poem from the magazine *Christian Reader* puts this in terms of letting go:

To let go is not to care for, but to care about.

To let go is not to fix, but to be supportive.

To let go is not to judge, but to allow another to be a human being.

To let go is not to be in the middle, arranging all the outcomes, but to allow others to affect their own destinies.

To let go is not to deny, but to accept.

To let go is not to nag, scold, argue, but instead to search out my own shortcomings and correct them.

To let go is not to regret the past, but to grow and live for the future.

To let go is not to cut myself off. It's the realization that I can't control another.

To let go is not to try to change or blame another. It's to make the most of myself.

To let go is to fear less and to love more.

I don't doubt that people need fixing, and it's certainly appropriate to pray such prayers. But before we start trying to make people better, we are wise to thank God for people as they already are. This prevents us from making friends into projects, or from being perpetually dissatisfied with them—a special temptation of spouses and parents, as I can attest.

This habit—beginning with thanks—will, more than anything else, transform your prayers for others. Even when you have no idea how to pray for them, you can certainly thank God for them. And many days, that's enough.

Knowledge

When Paul moves from thanksgiving into requests, his first request is this: He wants God, he tells his friends, "to give you spiritual wisdom and understanding, so that you might grow in your knowledge of God." (Ephesians 1:17)

If we need wisdom, so do our friends—in both the big decisions (school, marriage, moves, and jobs) and in the daily ones (how we use our time day by day). But Paul is thinking a bit more than this: He prays for "*spiritual* wisdom and understanding." He wants his friends not just to be healthy, wise, and successful, but also to grow in their knowledge of God.

Brother Lawrence, in his classic, *Practicing the Presence of God*, put it this way: "Let us give our thoughts completely to God. The more one knows him, the more one wants to know him, and since love is measured commonly by knowledge, then, the deeper and more extensive knowledge shall be, so love will be greater, and, if love is great, we shall love him equally in suffering and consolation."

Is there any more important prayer than this? And yet, if you're like me, it's a request I rarely make. I, too, readily assume that either loved ones are pursuing that already or that they really don't care about spiritual things, so why bother? But no matter their current spiritual state: They will have more joyful and meaningful lives if they get to know God better.

> **Snapshots of Answered Prayers**
>
> King Hezekiah fervently prayed that God would spare Jerusalem from the Assyrian troops that were ready to strike. That night an angel went to their camp and struck dead 185,000 of the troops! Read this amazing story in 2 Kings 19:29–36.

Hope

Another surprising request of Paul's is the next one: "I pray that your hearts will be flooded with light so you can understand the wonderful future …. I want you to realize what a rich and glorious inheritance he has given to his people." (Ephesians 1:18)

Paul isn't talking about a promotion at work or a new political administration. He's talking about ultimate things: the hope of the kingdom of heaven.

Let's get a little more specific, because when we talk about heaven in generalities, it may not seem to be an ultimate hope.

My ethics professor in seminary was Lewis Smedes, who later became well known for his books about forgiveness. He used to ask his students if they wanted to go to heaven. Everyone would raise his hand, of course. And then he'd ask, "Be honest now—who would like to go today?" Only a few would raise their hands. Most students, it seemed, wanted a rain check. They were ready to die, just not today.

Then Dr. Smedes would ask who would like the world set straight once and for all— no more common colds or uncommon cancers; no more hungry people or victims of AIDS; no more war and no more terrorism. And all this tomorrow. To this everyone would raise his hand. And then Dr. Smedes would remind everyone—that is what the kingdom of heaven is.

And that's the ultimate hope we want everyone to have. Here again, I find my prayers shortsighted. I'm constantly aiming for the here and now. But life is so fragile that we all need to have our hope pinned on something beyond this world, on something even more real than this present existence.

Power

Lest this whole business remain in the spiritual stratosphere, Paul adds one more request: "I pray that you will understand the incredible greatness of his power for us who believe in him." (Ephesians 1:19)

First, let's get a handle on this power: It is the power that created the world. It's the power that redeemed Israel from Egypt. It's the power that raised Christ from the dead. We're talking *power.*

> **Prayer Pearls**
>
> God never ceases to speak to us, but the noise of the world without and the tumult of our passions within bewilder us and prevent us from listening to him.
>
> —François Fenelon, French mystical theologian

Second, let's note that Paul assumes that something of this power is available to people like us—and to our friends.

Third, let's note that without this power being available to us, everything Jesus taught and Paul reiterated—including all this stuff about prayer—would be a big lie. It is not a new way of looking at things, not a new state of mind, not some helpful tips to make life easier: The radical promise of the Christian message is that people can be given a power, a strength, and an ability to actually move forward and upward in life. And this is nothing less than God's power working within us.

This amazing fact—God in us—is something we can pray about. The implication is that if we don't pray about it, the power will not be as available to us. If we do pray about it, for us and for our friends, we will experience it more and more.

One area in my life in which I've discerned God's power is my temper. In my younger days, it didn't take much to make me angry: misplacing my glasses, walking into a messy kitchen, arriving late. Over the years I've prayed about this, as have friends for me.

I'd say I'm now better at controlling my outbursts when I'm angry, but I chalk that up mostly to my own willpower. Where I think God has changed me is in getting angry in the first place. Over time, I have found myself unperturbed by situations that would have formerly incited an internal riot.

I remember one day sitting in a traffic jam—at one time a surefire rage producer— and feeling pretty much at peace. I was surprised at my reaction, but also pleased. I couldn't take much credit for it because I simply hadn't actually tried to *feel* calm. I knew I didn't have the power to do that. Instead, it was a gift, I believe from God— his power was working in my warped personality!

How Exactly to Use This Stuff

I am not able to pray Paul's prayer as I do the Psalms. For one thing, it's not as poetic. For another, Paul tends to like run-on sentences, which make me gasp for air by the end. Nor do I find it helpful each day to pray all four requests as modeled here. Frankly, the ideas are too rich to be expressed sincerely all at once.

Instead, I'd suggest that you take one of these ideas and run with it for a day or a week (depending on how you go about praying for others). For example, I might go down my prayer list like this: "Lord, I pray for John, that he might grow in spiritual wisdom and in knowledge of you. I pray for Elizabeth, that she might grow in spiritual wisdom and in knowledge of you." And so on. When I repeat the same words in the same way for each person, I find that the words sink deeper into me, and then I can pray them ever more sincerely.

When such a routine threatens to become monotonous, I'll pray for groups of people, whole families, before I repeat the phrase: "Lord, I pray for John and Elizabeth, and their children Joanna, Michael, and Stephen, that they might grow in spiritual wisdom …."

As I mention each name, I try to picture the person, and I also try to picture God doing something for them that will make *them* happy. This checks my tendency to pray only that people will be fixed according to my desires, but instead that they will be blessed by God in a way that will truly make them happy.

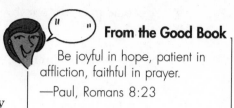

From the Good Book

Be joyful in hope, patient in affliction, faithful in prayer.
—Paul, Romans 8:23

Other Gold Mines of Prayer

If this is a practice you find you enjoy, you're not limited to the language and ideas of this prayer. You might want to meditate on some of Paul's other prayers, including Ephesians 3:14–21; Philippians 1:3–11; and Colossians 1:3–14.

Or you might simply pick a phrase from one of Paul's letters, or even a saying of Jesus', and use that as the key phrase by which you pray for others. Here are some phrases that immediately come to mind:

Prayer Hotline

We should always make room in our prayers for other people. It keeps our prayers from being merely selfish, and it's one practical way we can help others. As one writer put it, "Do not let us fail one another in interest, care, and practical help; but supremely we must not fail one another in prayer."

- ◆ "Lord, help Steven to become purer in heart, that he might see more and more of you." Based on Matthew 5:8, though you could do this with any of the Beatitudes. (Matthew 5:3–10)

- ◆ "Lord, help Kathryn to love you with her whole mind, her whole heart, her entire soul, and with all her strength." Based on Luke 10:27.

- ◆ "Lord, help Monica know that only faith, hope, and love endure, and that the greatest of these is love." Based on 1 Corinthians 13:13.

You get the idea. It's another reason the Bible is *the* book of prayer: Its resources are nearly infinite.

The Least You Need to Know

- ◆ The apostle Paul has a lot to teach us about how to pray for others.

- ◆ Spiritual blessings are of greater importance than material or physical benefits.

- We should pray that our loved ones grow in thankfulness, knowledge, hope, and power.

- We can take Paul's prayers for the churches and insert the names of our loved ones to receive the same blessings.

Part 5

The Greatest Resources of All Time

As has been noted a number of times, the Christian tradition is rich with prayer resources. Christians have been at this prayer stuff for nearly 2,000 years, and along the way they've learned a few things that have stood the test of time.

In this part, we'll look at some of the best prayer stuff Christians have come up with, as well as some that are very much the products of our modern age. And *some* is the operative word. Here are those resources we've found most helpful or interesting.

26

Let's Get Mystical

In This Chapter

- ◆ Mystical prayer in the Christian tradition
- ◆ The greatest mystics
- ◆ Exploring the five stages of mystical prayer
- ◆ How to begin following this way of prayer, including finding a spiritual director

There is a lot in prayer that is logical and rational, but there is a large part that is mysterious. And yet that mysterious part can be so captivating and so very personal. It's often called the mystical dimension of prayer.

Although a lot of pop-religion has focused on the mystical, this tradition is also one of the most misunderstood. At first glance, it seems like the Advanced School of Prayer, and in some ways it is. We are wise, though, to understand it as simply another way of prayer that has its own gifts to impart.

There's Mysticism—and Then There's Mysticism

Mystical prayer is prayer in which the pray-er seeks to experience God, or ultimate reality, in an immediate, direct, intuitive way—that is, you experience God more immediately than the chair you're sitting in. This is a broad definition, so many people who do not consider themselves mystics have had mystical experiences. For such people, including myself, the occasional experience (once or twice in a lifetime) is enjoyed but not sought after, remembered but not dwelt upon.

> **Snapshots of Answered Prayers**
>
> Ezra gave orders that the Jews should fast and pray for a safe journey to Babylon, the land of captivity. In Ezra 8:23 it says that God heard their prayer and they were rescued from their many enemies.

> **Prayer Pearls**
>
> Whether we like it or not, asking is the rule of the kingdom.
> —Charles Spurgeon, Baptist revivalist preacher

For the person pursuing the mystical way, more such experiences are sought, with the ultimate goal of ongoing or complete union with God. No one has understood mysticism better than Evelyn Underhill, an early twentieth-century Anglican writer who said this about a true mystic: "The central fact, it seems to me, is an overwhelming consciousness of God and his own soul: A consciousness which absorbs and eclipses all other centers of interest."

As such, mysticism can be found in every religion: in the Hindu metaphysical system known as the Vedanta, and in the philosophy of Yoga, which offers a rigorous discipline to encourage mystical experiences. Taoism, especially as expounded by its traditional founder, the Chinese philosopher Lao-tzu, has a strong mystical emphasis. The Muslim Sufi sect also practices a form of mysticism that closely resembles that of the Vedanta.

Some forms of Christian mysticism sound very similar to Eastern and Muslim mysticism. But in the best Christian mysticism (that is, the type that seeks to shape itself according to traditional Christian teaching), there are some important differences:

- Though nature can be a vehicle for experiencing God, nature never becomes God in Christian mysticism. For all their profound wonder at nature, Christian mystics always understand that there is a difference between creation and the creator.

- Mystics tend to be impatient with language that limits God—including the language of the Bible, in which God is understood in metaphors: Father, Redeemer, Rock, Lord, King, and so on. Mystics are fond of abstract language, which they believe more readily frees us from thinking about God in our "man-made" categories and allows us to experience God more truly. When they talk about God, they'll use words and phrases like these: Being, the Unknowable, Bare Pure One, Perfect Beauty, Love That Gives All Things Form, Reality, and so on.

Even many Christian mystics move in this direction. "God may well be loved but not thought," wrote the author of the mystical classic *The Cloud of Unknowing*. But in Christian teaching, the biblical metaphors for God—especially Father, Lord, and King—have been given to us by God himself. They are not intended to say everything there is to say about God, but what they do say should not be lightly set aside.

Furthermore, the democracy of history has determined that more people find God and have come to know him better by praying to "Our Father" rather than "The Ground of All Being."

♦ In some forms of mysticism, mystics become increasingly passive and isolated from society. In the Christian tradition, though, mysticism naturally leads to vigorous action in the world. In Christian history, you find mystics running monastic orders (Teresa of Avila), arguing politics with popes and kings (Catherine of Siena), and starting movements that electrify continents (Francis of Assisi).

♦ In non-Christian mysticism, often the goal is for the individual to be absorbed into the divine essence, to have his or her individual personality "obliterated" and united with the All-in-All. This is decidedly not the Christian goal, which is a relationship with God and demands that there will forever remain a distinction between God and us. If a Christian mystic speaks about "obliterating the self," it's usually hyperbole for getting under control those parts of the self that stand in the way of a relationship with God.

A Brief History of Mysticism

Let's go through the following history so that you can see some of the names associated with this form of prayer. This will give you an idea of the breadth and pedigree of the tradition. As a person who likes to know where things have come from, I need this sort of thing before I dip into something new. If you're not into history, though, just move along to the next section.

We start at the very beginning of Christianity: The apostle Paul was the first great Christian mystic. Though he didn't use the terminology or theology of later mysticism, he had his share of mystical experiences: He said he was once "caught up in the third heaven" (2 Corinthians 12:2–3), whatever that means.

Mysticism as we know it today was first articulated in the early Middle Ages, in the writings of Dionysius the Areopagite, a.k.a. Pseudo-Dionysius (because many scholars think someone else wrote this stuff and just attached Dionysius' name to it). He combined Christian theology with Neo-Platonist philosophy (which is where a lot of the abstract language of mysticism comes from).

From the Good Book

I have not stopped giving thanks for you, remembering you in my prayers. I keep asking that the God of our Lord Jesus Christ, the glorious father, may give you the spirit of wisdom and revelation so that you may know him better. I pray also that the eyes of your heart may be enlightened in order that you may know the hope to which he has called you, the riches of his glorious inheritance in the saints, and his incomparably great power for us who believe.

—Paul, Ephesians 1:16–19

In the Middle Ages, the most celebrated mystics were found among the monks of both the Eastern church and the Western church, particularly the "Hesychasts" of Mount Athos, Greece, and, in Western Europe; Bernard of Clairvaux; Hildegard of Bingen; Francis of Assisi; Teresa of Avila; and John of the Cross. Gerhard Groote, a Dutch mystic, founded the monastic order known as the Brothers of the Common Life, which Thomas à Kempis later joined and in which he produced his famous *The Imitation of Christ*, a prayer classic (see the next chapter).

Johannes Eckhart, also known as Meister Eckhart, was the foremost mystic of Germany. Some of his followers, members of a group called the Friends of God, wrote works that influenced the reformer Martin Luther.

Mysticism with an English touch, at least in the 1300s and 1400s, is exemplified by Margery Kempe, Richard Rolle, Walter Hilton, Julian of Norwich, and the anonymous author of *The Cloud of Unknowing*, another classic work on mystical prayer.

Prayer Pearls

You need not cry very loud; he is nearer to us than we think.

—Brother Lawrence, author of *Practicing the Presence of God*

Post-Reformation Catholic works include *The Spiritual Exercises* of Ignatius of Loyola; *The Practice of the Presence of God*, by Brother Lawrence; and the works of seventeenth-century French quietist Jeanne Marie Bouvier de la Motte Guyon, usually called Madam Guyon. On the Protestant side, there's Jakob Boehme's *Mysterium Magnum* (The Great Mystery) and William Law's *Serious Call to a Devout and Holy Life*.

In the twentieth century, the strongest mystical voices were Austrian Roman Catholic Friedrich von Hügel, British Anglican Evelyn Underhill, American Quaker Rufus Jones, French philosophers Simone Weil and Pierre Teilhard de Chardin, and American Trappist monk Thomas Merton. If any of these names have intrigued you in the past, their writings might be a place to begin your own exploration of mysticism.

The Five Stages of Mystical Prayer

Depending on whose material you read, there are as few as three and as many as seven (and sometimes more) stages in the mystical way. Though writers differ on the number, most seem to agree on the characteristic phases that people go through when they try to take up the mystical tradition.

"Stages" and "characteristic phases" are loose terms. These are stages in the same way that there are "stages" in grief. We each experience denial, bargaining, acceptance, and so on, but each stage has a way of returning again—in some ways, all stages are present in each one. Still, we recognize the stages as different types of experiences we have after a loved one has died. The same is true of stages in the mystical way.

Here we examine the classification of Evelyn Underhill as outlined in her now-classic *Mysticism:*

- **Awakening.** The person is first awakened to the reality of spiritual things and to the presence and love of God. This can happen suddenly, in an instant conversion, or it can take place over months or years. The person becomes aware of God's love as never before, and the experience comes with feelings of joy and even exaltation.

- **Purification, also called *purgation*.** Having experienced the love and holiness of God, the person before long recognizes how out of sync with God he is. Thus begins a period of mortification, the killing off of desires, habits, and states of mind that get in the way of God. Often serious disciplines are taken up— longer prayer, fasting, self-examination retreats, sexual chastity, relinquishing possessions—to conquer spiritual sloth and pride. The period is characterized by moral effort and spiritual pain.

- **Illumination.** Now more morally and spiritually honed, the person becomes joyfully aware of God at a new level. The knowing in the "awakening" phase is like enjoying the light of a full moon on a cloudless night; this is like basking in the noontime sun on a summer day.

These first three stages together are often called "the first mystic life," and this is about as far as most mystics travel along the way. As we'll soon see, it is not a perfect and ongoing experience of God, but one in which purgation is still necessary. Still, it is an experience far richer than awakening and is characterized by ongoing peace and joy.

- **Dark night of the soul.** This most terrible experience of the mystical way is sometimes experienced at various points in each stage, and sometimes as an extended period of its own. It is sometimes called "mystic death," for it entails the final and complete purification of the self. It takes its name from a book by this title, written by John of the Cross, in which John describes the new experience.

  The chief characteristic is absolute loss of God, a sense that the sun has been completely obliterated. Desolation and despair are the usual emotions the seeker experiences. It isn't that God literally withdraws—the omnipresent God cannot do that—but he does withdraw every emotional benefit the seeker has so far derived from faith. The seeker continues through the spiritual loneliness knowing that this "spiritual crucifixion" is necessary: One must learn to seek God for God's sake, not for the sake of the happiness God brings.

- **Union.** In this stage, the seeker enjoys God not as in illumination, in which God shines down upon him: Here he becomes one with God. Again, this is not one in the sense that the seeker is destroyed, but one in the sense that husband and wife become one in sex. I'm not being disrespectful here; in fact, sexual imagery is common in mystical teaching, and this stage is often called "mystical marriage."

Books to Get You Started

This is only the briefest of overviews. Underhill's classic is more than 500 pages and is only one book of many on the subject. But if this approach intrigues you still, you might look for others.

> ### Prayer Pearls
>
> He causes his prayers to be of more avail to himself, who offers them also for others.
>
> —Pope Gregory I

For starters, read one of Underhill's books (*Mysticism* or *The Essentials of Mysticism*), or a more modern treatment such as Father Benedict Groeschel's *Spiritual Passages: The Psychology of Spiritual Development* (Crossroad, 1990). Whereas Underhill's book describes all of mysticism, Groeschel's book concentrates on discussing the stages (he has three)—how they are experienced psychologically and spiritually, as well as some of their dangers and opportunities.

You may also want to read a classic in mystical writing: Teresa of Avila's *The Interior Castle,* or John of the Cross's *Ascent of Mount Carmel.*

Getting "Professional" Help

If you're going to embark on this way, you also are wise to find a spiritual director—all the great mystics had them. These are people skilled in the art of discerning the spiritual life. You meet with them as you would a counselor (though not at the cost!), and you discuss your spiritual life. Some are more directive, giving assignments each week (or month—however often you meet); others are nondirective, asking questions to help the seeker to understand better how God is speaking.

Spiritual directors are not listed in the phone book as such, but many monasteries have people who specialize in spiritual direction. You might also contact a local Roman Catholic or Episcopal priest, who may know other places in your area where you can find a spiritual director.

You are better off not using your own pastor or priest, because the relationship with the spiritual director is more intimate than most people feel is appropriate with their clergy person. In fact, I believe that it's best to not know your spiritual director in any other setting. Let this person's one job be as your spiritual director—not pastor, teacher, friend, or whatever. This way he can focus on you in just this one capacity.

Furthermore, you are probably wise to select a spiritual director of your own gender. First, there's the matter of intimacy; you don't want to start becoming confused about your feelings for your spiritual director. Enough said. Second, the spiritual life is a gendered life. How we experience God is in many ways shaped by our gender and how we relate to people of the same and opposite sex. In most circumstances, these aspects of spirituality are best discerned by someone of your own gender.

Prayer Hotline

You may want first to visit a few individuals to discuss their philosophy and approach before settling on the one person who is going to help guide your spiritual life. And there is no law that says you can't change your spiritual director if you're not being helped.

Don't expect your spiritual director to pamper you. Sometimes he or she will challenge you to the point of discomfort, though it is ultimately for your own good. A pamphlet, "O God, Revive Us Again" by Harold Voelkel (revised by Will Bruce), describes one such encounter.

Miss Aletta Jacobsz had a profound spiritual impact in Korea in the 1940s. She was never happy encouraging a general confession of sins when she talked with individuals. Her dealings with one prominent Presbyterian missionary are a case in point.

She asked him, "Have you considered Matthew 6:33, 'Seek ye first the kingdom of God'?"

The missionary said he preached on it often.

"Are you willing to face this truth squarely," she continued, "and see if you are actually seeking God's will first in all things?"

After a few moments of reflection, he replied, "Well, I suppose I am not seeking God first in everything. Yes, I will have to admit I am not always putting Christ first in my life."

The relentless Jacobsz continued: "Now, since you say you have preached this truth frequently, and you now recognize you are not fulfilling it in your life, what would you consider anyone, who, while urging others to do something, is not doing it himself?"

"A hypocrite," the missionary replied.

"Then how do you characterize yourself?"

"A hypocrite."

Soon he had listed not only hypocrisy, but a long list of sins that had been weighing him down but which he hadn't confronted. This painful process led him to a new sense of God's forgiveness and peace.

In any event, having a guide is crucial—and even if you're not going to embark on the more strenuous mystical way, it can be a big help. Climbers of Mt. Everest don't go without a guide, for sure. But even those who simply want to take a nature walk through Yosemite Valley find that a ranger's company can make the experience more meaningful.

The Least You Need to Know

♦ The mystical way is a powerful strand in the history and practice of prayer.

♦ There are some key differences between Christian and non-Christian mysticism, especially related to who God is and how we relate to him.

♦ There are five stages common to much mystical experience, from first being aware of spiritual reality to experiencing final union with God.

♦ If we get involved in the complex world of mysticism, we should find an experienced spiritual director.

Chapter 27

The Imitation of Christ

In This Chapter

- Thomas à Kempis's *The Imitation of Christ*, one of the greatest devotional works of all time

- A look at how one of the most devout men in history thought about his relationship to God

- Understanding what the classics of devotional literature are about

- How devotional literature benefits our spiritual lives

Sir Thomas More, England's famous Lord Chancellor under Henry VIII (and the subject of the film *A Man for All Seasons*), said it was one of the three books that everybody ought to own. Ignatius of Loyola, founder of the Jesuits, read a chapter a day from it and regularly gave it as a gift. Methodist founder John Wesley said it was the best summary of the Christian life he had ever read, and he translated it for his followers. Thomas Merton, America's best-known writer on the spiritual life, said it was one of the first works to begin his conversion.

The Imitation of Christ by Thomas à Kempis has been translated into more than 50 languages, in editions too numerous for scholars to keep track of. (By 1779, there were already 1,800 editions.) Not counting the Bible, it has been the most popular of Christian classics. If you're going to get serious about prayer, this is one book you'll want to become familiar with.

A Book for Spiritual Novices

"When you read the opening lines of *The Imitation of Christ*, a clear voice reaches you with a promise that is as compelling today as it was in the fifteenth century." So writes Sally Cunneen in her preface to a recent edition of *The Imitation of Christ*.

That voice has been heard clearly by people of all stations and callings of life, but it was originally written for a select audience: men who desired to become monks. It was written as a guide to help them mature spiritually. But it wasn't long after its author's death that a larger audience was invited to consider its contents, for it quickly became apparent that the book made a whole lot of sense to anyone seeking to grow spiritually.

Thomas à Kempis (1379–1471) was a German monk who spent most of his life in a Dutch monastery with a group called The Brethren of the Common Life. When he became the prior's assistant, à Kempis was charged with instructing novices in the spiritual life. In that capacity, he wrote four booklets that were later collected and named after the title of the first booklet.

À Kempis wanted to help his readers become more like Christ—that is, more virtuous, with a fuller interior life and with a closer relationship with God. He does not teach by way of reason (though what he says makes a lot of sense); instead, he attempts to speak to our hearts and our yearning to be like Christ. It's not intellectual insight but spiritual strength and encouragement that he tries to impart.

The power of *The Imitation of Christ* comes from at least three sources. First, it is an encyclopedia of spiritual wisdom of the ages. It is the fruit of à Kempis's lifelong pursuit of spiritual perfection and his deep reading of the Bible, Augustine, Bernard of Clairvaux, and other great spiritual writers. The book is littered with quotes and paraphrases from rich spiritual resources.

Second, à Kempis expresses his thoughts in language that is unusually simple and to the point. Many writers easily fall into vague language and abstract terminology if they attempt to capture the essence of the spiritual life. Not this one. À Kempis speaks in a language that is accessible to a novice and yet that contains wisdom that the most spiritually advanced can learn from.

Snapshots of Answered Prayers
When Daniel heard that King Darius signed an edict that he could not pray to God, he went and did exactly that. When Daniel was later thrown to the lions, he was unharmed. The king then threw in his enemies, who were devoured. Read this story of faith and heroism in Daniel 6.

Third, à Kempis has a profound understanding of human nature. Some are surprised that a man who spent his whole life confined to a monastery could understand the dynamics of human behavior so well. But we forget that monks live in an intense form of human community—with all its joys, sorrows, sins, virtues, daily irritations, and profound wonder. And à Kempis happened to have been better than most at expressing the complexities of the human heart.

The Essence of *Imitation*

A quick overview of the contents may help you decide where you want to dip in first. *The Imitation of Christ* should not be read like a novel, in which you race through many chapters at a sitting. Instead, it should be read as we read the Bible devotionally, one chapter at a time at most. After that you'll want to meditate patiently on what you've read until the words enlarge you in some way.

Book One is titled "Helpful Counsels for the Spiritual Life." À Kempis advises us to renounce superficial pursuits and pleasures and to give ourselves to humility as we pursue the interior life. "If you knew the entire Bible inside and out and all the maxims of the philosophers," he writes, "what good would it do you if you were, at the same time, without God's love and grace? … This is the highest wisdom: To despise the world and seek the kingdom of God." (More on this business of "despising" the world in a bit.)

In Book Two, titled "Directives for the Interior Life," à Kempis develops the themes introduced in Book One. Because the kingdom of God is within, he argues, it cannot be perceived with the senses:

> Why look about you? This place is not the place of your rest. Your dwelling place is to be in heaven, and you should view all earthly things as passing shadows. Everything is transitory and so are you. So do not cling to ephemeral things, otherwise you will get caught in their webs and perish.

Or, more positively:

> He who sees all things as they really are, and not as they are said to be or thought to be, is truly wise, for God is his teacher and not man. He who knows how to walk with the light from within and makes little of outward things needs no special place nor definite time to perform religious exercises.

Throughout the book, we are told to listen attentively to God's call, and that to do so we need humility, inner peace, pure intentions, a good conscience, and constant attentiveness. À Kempis also spends much ink on what it means to be a friend of

Jesus: "Love Jesus and keep him as your friend. When all others forsake you, he will not leave you nor will he allow you to perish on the last day."

Book Three, the longest of the four books, is titled "On Interior Consolation" and treats the book's themes afresh, just as a composer does with the themes of his symphony. This book is cast in the form of a dialogue between Jesus and the disciple, and it concentrates on the disciple's desire to reach new spiritual heights.

Jesus: My son, you must give all for all and keep nothing back for yourself. Realize that there is nothing more harmful to you in this world than self-love ….

If your love be pure, simple, and properly ordered, then nothing can ever hold you captive. Neither desire what you should not have, nor possess anything that could hinder you or rob you of your interior freedom ….

From the Good Book

And pray in the Spirit on all occasions with all kinds of prayers and requests. With this in mind, be alert and always keep on praying for all the saints.

—Paul, Ephesians 6:18

Disciple: Uphold me, Lord, with the grace of your Holy Spirit. Give strength to my inner self and empty my heart of all useless cares and concerns.

Finally, Book Four, "An Invitation to Holy Communion," is a guide to preparing for and taking communion, and it emphasizes the healing powers of the sacrament.

On Not Despising Thomas

Before we consider a sample chapter, I should address a couple of matters that will probably concern modern readers. Some, for example, may find à Kempis's exclusive use of male pronouns a problem. Then again, à Kempis meant them literally: He was writing to monks. Besides, plenty of female saints, including Thérèse of Lisieux, have been able to translate the material so that it has become meaningful for them.

Then there is à Kempis's stark dualism between this world and the kingdom of God, with the repeated instruction to "despise" the world or one's self, to forsake human friendship, and so on. Before we reject such extreme counsel too quickly, we might first consider his reason for speaking so forcefully and look for the grain of truth.

It may be that à Kempis has taken things a bit far—after all, we are commanded in the Bible to love ourselves, to thank God for his creation, and to seek the solace of friends. Then again, we may be clinging to creation so tightly that we are unable to experience the creator.

Finally, there is à Kempis's economy of expression. He often says things that demand elaboration—and then he doesn't bother to elaborate. He acts as if we know exactly what he was talking about. For example, in Chapter 13, "How to Resist Temptation," he says, "Many attempt to flee temptations, but they only sink more deeply into them. Conflicts are not won by running away; rather it is by humbly and patiently standing up to them that we gain strength against all our enemies."

This is a profound thought, but it leaves a number of questions unanswered: What exactly does it mean to "flee" temptation? How is "standing up" to it different? How can we "gain strength" from standing up to temptation if we don't feel we have the strength to stand up to it in the first place? And so on.

À Kempis speaks so tersely and leaves so many questions unanswered that we will be tempted to toss the book aside as the idealistic ramblings of a medieval mystic. But we mustn't read à Kempis, or any deep writer, as we would a modern how-to book (like this one!). How-to books are intended to explain. Books of spiritual devotion are intended to prod, probe, and force us to pray more deeply. The best ones will sometimes leave us wondering, pondering, and even a little irritated that we can't quite get a handle on things. That tension is precisely the thing that makes us want to give up—or that allows us to go deeper than we could have imagined.

> ### Prayer Pearls
>
> Prayer is naught but a rising desire of the heart into God by withdrawing of the heart from all earthly thoughts.
>
> —Walter Hilton, English mystic

Love of the Alone

To give you a flavor of *The Imitation of Christ*, let's look more closely at one of the chapters, "The Love of Silence and Solitude" (Chapter 20, in Book One). This chapter directly concerns the theme of this book, and I'd like to work through it as I would a prayer journal. This will give you one example of how to use *The Imitation of Christ* in your prayer life. Thomas's words (the really good stuff) are indented; my reflections are in *italic*.

> Set aside an opportune time for deep personal reflection and think often about God's many benefits to you. Give up all light and frivolous matters, and read what inspires you to repentance of soul and not what just entertains the mind.

Lord, on the one hand, I'm not very good at thinking about the "many benefits" you bestow on me. On the other hand, I'm pretty good at reading what inspires "repentance." But I'm tired of doing things that way. It's so self-punishing. I'm not doubting that there's a lot to repent of, and to repent of time and again (greed, lust, sloth, selfishness, and so on). It's just that it's a vicious cycle. Perhaps if I focused more on the many blessings you grant me, I'd be more joyful and have more energy to deal with repentance issues.

If you abstain from unnecessary conversation and useless visiting, as well as from listening to idle news and gossip, you will find sufficient and suitable times for your meditations. The great saints avoided the company of men as much as they could, because they wanted to live for God in silence.

Lord, there is wisdom here, but I'm confused how to put it into practice. I am indeed weary of "useless visiting" and "listening to idle news and gossip," but it does seem to be what many people want to talk about. If I refuse to participate in such conversations, I'll seem aloof, won't I? People won't think I really want to talk with them because I think they are superficial. But isn't one of the gifts of life to enjoy "useless" conversation with friends? Does everything I do and say have to be "useful"?

Then again, there is enough truth here to move forward. I admit to spending too much time in useless and unnecessary activities, and they do take time away from you. Help me to be better disciplined with my time.

If you aim at a fervent spiritual life, then you too must turn your back on the crowds as Jesus did. The only man who can safely appear in public is the one who wishes he were at home. He alone can safely speak who prefers to be silent. Only he can safely govern who prefers to live in submission, and only he can safely command who prefers to obey.

Lord, at first I balked at the sentence about Jesus. For it seemed to me that this— turning his back on the crowds—is precisely what Jesus did not do. And then I remembered that there were definite moments when he went off by himself, away from the crowds and even away from the disciples. And then he just prayed—all through the night, no less.

I tend to think of Jesus as a man of the people and a man of action. But I forget that he was a man of prayer first. I keep seeing the world in dichotomies that don't exist—as if one could not be a person of prayer and a person of action. It's not either/or, but both/and.

I go through periods when I yearn to be one or the other. Sometimes I want to become a monk and pray the rest of my life. Other times, prayer seems like such a waste of time compared to writing or building a bookcase. Maybe if I could get some balance in my life—with an ongoing and steady diet of both prayer and action—I wouldn't swing back and forth as I do.

> **Prayer Pearls**
>
> He who has learned to pray has learned the greatest secret of a holy and happy life.
>
> —William Law, Anglican author

Recommended Editions

You get the idea: À Kempis's *The Imitation of Christ* is a wise book that can provoke you into deeper thought and prayer. As I mentioned, there are many editions and many translations of *The Imitation of Christ.* You'll probably find more than one edition at your local library alone, not to mention your local bookstore. Read through a chapter or two before you choose an edition. Read also the introductory material, and notice the type of footnotes or end notes the edition has. Make sure they are at the level (some are more scholarly, some more devotional, some are nonexistent!) that you desire.

There is no one right edition, of course, but I've enjoyed (and used in preparing this chapter) the one published by Vintage, in the Vintage Spiritual Classics series. This *Imitation* was edited and translated by Joseph N. Tylenda, S.J., and includes a splendid preface by Sally Cunneen; it was most recently published in 1998.

The Least You Need to Know

- *The Imitation of Christ* is a perennial spiritual classic filled with the wisdom of the ages and a profound understanding of human nature.

- Devotional books are not how-to books, but rather are intended to motivate us to draw closer to God.

- We should interact with these books, even argue with them, to get the most out of them.

- Thomas à Kempis emphasizes the need to be alone with God in silence so that we may learn how to better please him.

Chapter 28

The Jesus Prayer

In This Chapter

◆ The history of the Jesus prayer

◆ How to use this ancient practice in your own prayer life

◆ How to repeat this prayer without it becoming rote

◆ The meaning of each word and phrase of this prayer

It seemed like the most unimaginable idea for a national commemoration: a rectangular granite block with a bunch of names chiseled into it. But it has turned out to be our nation's most moving monument. I'm referring, of course, to the Vietnam Memorial in Washington, D.C. If you've been there, you know what I mean. It's a typical experience: Someone walks along the wall searching. He stops, runs his finger over the letters of a name, and begins to weep. Such is the power of a name.

We tend to think of names as mere labels. We call the skinny thing we use to write "pen"; we call the thing we sit in "chair"; and we call our newborn "Luke." But it's not quite the same because as "Luke" grows and interacts with us and others, he creates relationships and memories. It doesn't take long before "Luke" is a history of relationships and memories, and when we say "Luke," something happens inside us, however subtle, so that all this comes back to us, mostly unconsciously.

This is especially true when a certain young woman meets Luke and creates her own history with him. She begins to find herself thinking of Luke often. And there comes a time that whenever "Luke" is mentioned, she is very conscious of what is happening: She is stabbed with that most delirious of feelings that we call being in love.

Names are not labels, at least not with people we know and love. And the mere mention of a loved one's name is enough to remember our love and even to make it grow deeper. This is the idea behind one of the most venerable prayer practices in the Christian tradition, called the Jesus prayer.

The Way of a Pilgrim

As told in the Russian spiritual classic *The Way of the Pilgrim*, the story goes that a poor, lame Russian peasant was traveling all over Russia and Siberia, with a knapsack that contained only dried bread, a Bible, and a heart that yearned to discover what the apostle Paul meant when he advised, "Pray without ceasing."

> **From the Good Book**
>
> Do not be anxious about anything, but in everything, by prayer and petition, with thanksgiving, present your requests to God. And the peace of God, which transcends all understanding, will guard your hearts and your minds in Christ Jesus.
>
> —Paul, Philippians 4:6

One day this pilgrim met a *starets*, a spiritual father, who taught him the Jesus prayer: "Lord Jesus Christ, have mercy on me." The spiritual father told him to pray it 3,000 times a day. After the pilgrim obliged, the spiritual father told him to do it 6,000 times a day—then 12,000.

What happened eventually was this: The pilgrim stopped counting because the prayer had become a part of him, and he prayed it with every breath. Finally, he spoke no words; as he put it, "The lips stopped moving, and the only thing left to do was to listen to the heart speak."

The pilgrim continued on his way, and he met many others—peasants, civil servants, landowners—who shared his desire for a life of ceaseless prayer. On his journeys, he often faced hunger, thirst, cold, and hostile people. At such times, he said, the prayer saved him:

> When the bitter cold cuts through me, I repeat my prayer with even more fervor, and I feel warmed up. When hunger begins to torture me, I invoke the name of Jesus Christ more often, and I forget that I want to eat …. If someone hurts me, I just think, 'How sweet is the Jesus prayer,' and the offense and the resentment fly away and are forgotten.

He then summed up his experience with the Jesus prayer:

> I have nearly lost all feeling; I have no cares; I have no desires; nothing attracts me. The only thing that I desire is to pray, pray without ceasing, and when I pray, I am filled with joy.

It is debated whether this story is fiction or fact, but in either case, it was written to inspire others to learn to pray without ceasing and to introduce them to the centuries-old practice, especially in the Eastern Orthodox tradition, of invoking the name of Jesus in prayer.

> **Snapshots of Answered Prayers**
>
> When the Israelites began to complain to the Lord about their hardships, God's anger blazed and he sent fire among their camp. In Numbers 11:1–3 they asked Moses to pray; after he did, the fire stopped.

The History of Jesus' Name

The idea of praying in or with Jesus' name goes back to Jesus himself, who told his disciples, "You can ask for anything in my name, and I will do it." (John 14:13) Early Christians would often chant, "Kyrie eleison," which means "Lord, have mercy." Over the centuries this developed into the practice of what are called "ejaculatory prayers," short prayers said many times during the day, and finally into a prayer we know as the Jesus prayer: "Lord Jesus Christ, son of God, have mercy on me."

The prayer has always been flexible. Some make it more confessional, adding "a sinner" at the end. Some make it more communal, praying, "have mercy on *us.*" But the basic idea is the same: a repeated invocation of the name of Jesus.

Exploring the Prayer

This prayer is not a magical formula, as if the more times you say it, the more holy you become. But it is like the Lord's Prayer, a prayer that sums up so much of what we long to say. It is also a prayer that, because it invokes the name of Jesus, begins to do something to us without our being aware of it.

The idea here is similar to invoking the name of a loved one now dead. To invoke the name "Ruby" at a Galli family gathering is to invoke memories of my mother—and smiles and laughter as we remember her passion, her flair, her dramatics, her energy.

To invoke the name of Jesus is to invoke the memory of the God-man who walked among us, whose story we recall in the Gospels, stories of compassion, wisdom, authority, mercy, and love. But there's one big difference: Jesus is not dead. So to invoke the name of Jesus is also to make us aware of his ongoing presence in our lives.

To make the Jesus prayer an integral part of our day is to make the living reality of Jesus an integral part of our day.

This prayer hints at a lot of theological truths. In it one finds a reference to God's sovereignty ("Lord"), to the incarnation ("Jesus"), salvation ("Christ"), the Trinity ("Son of God" implies a Father and the Spirit who proceeds from the Father) grace ("have mercy")—I could go on and on. But for the purposes of this book, it also covers a lot of ground in terms of prayer:

> **Prayer Pearls**
>
> There is not in the world a kind of life more sweet and delightful than that of a continual conversation with God.
>
> —Brother Lawrence, author of *Practicing the Presence of God*

- ◆ **Adoration.** To begin, we praise Jesus for being "Lord," the one in control of history, who is driving all the apparent chaos of life to a glorious end. In calling him the "Son of God," we imply a prayer to the Father, and thus, to the Holy Spirit, and inadvertently we recognize the mystery of the Trinity. In seeking his mercy, we imply that he is merciful.

- ◆ **Confession.** To seek mercy—and especially if we add at the end, "a sinner"—is to go before Christ penitent, weak, helpless, in need of his healing touch.

- ◆ **Thanksgiving.** To pray this prayer is to acknowledge that not only can Jesus heal our hearts but that he will do so. As such, this is a prayer of thanksgiving for all the healing he has accomplished in our lives and all the healing he will bring to us in the future.

- ◆ **Intercession.** Some people try to pray the Jesus prayer silently whenever they meet another during the day, some changing it to "have mercy on us." In this way, it becomes a prayer that reaches out to others and pulls us closer to others.

Doing It

There are two principle ways of using this prayer: prayer of the heart and prayer of daily life.

Prayer of the heart has been emphasized by those of the "hesychast" tradition, the mystical tradition within the Eastern Orthodox Church. In this method, the person sits alone, with head bowed and mind focused on the stomach or chest (that is, the "center" of one's being). He empties his mind of all rational thoughts and eliminates every picture or image. Then "without thought of imagination," but with concentration, he repeats the Jesus prayer silently. (The Greek word *hesychia* means "silence.")

This method, if practiced faithfully and in the context of participation in the larger life of the church, is said to unite the pray-er with God so that she experiences the "uncreated divine Light" and "unspeakable joy of the soul."

Everything I've read on the Jesus prayer firmly states that this practice should never be undertaken without a spiritual director. As Father Thomas Hopko, a leading Orthodox theologian, put it, "To use this method without guidance or humble wisdom is to court spiritual disaster." (For that matter, anyone whose prayer life transports them into more mystical dimensions should seek out a spiritual director. The spiritual is a powerful dimension and can become destructive if not guided by someone with experience and wisdom.)

In the *prayer of daily life*, the Jesus prayer is said in the normal course of one's prayer and life. You might pray it verbally or silently for a few minutes at the beginning and/or the end of your daily prayer. You might repeat it a few times at lunch or before you retire for the night (saying the Jesus prayer instead of counting sheep!). You can say it silently whenever you meet someone during the day or as you pick up the phone as a way of praying for the person you are about to speak with.

The key in this method, as with any prayer repeated over and over, is to avoid what Jesus himself called "vain repetitions." To pray it unthinkingly, as if it were a good luck charm, is to misuse the prayer. But you can repeat it, over and over, rolling it around in your mind, savoring every part of it, concentrating on one word and then another—"enjoying" it as one would a glass of fine wine. That's not "vain repetition," but meaningful immersion in the prayer.

Prayer Hotline

I try to make the Jesus prayer the first thing on my lips in the morning, and I often repeat it as I fall asleep at night. It's a very good way to bookend one's day.

Getting the Most out of It

One more thing that has already been mentioned but is worth highlighting: This prayer is not the property of the individual. It belongs to the entire church. It arose out of the church's history and will become most meaningful if prayed in the context of the church. That means participating in the worship and life of a local congregation, with people who regularly worship the "Lord Jesus Christ" as the "Son of God," and who together experience his "mercy."

Of course you *can* pray it by yourself. There's no law against it. But the experience of those who have been most transformed by this prayer suggests that it needs to be balanced with corporate prayer. More of this will be discussed in Part 6.

The Least You Need to Know

♦ Praying with the name of Jesus goes back to when he told his apostles to ask for anything in his name.

♦ The purpose of the Jesus prayer is to unite us in a close relationship with Christ on an ongoing basis.

♦ You should not just repeat this prayer without thinking.

♦ Periodic meditation on the parts of the prayer will keep it from becoming rote and meaningless.

29

An Uncommon Prayer Book

In This Chapter

- ◆ How *The Book of Common Prayer* came to be
- ◆ How *The Book of Common Prayer* can be a rich resource for your personal prayer life
- ◆ A study of one service in that book, Morning Prayer
- ◆ Some of the finest prayers in *The Book of Common Prayer*

The works of Shakespeare, the King James Bible, and *The Book of Common Prayer* were all written within decades of one another (in the late 1500s and early 1600s), and each was destined to become a classic of the English language.

Most people know the lasting influence of Shakespeare and the King James Bible, but not as many know that *The Book of Common Prayer*, the official prayer book of Anglican and Episcopal churches, continues to be used by millions of people to guide their individual and corporate prayer. It is a book rich in biblical allusions and historic prayers that have stood the test of time. Even non-Anglicans have found it a treasure—I certainly have.

Prayer for the Ages

I first began using *The Book of Common Prayer* (abbreviated BCP from now on) when I was a Presbyterian. In that tradition, which was strongly colored by my early experiences in the evangelical community, prayer is the spontaneous expression of one's thoughts to God. I discovered, though, that after years of daily praying, my spontaneous expressions were trite, boring, and predictable. I was ready to give up prayer when I discovered the BCP.

> **Prayer Pearls**
>
> Prayer is the service of the heart.
> —Talmud, the written collection of Jewish law and tradition

It's not that I gave up spontaneous prayer—which to me still must be the staple of one's prayer life—but the BCP did help me move out of my boredom and triteness and taught me to pray better.

Long History

The first full edition of the BCP was composed by Archbishop Thomas Cranmer in 1552 for use in the new Church of England. The English church had just broken away from Roman Catholicism, and the English wanted to worship in, well, English, not Latin. Cranmer condensed five huge Latin volumes that guided Roman Catholic worship into one. The BCP has been revised in minor ways a couple of times since.

In 1979, the Episcopal Church in the United States updated the Elizabethan English (though still keeping an Elizabethan version of some prayers and services, which are usually referred to as "rite I"). In large measure, the BCP we use today is the BCP of Cranmer's day. For the rest of this chapter, it is this American version to which I am referring.

Because the BCP is the official prayer book of the Episcopal Church, it includes the order for all sorts of services—not only Sunday morning worship, but also baptisms, weddings, funerals, ordinations, and so on. For the individual pray-er, it's not those sections that are most helpful, but the services called Morning Prayer, Evening Prayer, and Compline.

As its name suggests, Morning Prayer is to be said in the morning and can be used for Sunday worship. Evening Prayer is designed for early evening, and Compline is ideal for the very end of the day. I'll let you explore Evening Prayer and Compline on your own. For this chapter, let me take you through Morning Prayer (specifically, Morning Prayer II, which is the rite that uses contemporary English).

Though Morning Prayer is designed for group worship, many people use it to guide their personal morning prayer. Some change every "we" and "us" to "I" and "me," but I prefer to keep the first-person plurals to remind me that others worldwide are using this to guide their prayers. This helps me experience in some small way my essential connection with these pray-ers.

This more formal approach to daily prayer may not be for you, or not for you at this time in your prayer life. If so, just skip the rest of this chapter and move on to the next section of the book.

If you're sticking with me, you'll be reading many quotes from Morning Prayer because you can't really get a feel for it otherwise.

> **Prayer Pearls**
>
> I have not the courage to search through books for beautiful prayers …. Unable either to say them all or choose between them, I do as a child would do who cannot read—I just say what I want to say to God, quite simply, and he never fails to understand.
>
> —St. Thérèse of Lisieux

To Begin

Morning Prayer begins with an opening sentence, a number of which are printed at the beginning under the headings of church seasons (see Chapter 35 for more on church seasons) or "At any time." These are brief affirmations from Scripture that set the tone for worship, such as these:

- I was glad when they said to me, "Let us go to the house of the Lord." (Psalm 122:1)

- "Let the words of my mouth and the meditations of my heart be acceptable in your sight, O Lord, my strength and my redeemer." (Psalm 19:14)

Then follows a confession of sin, which is a fuller way to prepare oneself:

> Most merciful God, we confess that we have sinned against you in thought, word, and deed, by what we have done, and by what we have left undone ….

I'll stop here because I've quoted this prayer in full already. As I said earlier, I try to pause after each phrase, however briefly, to allow my mind to let one specific sin come to mind. Then follows the pardon:

> Almighty God, have mercy on us, forgive us all our sins, through our Lord Jesus Christ, strengthen us in all goodness, by the power of the Holy Spirit keep you in eternal life. Amen.

Psalm Prep

Next comes the morning Psalm, which is introduced with these lines:

> Lord, open our lips.

> And our mouths shall proclaim your praise.

This frame follows:

> Glory be to the father, and to the son, and to the Holy Spirit, as it was in the beginning, is now, and will be forever. Amen.

Next comes another short sentence called an "antiphon," (which acts like a theme sentence) followed by a special psalm called "Venite" or another called "Jubilate." Don't let the Latin terms intimidate you; they are merely the first words of each Psalm in Latin. You can read either Psalm, but I like Venite better. The first stanza goes like this:

> Come let us sing to the Lord,

> let us shout for joy to the rock of our salvation

> Let us come before his presence with thanks-giving

> and raise a loud shout to him with psalms.

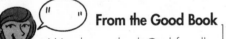

From the Good Book

We always thank God for all of you, mentioning you in our prayers. We continually remember before our God and father your work produced by faith, your labor prompted by love, and your endurance inspired by hope in our Lord Jesus Christ.
—Paul, Silas, and Timothy, 1 Thessalonians 1:2, 3

Again, all this is designed to shape one's heart and mind to prepare for the hearing of Scripture, which is the heart of this service.

In the back of the BCP, you'll find suggested Scripture readings for each day, including a suggested Psalm, which is to be read next. After the Psalm is read, the "frame" is completed, as above, with: "Glory be to the father, and to the son, and to the Holy Spirit, as it was in the beginning, is now, and will be forever. Amen."

Prayer Central

The next part, called "The Lessons," is comprised of three readings, one each from the Old Testament, New Testament epistles, and the Gospels. Here is the climax of Morning Prayer. The idea is that through Scripture God speaks to us, thus completing the dialogue of prayer. This is why the service spends a great deal of time preparing for this part: We want to be mentally and spiritually alert when God speaks.

Again, the specific readings for the day are found at the back of the BCP. Daily readings are divided into two years, so if you were to follow this guide, you would read nearly the entire Bible in two years.

After each reading, it is appropriate to say, "The word of the Lord. Thanks be to God," and then wait in silence, for sometimes in the silence of meditation, a feeling or a thought comes that makes the passage just read speak to your personal situation—this is indeed a word from the Lord that is to be listened to closely. But even when no specific word comes as such, the simple act of meditating on Scripture reveals general truths that can enrich us.

After each reading and meditation, (or for me, after all three readings), a "Canticle" is said. A canticle is merely a passage of the Bible that is songlike (in fact, when Morning Prayer is said in church, these canticles are often sung). One of my favorites is Canticle 15, "The Song of Mary," also called the *Magnificat*, which was the prayer of Mary after hearing the news that she was pregnant with Jesus. Yet her words transcend that setting. The first lines go like this:

> My soul proclaims the greatness of the Lord,
>
> my spirit rejoices in God my savior;
>
> for he has looked with favor on his lowly servant.
>
> From this day all generations will call me blessed,
>
> the Almighty has done great things for me,
>
> and holy is his name.

There are 21 canticles to choose from, so it is easy to say one after each reading and not become repetitive.

This section ends with a reciting of the Apostles' Creed, which is one of the oldest summaries of Christian teaching. This is a concise and poetic way to rehearse the main story line of the entire Bible, from creation to ultimate redemption:

> I believe in God, the Father almighty,
>
> Creator of heaven and earth.
>
> I believe in Jesus Christ, his only Son, our Lord,

He was conceived by the power of the Holy Spirit

and born of the Virgin Mary.

He suffered under Pontius Pilate,

was crucified, died, and was buried.

He descended to the dead.

On the third day he rose again.

He ascended into heaven,

and is seated at the right hand of the Father.

I believe in the Holy Spirit,

the holy catholic church,

the communion of saints,

the forgiveness of sins,

the resurrection of the body,

and the life everlasting. Amen.

> **Prayer Pearls**
>
> A good prayer, though often used, is still fresh and fair in the eyes and ears of heaven.
> —Thomas Fuller, English clergyman

There is a certain amount of jargon here, and not every part is equally comprehended, even by the best of theological minds. It is not critical that you understand everything, but as you say it, you affirm that this, in fact, is the teaching of Scripture and that in saying it, you desire to "grow into" the creed over time.

The Prayers

"The Prayers" is the prosaic title of the last part of Morning Prayer, which opens with the Lord's Prayer followed by one of two "suffrages" or petitionary prayers set in responsive form. One person or group says the first line up to the semicolon, another person or group responds to the end of the sentence. For private prayer, though, Suffrage A would be said simply, like this:

Show us your mercy, O Lord;

And grant us your salvation.

Clothe your ministers with righteousness;

Let your people sing with joy.

Give peace, O Lord, in all the world;

For only in you can we live in safety.

Lord, keep this nation under your care;

And guide us in the way of justice and truth.

Let your way be known upon earth;

Your saving health among all nations.

Let not the needy, O Lord, be forgotten;

Nor the hope of the poor be taken away.

Create in us clean hearts, O God;

And sustain us with your Holy Spirit.

As you can see, this prayer includes petitions for the church (both ministers and people), for the nation, for the world, for the poor, and for hope. I find this an elegant way to pray for these larger issues.

This is followed by the daily "collect," a prayer that sums up a theme for the day. Some of these are listed by the day of the week and others by theme. One of my favorites is the Collect for Guidance:

Heavenly Father, in you we live and move and have our being: We humbly pray you so to guide and govern us by your Holy Spirit, that in all the cares and occupations of our life we may not forget you, but may remember that we are ever walking in your sight; through Jesus Christ, our lord. Amen.

Grand Finale

Near the end of Morning Prayer comes one of the finest prayers in the entire BCP, "The General Thanksgiving":

Almighty God, Father of all mercies,

we, your unworthy servants, give you humble thanks

for all your goodness and loving kindness

to us and to all whom you have made.

We bless you for your creation, preservation,

and all the blessings of this life;

but above all for your immeasurable love

in the redemption of the world by our Lord Jesus Christ;

for the means of grace and the hope of glory.

And, we pray, give us such an awareness of your mercies,

that with truly thankful hearts we may show forth your praise,

not only with our lips, but in our lives,

by giving up our selves to your service,

and by walking before you

in holiness and righteousness all our days;

through Jesus Christ our Lord,

to whom, with you and the Holy Spirit,

be honor and glory throughout all ages. Amen.

Prayer Hotline

In case you're wondering: Morning prayer takes anywhere from 10 to 20 minutes or longer, depending on how much meditation you do after each Scripture reading and how many canticles and the like you include.

This is packed; each phrase has a wealth of meaning that can take a lifetime to uncover. You may want to commit this to memory. I've found no better full and yet concise expression of my thankfulness to God.

The service then concludes with one of three final sentences of Scripture, like this one: "May the God of hope fill us with all joy and peace in believing through the power of the Holy Spirit. Amen." (Romans 15:13)

A Rich Resource

The BCP has more prayer resources still. In addition to Evening Prayer and Compline (which are not as full as Morning Prayer), there is a section of "Prayers and Thanksgivings" useful for all sorts of occasions. There are collects for each week of the year, and then some. All 150 Psalms, in a very readable translation, are included. And, as I mentioned, there are guides to Scripture reading, both daily and weekly, that will get you through the Bible in an orderly way.

Perhaps you can see why the BCP is not merely the official prayer book of Episco-palians but is also a resource for anyone interested in deepening his prayer life. Most major bookstores carry a copy in their "Religion" or "Spirituality" or "Prayer" sections, or you can order it through Amazon.com or some other online book dealer. (It is published by Oxford University Press, and its full title is *The Book of Common Prayer and Administration of the Sacraments and Other Rites and Ceremonies of the Church*—but I've never heard anyone call it that!) Also, your local Episcopal church might have copies it would be willing to give or sell you.

The Least You Need to Know

- *The Book of Common Prayer*, the prayer book of the Anglican Church, is a rich deposit of Psalms, Bible readings, and prayers.

- The Morning Prayer section of the BCP is a helpful guide to one's daily prayer.

- Written prayers can be personally very meaningful.

- When you use the BCP, you are in touch with the history of believers, sharing in their prayers going back centuries.

Singing Prayer

In This Chapter

- Song as a form of prayer
- What song does for our prayer life
- A handful of "the greatest hymns of all time"
- Why singing is so important to the life of prayer

If you want to throw a church into chaos, get people furious with one another, or even cause a church split, then change the worship music. There are few topics more volatile in churches. It's not that Christians are petty—well, no more petty than the rest of the world—it's just that music is more than music for them: It is the most meaningful form of prayer. When you tamper with music, you're tampering with how people relate to God.

Church fights aside, we need to look at how music—especially singing—is one of the most profound forms of prayer available to us.

What Song Does for Us

It's hard to know where to begin—and where to end—when it comes to this topic. Music is a mystery. It helps us express and experience things beyond words. But song adds the dimension of words and so combines the mysterious with the rational. It is this combination that has the potential of infusing our lives with incredible meaning and joy. Two examples will suffice.

Writer Florence Parkes tells this story in *Christian Reader:*

> It was early January and in the doctor's waiting room every seat was occupied. There was the usual atmosphere of tension, each person concerned with his own problems. We looked down at our feet, flipped through old magazines, gazed at the pictures on the walls. Suddenly a woman sitting across the room from me spoke up. "Why don't we sing? Are you tired of Christmas carols?"

> Every head turned in her direction. Startled at such an idea, we couldn't help returning the smile on her happy face. Without waiting for an answer, her strong soprano voice began, "O Come, All Ye Faithful." My husband, always ready to sing, joined in with his tenor. A bit more timidly, I added an alto and soon others joined in. We sang one carol after another, filling the room with joyous music.

The other example comes from the other end of life. Anne Chapman, in *Decision* magazine, tells about a woman she met at a conference she spoke at:

> All alone, she sat in the back of the church. The rest of the 500 women at the women's conference that weekend had already exited the auditorium. I was gathering up my books, papers, and props when I saw her at the back of the room. I walked over to where she was sitting; her head was bowed low, and her shoulders were drooping. I sat down, and she began to tell me her story. She was the mother of three. Her oldest son, suffering from muscular dystrophy, had been confined to a wheelchair for most of his 17 years. Her other two children had a variety of learning and emotional challenges.

> With her head still bent, she whispered, "I'm married to a mean, hateful man who makes my life miserable. He won't help me with our son. He even refuses to help while I hold our son when he goes to the bathroom."

> "I buried my father this week," the woman continued. "At the funeral I learned that my father had disinherited me from his estate because he hated my husband." Then she told me something that still haunts me: "I came this weekend with one prayer. I asked God to kill my

From the Good Book

I urge, then, first of all, that requests, prayers, intercession and thanksgiving be made for everyone—for kings and all those in authority, that we may live peaceful and quiet lives in all godliness and holiness. This is good, and pleases God our savior, who wants all men to be saved and to come to a knowledge of the truth.

—Paul, 2 Timothy 2:1–4

husband. I prayed, 'Lord, I need a way out! I feel like a bird in a cage.'" Finally she lifted her eyes and said, "When I prayed that prayer, God spoke to me as clearly as I've ever sensed His voice. He said, 'Even a bird in a cage sings.'" With tears running down her face she asked, "What am I supposed to do with that? How do I live with that answer?"

Feeling utterly impotent, I replied, "If God says, 'Sing,' you need to find your song."

Whether we are living on the mountaintop of joy or in the valley of despair, there is a song we can sing, and if that song is directed toward God, it becomes a form of prayer.

The Categories of Church Music

If you talk to people who are really into church music, the categories of songs multiply like rabbits. For now, let's look at the major categories.

First, there's the *Gregorian chant.* Just when this type of song had been relegated to the dustbin of history, along come the Benedictine Monks of Santo Domingo de Silos, who recorded the best-selling *Chant.* The huge fad has passed, of course, but Gregorian chant will never pass away. It will always express something that no other musical form can.

A musical chant is *a cappella* singing that closely resembles the spoken word. Chants have been used in religious ceremonies since ancient times. To create their own chants, early Christians borrowed from Hebrew melodies and used the words of the Psalms. Gregorian chants are named after Pope Gregory I, who compiled chants for the Roman Catholic liturgy and helped to disseminate them in churches all over Europe in the late 500s. You'll find them mostly used in Roman Catholic and Anglican churches.

> **From the Good Book**
>
> Speak to one another with psalms, hymns and spiritual songs. Sing and make music in your heart to the Lord, always giving thanks to God the father for everything, in the name of our Lord Jesus Christ.
>
> —Paul, Ephesians 5:19, 20

Having arisen in medieval Europe, these chants are usually sung in Latin and rely on phrases from the Psalms and other biblical books for their words. Often the entire song is an elaboration on a single phrase. Some titles and their English translations are listed here:

♦ "Venite, exsultemus Domino" ("Come, let us sing to the Lord")

♦ "Veni Sancte Spiritus" ("Come Holy Ghost")

♦ "Benedictus Dominus, Dues Israel" ("Blessed be the Lord God of Israel")

Then there are *spirituals*. Though the term can refer to religious folk music found in both white and African American traditions, it usually refers to the musical genre first created by African American slaves. Some spirituals were used as work songs, and others contained coded information for slaves to communicate secretly to one another, but those that have survived in churches are prayers.

Some of the more famous include "Jericho," "Swing Low, Sweet Chariot," and "When All the Saints Come Marching In." One of the most moving, which you'll hear sung during communion services, is this one:

Were you there when they crucified my Lord?

Were you there when they crucified my Lord?

Oh! Sometimes it causes me to tremble, tremble, tremble

Were you there when they crucified my Lord?

Were you there when they nailed him to the tree?

Were you there when they nailed him to the tree?

Oh! Sometimes it causes me to tremble, tremble, tremble

Were you there when they nailed him to the tree?

Were you there when they laid him in the tomb?

Were you there when they laid him in the tomb?

Oh! Sometimes it causes me to tremble, tremble, tremble

Were you there when they laid him in the tomb?

Praise choruses are a modern version of Gregorian chant, in some respects. Like Gregorian chant, praise choruses usually rely directly on the Bible verses and phrases for their texts, but the melodies are usually folk or soft rock.

Hymns are older songs that address God or that speak about him and his ways. The first hymns in the Judeo-Christian tradition are the Psalms, and the earliest Christians sang hymns, some of which are found in the New Testament. All through their history, Christians have composed and sung hymns. The first book published in America, *The Bay Psalm Book*, was a hymnbook.

Many, many hymns have stood the test of time—we still sing versions of hymns from all periods of Christian history. Probably the best way to introduce you to this incredible heritage is simply to show rather quickly the feelings and attitudes hymns can help you express.

> **Snapshots of Answered Prayers**
>
> Hannah desperately prayed for a child, and when God finally answered her prayer by giving her the future prophet Samuel she recited a beautiful prayer of praise found in 1 Samuel 2:1–10.

Poetry of Prayer

The church's hymns function like great poetry: They help us articulate what's going on deep inside us, and they do so succinctly, accurately, and beautifully.

For starters, some hymns express praise and adoration. Praise of God is probably one of the most difficult things to articulate. "God, you're great!" has the advantage of being simple and to the point; however, it doesn't quite express everything I want to say a lot of the time. Reading the Psalms can help here, but reading or singing hymns can also help.

For example, some hymns can help express praise for the simple pleasures of life:

> For the beauty of the earth,
>
> For the beauty of the skies,
>
> For the love which from our birth
>
> Over and around us lies
>
> Lord of all, to thee we raise
>
> This our hymn of grateful praise.
>
> For the wonder of each hour,
>
> Of the day and of the night,
>
> Hill and vale, and tree and flower,
>
> Sun and moon, and stars of light,
>
> Lord of all, to thee we raise
>
> This our hymn of grateful praise.

The hymn goes on to praise God for the gifts of sight and hearing, for family and friends, and for the church. Other hymns express praise for God's steadiness, power, and eternity:

Prayer Hotline

Quietly singing a hymn can be a great way to start or end your daily prayer. It also becomes a way to memorize the hymn, which can then become a prayer that stays in your head and heart throughout the day.

> O God, our help in ages past,
>
> Our hope for years to come,
>
> Our shelter from the stormy blast,
>
> And our eternal home.
>
> Before the hills in order stood,
>
> Or earth received her frame,
>
> From everlasting thou art God,
>
> To endless years the same.

Hymns also can express hope: More than once in a while, life deals us a left hook. One minute we're standing proud and tall and feeling invincible; the next, we're flat on our back wondering how we're going to start breathing again, let alone get up. "O God, help!" is another simple prayer, but sometimes you just want to express something deeper—like this:

> If thou but suffer God to guide thee,
>
> And hope in him through all thy ways,
>
> He'll give thee strength, whate'er betide thee,
>
> And bear thee through the evil days;
>
> Who trusts in God's unchanging love
>
> Builds on the rock that nought can move.

As Miguel de Cervantes, author of *Don Quixote*, put it, "He who sings frightens away his ills."

Like praise, joy is a hard thing to express with much detail. "Hooray, God!" just doesn't cut it for me, but a hymn like this does:

> The strife is o'er, the battle done;
>
> The victory of life is won;
>
> The song of triumph has begun.
>
> Alleluia!

The powers of death have done their worst,

But Christ their legions hath dispersed:

Let shouts of holy joy outburst.

Alleluia!

Of course, there also are dedication hymns. Once in a while I snap out of my ongoing daze and decide that it's time, once more, to get serious about this God stuff. So I want to tell God I'm going to try to start acting like a follower of Jesus. When I get tired of repeating "God, I'm going to do better," I'll turn to a hymn like this:

O Master let me walk with thee

In lowly paths of service free;

Tell me thy secret; help me bear

The strain of toil, the fret of care.

> **Prayer Pearls**
>
> The wish to pray is a prayer in itself.
>
> —Georges Bernanos, French writer

Or another, like this:

Take thou our minds, dear Lord, we humbly pray;

Give us the mind of Christ each passing day;

Teach us to know the truth that sets us free;

Grant us in all our thoughts to honor thee.

The next verse begins "Take thou our hearts ..." and the one after that, "Take thou our wills ..."—which pretty much covers the waterfront of how a person can dedicate himself to God.

Hymns have been around so long that there is hardly a topic that someone hasn't written a hymn about. One of my favorite hymnals, the 1955 Presbyterian *The Hymnbook*, classifies hymns in more than 50 headings. Under "Life in Christ" alone, you'll find a number of hymns on each of these topics:

◆ The Call of Christ

◆ Repentance and Forgiveness

◆ Discipleship and Service

◆ Dedication and Consecration

" " **From the Good Book**

For everything God created is good, and nothing is to be rejected if it is received with thanksgiving, because it is consecrated by the word of God and prayer.

—Paul, 1 Timothy 4:4, 5

- ◆ Stewardship
- ◆ Hope and Aspiration
- ◆ Pilgrimage and Guidance
- ◆ Loyalty and Courage
- ◆ Trial and Conflict
- ◆ Faith and Assurance
- ◆ Prayer and Intercession
- ◆ Love

- ◆ Joy
- ◆ Peace
- ◆ The Life Everlasting

In other words, hymns are an astoundingly rich resource of prayer. Certainly, some are pretty schmaltzy, others terrible poetry, and others still nearly indecipherable today ("Here I raise my Ebenezer, Hither by thy help I'm come …"). But there are enough hymns left to pray through a lifetime.

The Prayer of Music

"Next to theology, I give music the highest place and honor," wrote Martin Luther. "Music is the art of the prophets, the only art that can calm the agitations of the soul; it is one of the most magnificent and delightful presents God has given us."

Music not only helps us express our innermost thoughts and feelings to God, but it can also do something else. There is the story of a little French girl hearing music for the first time, who cries out, "It's God speaking to us!" If prayer is communication with God, then music is certainly one way to do that.

The Least You Need to Know

- ◆ Whether we are living in joy or despair, there is a song we can sing, and if that song is directed toward God, it becomes a form of prayer.
- ◆ Chants and spirituals precede the more contemporary praise songs and hymns, which all comprise prayer in song.

◆ Hymns can also double as great poetry, reaching the heights of adoration and dedication as a form of prayer.

◆ Music is an added dimension to prayer that allows us to express our worship in a deeper way.

Chapter 31

Technology for the Spirit

In This Chapter

- Harnessing technology to enhance the life of prayer
- How computers, cell phones, and even TV and radio can supplement one's prayer routines
- Personal digital assistants (PDAs) and prayer
- The dangers inherent in technology

The resources for prayer are countless. That only makes sense. If prayer encompasses all of life, it only makes sense that all of life can become a resource for prayer.

At first blush, the words *prayer* and *technology* seem miles apart. What could they possibly have to do with one another? It turns out, quite a bit.

Many of the matters already raised in this book are grounded in some technologies we've gotten used to ("technology" here simply meaning any manufactured item that helps us accomplish tasks). To write with a pen in a notebook called a prayer journal is using two relatively recent inventions. Icons and candles are another type of technology. Cathedral bells called people to prayer many times a day for centuries. So it's really not all that strange to say that computers, cell phones, and digital watches, among other things, can be used to enhance one's prayer life. In this chapter we'll look at some examples.

Setting Time to Pray

This is, day in and day out, the most useful piece of technology for a life of prayer. Most of us pray in the mornings. It is the time when—after a cup of coffee anyway!—we are most alert. And it seems to make the most sense to start the day in prayer—to pray through the challenges the day will present.

But morning prayer is not going to happen without adding an extra 15 to 30 minutes to the morning routine. That means setting that alarm a little earlier. And it means getting up when it goes off.

A New Way to Record Your Thoughts

If you use pen and paper to keep a prayer journal or to write prayers, it's probably already occurred to you that you could do this on a computer. What you may not have thought through is the advantages of doing such with a word processor.

To begin with, you may not like the physical act of writing all that much. I know I don't. My thoughts tend to run faster than my hand can write, and this can be frustrating at times, as fresh thoughts start to slip away as I labor along trying to get down my last thought. On top of that is my handwriting, especially when I'm trying to write quickly. Most people cannot read my handwriting when I'm trying to be careful, but *I* can't even read it weeks or months later after I've jotted down ideas in a rush.

And if you're trying to craft a prayer—as opposed to writing an extemporaneous prayer—the advantages of a word processor are enormous because of its editing features.

One other advantage of creating an electronic journal: You can quickly find a reference to a thought, dream, idea, or insight that you had months ago. I can't tell you how many hours I've wasted trying to find a passage in my handwritten journal. If I had entered them in a word processor, I'd only have to come up with a keyword or two, and I'd be able to go right to it.

At the same time, I'll be the first to acknowledge the disadvantages of the electronic journal. The main one for me—and the reason I don't do it still—is that I don't find typing on a computer conducive to prayer. I like it for generating ideas, even ideas about prayer. But when it comes to an atti-tude and mood that I like to establish in prayer, the computer works against it. There's the bright screen staring at me, the click of the keyboard, and the hum of the fan and hard drive.

Then again, I have many good friends who tell me I'm being ridiculous, Neanderthal, and all that. Whatever. To each his own.

> **From the Good Book**
>
> I have set God always before me: for he is on my right hand, therefore I shall not fall.
>
> —Psalm 16:8

E-Mail and Prayer Chains

Naturally, many things that a letter or phone call can accomplish, an e-mail can ac-complish as well. I noted how a prayer chain can enrich one's prayer life. Many of these are conducted by phone still, but more and more, they are conducted by e-mail.

Again, the nature of this medium has certain advantages. For one, there is no need for three people to phone three more people and so on. The person through whom the church or community funnels prayer requests simply compiles a mass mailing list. When a prayer request comes through, she writes one e-mail, enters the group name in the address line, and before she knows it, ten, one hundred, or one thousand peo-ple have a prayer request in their inbox.

In addition, with an e-mail prayer request, you have a record of the prayer request—assuming you don't delete that e-mail after you've read it. This is important for two reasons. First, when you get a fresh e-mail about someone who is having a long-term bat-tle with cancer, and it's been some time since you prayed for that person, it's easy to go back and remind yourself about the length, severity, and progress of their illness.

It's also nice to have a record of the things that you've prayed for. Not that we should keep score with God, but it always amazes me how many times prayers are answered, and how they are answered in unusual ways—at least when I take the trouble to recall what it is I've prayed for.

> **Prayer Pearls**
>
> There are whole periods when you are neither at the bottom of the sea nor at the top of the peak, when you have to do something about praying, and that is the period when you can-not pray from spontaneity but you can pray from conviction.
>
> —Anthony Bloom, writer on Orthodox spirituality

One other advantage: I belong to a few missionary e-mail prayer lists. I get regular updates about what is going on in other nations, how Christians are faring, and of course, how I can pray specifically. Often, I learn about breaking world events earlier from the e-mail prayer lists—often generated by people on the front lines of third-world missions of mercy—than I do from newspaper or television.

Prayer and the Internet

Here I'm thinking particularly of the many, many websites devoted to prayer and the spiritual life. See Appendix C for a starting list. Why get bundled up, start the car, drive to the library or bookstore, browse, stand in line, drive home, and get unbundled when you can often find great resources at the touch of your fingertips?

Naturally, as with all things on the web, let the browser beware. Just because it says it's "Christian" or "orthodox" or whatever doesn't mean it's something you can trust. All sorts of people are shouting all sorts of things about the spiritual life, especially on the web. The caution given about resources like books and conferences applies here. Weigh the information against the teaching of the Bible—*the* prayer book of prayer books—and get the good advice of people who know something about prayer as practiced traditionally by the Christian church.

Cell Phone Spirituality

Some days, I can't imagine any spiritual value in cell phones, especially when they ring in a movie theater or church service! But in other contexts, a cell phone is a nice addition to life. I was watching my youngest daughter run in a cross-country event one morning recently, her first run after having been promoted to the varsity squad.

I was pretty excited, so as I was waiting for the race to begin, I phoned my oldest daughter, now away at school, to tell her about it.

I do that sort of thing a lot—a spur of the moment call to tell someone good news, or a piece of information, or to say hello. No reason I can't use that same technology to, on the spur of the moment, tell someone I could use some prayer right now, or to say, "I've been praying for you lately; how's it been going?"

> ### Snapshots of Answered Prayers
>
> Abraham's servant went in search of a wife for Isaac and prayed that the one who wished to water his camels would become Isaac's wife. The result was Rebekah, who did indeed wed Isaac. Read about it in Genesis chapter 24.

An Hourly Reminder to Pray

I used to have a friend who would ever so casually mention how much time he was spending in prayer. "When I was praying from 8:00 to 10:00 this morning …." Or "I found myself bogged down as I came to the third hour of my morning prayer …." He was a young Christian, enthusiastic, and in need of affirmation. But it still irritated me.

In the circles I travel—evangelical ones—there is a tendency of some to rate one's prayer life by the amount of time spent in morning devotions, or "quiet time," as many of us like to call it. It's easy to see how quickly that can lead to self-righteousness, not to mention a rather juvenile faith. So let me begin this section by saying that I probably think it a good idea *not* to wear a watch or be near a clock when you're having prayer.

On the other hand, I've recently rediscovered a feature of my digital watch that is actually enhancing my prayer life. For years, I've immediately shut off the hourly chime as soon as I bought a new watch. I've just begun turning it back on. The reason? It has become for me an hourly reminder to pray.

I have written much about the value of "arrow prayers": quick, one-phrase prayers that can be made throughout the day. Well, if your schedule is like mine, you'll find that an entire day can pass as you meet one crisis after another, and you've not given one second of thought to God.

So I use that hourly chime, if nothing else, to stop for just five seconds and say, "Thank you God for being with me in this hectic day." Not much, it seems, but it's huge if I do that every hour all day long. Often, I find, I'm not in the middle of a crisis, and I can actually take a minute or two to take a deep breath, recall God's presence, and think about someone in my office I could pray for briefly.

Once I was in the middle of a conversation with a co-worker and my chime went off. Immediately I repeated inward the verse from the Psalms that I had said I would repeat that day during the chime: "The earth is the Lord's and the fullness thereof." As my friend continued to talk (he didn't notice the chime), I suddenly became aware that God was fully present with us in that conversation, and that my friend was created in the image of God. At that

> **Prayer Pearls**
>
> People who are in the habit of praying—and they include the mystics of the Christian tradition—know that when a prayer is answered, it is never answered in a way that you expect.
>
> —Kathleen Norris, American spiritual writer

moment, something of the fullness of God touched me ever so briefly. It was quite a startling moment.

I don't know how long I'll be able to keep this up. I've noticed that after only a few weeks, my mind often blocks out the chime, and I can go four, five, or six hours without hearing it. I think I'm way too busy, if that's the case. And maybe that deafness should signal something to me!

Personal Digital Assistants (PDAs) and Prayers

This to me is the greatest invention since the wheel. I use it to keep my address book, my calendar, my finances, my photo album, my memo pad—and on it goes. If I were to lose it (and if my backup on my computer were to disappear), it would take me days just to figure out who I am! My fondness for the PDA is probably verging on addiction, but instead of this addiction pulling my life out of control, it's giving me control. That's my justification, anyway.

As you can probably guess, my PDA has helped my prayer life. At a very basic level, I keep prayer lists on it. As I noted with e-mail, keeping a record of prayer requests can be really helpful. But the PDA calendar and to-do feature is a tremendous boon to prayer. You can set alarms minutes, hours, days, weeks, or months in advance to remind yourself to buy a birthday card, or send in an application, or, you guessed it, to pray for someone.

Television Visionaries

The same medium that brings you All-Star Wrestling and the Playboy Channel also brings you prayer. Television is a mixed blessing to say the least. Television Christianity, of course, runs the gamut from traditional Catholic Masses to Black Pentecostal preaching services to right-wing religious talk shows.

My temptation is to dismiss it all. We've heard about the hypocritical televangelists who preach simplicity and purity and then live in plush homes and commit adultery left and right. Morality aside, how can a television worship service even begin to compare with participating with others in the flesh? Well, there is no comparison.

Then again …. I have listened to a few television preachers and come away with a new insight or understanding about my faith. And I do recall that my own mother turned her own life around when she became a Christian after watching Billy Graham on TV. That led to my own commitment of faith. So in some sense I am a product of televangelism, as are many others.

The point is don't reject television Christianity outright, even the programs that showcase flamboyant preachers. For in spite of their showbiz ways, they sometimes have important things to say. Aside from the flamboyant, there still are moderate voices that you might find helpful from time to time.

Christianity on the Radio

The same warnings apply here regarding radio preachers. But radio Christianity has an additional dimension worth noting: Christian music.

The type of music most Christian radio stations play tends toward the soft-rock end of things, and the songs are mostly about praise and worship. They'll often include some nationally syndicated programming from Christian psychologists or well-known and sensible preachers. But it's mostly about the music.

Prayer Hotline

I'm a fan of country-western music and oldies rock, but I go through periods where I want to extend my morning prayer time as I head toward work. That's when I'll press my preset for the local Christian station and take in some praise music as I make my way through traffic.

The Limits of Technology

Of course, one can have a vibrant, active prayer life without using technology. But by God's providence we live in a technological age, and there is no reason why we should not use the available technology to deepen our relationship with him.

That said, we are also wise to consider how technology can undermine that relationship. Some of the technologies I've just discussed are expensive, and it is sometimes poor stewardship to spend money for expensive gadgets when you might be giving more to the needy. Some technologies can begin taking over our lives so that we become dependent on them—we can't imagine living without them. And using some technologies—because they are in themselves impersonal and allow us to control or manipulate our world—can ever so subtly shape us so that we become increasingly impersonal and begin to use them to control or manipulate others or even our spiritual lives.

In the end, prayer is about abandoning control and refusing to manipulate. It is to put oneself in the hands of a loving and sovereign God who will guide you as and how he sees fit. When technology helps us move in that direction, so much the better.

The Least You Need to Know

◆ One can use technology creatively to enhance one's prayer life.

◆ The technologies that include automatic alarms or reminders are especially useful because they can help discipline one's prayer life.

◆ Technology is helpful only when it helps us organize our lives for prayer.

◆ Technology undermines the spiritual life when it becomes a means to control life, rather than a tool to teach us how to let go.

Part 6

Praying with Others

I hope you didn't pick up this book hoping that with it as your constant companion, you could learn everything you needed to learn about prayer on your own. Thanks for the compliment, but a book can take you only so far. And as important as praying by yourself is, it also can take you only so far. We're getting to that part of the book where you need to start thinking about long-term learning, and one key to learning Christian prayer more deeply and for the long haul is learning to pray with others. In this part, we'll look at the various ways to do that.

32

Going One-on-One

In This Chapter

- ◆ How to pray with your children
- ◆ How to pray with your spouse
- ◆ Prayer chains: what they are and how they work
- ◆ Finding a prayer partner
- ◆ The need for the occasional prayer retreat

I've played basketball since high school, and I've enjoyed the many ways the game can be played. Full-court, five-on-five is what it's all about, of course, but three-on-three half-court can be a lot of fun. And then there's one-on-one, in which you pit your skills against another's. No excuses now: You can't blame your teammates if you lose—it's just your skills against your opponent's skills.

Prayer has a one-on-one dimension, too: Lots of people get a great deal out of sitting down with a friend or a spouse or whomever and praying together. Sometimes that means praying with another individual. Other times it means praying in the context of other individuals. In this chapter we'll look at both expressions.

Out of the Mouths of Babes

Let's start with the easy one: praying with your kids. Even if you are shy about praying with other adults, you may not be shy about praying with your own children. This is good, because praying with your kids is not only a great way to introduce them to prayer, it's a great way for adults to learn more about prayer and about God.

Praying with children usually begins with saying rote prayers with the child. The classic is this one:

> Now I lay me down to sleep,
>
> I pray the Lord my soul to keep.
>
> If I should die before I wake,
>
> I pray the Lord my soul to take.

Some adults are freaked out by this prayer—all this talk of dying before they get up the next morning. But many children are more matter-of-fact about such matters. In this regard, they are wiser than adults who spend a great deal of energy denying death. If all of us prayed—and lived—as if this were our last day, I dare say this would be a better planet. In this respect, this is a profound prayer indeed.

Be that as it may, some children are indeed frightened by such a prayer, and so it should not be used indiscriminately.

Of course, another prayer that can be said with children is the Lord's Prayer. You'll find other samples in Appendixes A and B, which offer some suggested prayers for particular times.

Prayer Pearls
Prayer for many is like a foreign land. When we go there, we go as tourists. Like most tourists, we feel uncomfortable and out of place. Like most tourists, we therefore move on before too long and go somewhere else. —Robert McAfee Brown, American theologian

You can also pray conversationally with your child. My wife and I have done that with all three of our children when they were younger. We began by asking them the type of things they would like to pray for. They were often stumped, so we'd make suggestions, perhaps rotating the people we would pray for (immediate family one night, relatives the next, friends the next, and so on).

Then parent and child each took a turn saying a prayer. On the adult side, this often amounted to two or three sentences, in very simple language— you don't want to overwhelm your child. For example: "Dear God, we thank you for this day, that Luke was able to play soccer with his friends. Thank you for giving him the skills to play such a fun game. We pray tonight for his friend, Zach, and for Zach's family, since their mother is in the hospital. Heal her, and help Zach and his family know of your presence in their lives. In Jesus' name. Amen."

Praying with a child teaches you that the simplest language and requests will have to do—that's all a child is capable of. And if God accepts those prayers, then he'll accept any prayers. I don't know how many nights I've prayed for sick guinea pigs or what present should be bought for somebody's birthday.

Praying with children is a form of theological education. There are a number of issues we do a very good job of avoiding day by day, but as you talk with your child before praying, you'll often be confronted with these:

♦ "Dad, will my parakeet go to heaven when it dies?"

♦ "Mom, why did God create people with so many different colors of skin? Wouldn't it have been simpler to create just one color?"

♦ "Dad, what is heaven like?"

♦ "Mom, you're always saying how God creates us. How exactly did God create me?"

I've heard of more than one parent having to consult the local minister to figure out how to answer a question the child has asked.

 **From the Good Book**

Let us then approach the throne of grace with confidence, so that we may receive mercy and find grace to help us in our time of need.

—Hebrews 4:16

The Family That Prays Together ...

Family prayer is not quite "one-on-one," but while we're on the subject of praying with children, we ought to look at it. Many families not only pray with children at bedtime, they also have a family prayer time during the week, especially during special seasons of the year. Our family, for instance, tries to pull this off during Advent (the four weeks leading up to Christmas) and Lent (the six weeks leading up to Easter).

We aim to do something every night just as we're sitting down to eat. So, with the food steaming before us and smaller children squirming away, we're inclined to keep it short. We've also done it after dinner, giving ourselves more time to go in depth (the disadvantage then is that everyone is anxious to get on with their evening plans).

The structure is simple: A Bible passage and/or a devotional story is read, songs are sung, and prayers are said. For example, during Advent, we might read a Bible passage that speaks about the coming of Christ: "Out of the stump of David's family will grow a shoot—yes, a new Branch bearing fruit from the old root. And the Spirit of the Lord will rest on him—the Spirit of wisdom and understanding, the Spirit of counsel and might, the Spirit of knowledge and fear of the Lord .... He will defend the poor and the exploited .... He will be clothed with fairness and truth." (Isaiah 11:1–4)

Then we'll talk about how new branches grow out of old stumps and how that is like Christ coming. Or we'll try to figure out what it means to have a "Spirit of wisdom and understanding." And so on. We're not left on our own, of course. There are family devotional guides available in most religious bookstores that will either guide such a discussion or that contain a reading that will explain the biblical reading.

Then we might sing a hymn about Christ's coming, something like, "O Come, O Come Emmanuel." Or we might pray together, either reciting a prayer found in the devotional guide, or praying extemporaneously with one leader, or going around the circle and each saying a sentence or two.

Sometimes, such as during Advent, we light a candle during the service, and this can be a highlight for the smaller child who gets to do that—although having a fight erupt over whose turn it is to light the candle can put a damper on the devotional mood!

You can slice and dice family prayer in all sorts of ways. The key is to find a routine that isn't routine, that involves the children, and that stays on the short side. Our devotional times before dinner are maybe five minutes at most. But even a short dip into family prayer, even if for just two seasons of the year, can set a tone, create memories, and help everyone focus themselves a little more deliberately on larger themes. It sure beats hearing about how boring school was that day.

More Intimate Than Sex

If you think you're intimate when you're having sex with your spouse, wait until you pray with him or her. Joint prayer can allow a couple to share a spiritual intimacy that sex cannot touch. That's why many couples make it a practice to pray with each other once a day, or at least a few times a week.

This doesn't work for every couple, though—or it doesn't work all the time. There have been a few times in our marriage when my wife and I have prayed together. But, to be frank, the practice has not been particularly helpful for us, so we've not stuck with it. We tend to be individualists when it comes to prayer, so we never can quite agree on a time or method. Still, there have been occasions when we've prayed together when it has been a significant time for us.

At its best, praying with one's spouse can reap immense benefits. The late psychologist Paul Tornier wrote about them in an article in *Leadership* journal:

> It is only when a husband and wife pray together before God that they find the secret of true harmony: that the difference in their temperaments, their ideas, and their tastes enriches their home instead of endangering it. There will be no further question of one imposing his will on the other, or of the other giving in for the sake of peace.

> Instead, they will together seek God's will, which alone will ensure that each will be fully able to develop his personality …. When each of the marriage partners seeks quietly before God to see his own faults, recognizes his sin, and asks the forgiveness of the other, marital problems are no more. Each learns to speak the other's language, and to meet him halfway, so to speak. Each holds back those harsh little words which one is apt to utter when one is right, but which are said in order to injure.

Snapshots of Answered Prayers

David sinned by having sexual relations with Bathsheba, Uriah's wife. In Psalm 51 he acknowledges his sin, asking forgiveness, and God restores him.

Prayer Chains

Many churches use prayer chains to encourage people to pray for one another. It's a very simple idea, an adaptation of a phone chain used to communicate information. Prayer requests in the church are funneled to one person, who phones three people to tell them to pray about this concern. Those three each tell three others, and those three, three others still, and on it goes.

To be a part of a prayer chain does a number of things. First, it puts you in touch with the needs of the community you are a part of. It's easy to get lost in the life of a church, to feel disconnected. There are a lot of things going on with a lot of people, and it's easy to feel out of touch. Prayer chains help you to stay in touch.

Prayer chains also connect you more intimately to a few other people in the church, especially those whom you call or who call you. When you see them in church, there's an automatic topic of conversation available, making it easier to build a friendship.

Prayer Hotline _____

Prayer chains help you to pray. In the daily flurry of life, it's easy to put off prayer for days. Before you know it, a week or two have gone by and you haven't been in private prayer. And if you have, it may have been all focused on yourself. A call from the prayer chain can be a nice interruption to your hectic life, giving you an excuse to spend some time in prayer!

Prayer chains are a way to participate in the life of the church, that is, to be of real help to people in need. We may not know Mary, who we've been told has cancer. But once we hear about it, we feel like we want to do something for her. Well, we can pray for her. As has been documented many a time throughout this book, prayers can work miracles in people's lives.

But one more story of answered prayer won't hurt. A woman we'll call Anne sent the following story to co-author Jim Bell in the course of preparing this book. Anne had been praying about how to confront her son, who she was sure was hooked on drugs. The problem was she had no hard proof. She told her support group about her concerns, and after she was done, another member of the group spoke up. This member said she was there to find support to help her deal with *her* son's drug problem. She said she had caught her son red-handed while speaking on the phone to someone who could lead him to a drug dealer. She added that if she ever caught this perpetrator, whose name was ….

Anne gasped. It was her son! Her prayer for proof positive was positively answered. The next day she confronted her son, and he was humbled. He turned his life around, and now, many years later, he is a responsible father and has a steady job.

Prayer can change things, and being in a prayer chain gives us the privilege of praying for all manner of people in all manner of situations.

Prayer Partners

In some Christian circles, you'll find that people have "prayer partners." This can mean one of two things. At a minimum, you have someone you check in with every few days or every week. You each discuss the types of challenges you'll face in the coming week, things you are especially thankful for, and areas in your spiritual lives that need attention. Then you promise to pray for one another. Many prayer partners take it to the next level: They actually meet (sometimes just over the phone) and pray with and for one another.

As you can see, this also can be a scary proposition, but it does have a few salutary effects. It helps you develop deeper friendships; the bond you develop with people you pray with is a unique one. It also helps you be accountable for your prayer life. It's like having a spiritual director, except that each of you is acting as a spiritual director to one another.

In an article in *Men of Integrity* magazine, Gregg Lewis tells about the power of prayer partners in one man's life. Kurt Stansell was a man who seemed to have it all together: a 16-year marriage, two great kids, a successful investment counseling service, and an active church life. But at the same time he was a sex addict.

For years he struggled with his addiction to pornography. It started with magazines, then evolved into visits to strip joints. Kurt kept going through a cycle of guilt and remorse, then prayer and repentance—only to find himself back at it again.

He eventually found a prayer partner named Stan with whom he would talk and pray. At first, Kurt held back; he found it difficult to be completely honest about his problem. But when he finally confessed the whole truth, he immediately felt a weight lift off his shoulders. That was the first step on his road to recovery.

If prayer partners can help with that level of problems, it's easy to see how it can help in the day-to-day struggles we face.

Prayer Retreats

A prayer retreat is just that—you "retreat" from your daily life and spend a day or two, or more, mostly spent in prayer. This can be done by oneself or in a group. But often one spends most of the time in private prayer while in the context of others.

The practice for many is to visit a monastery in the area. Many monasteries are set up to do this sort of thing. They offer a very simple room and often meals in their kitchen (which may be taken with the monks or nuns), and all for a very modest price.

Some of the monks may be trained as spiritual directors and are available to talk with the visitor. Visitors are also usually welcome to join the monks or nuns in the daily prayer routine, which can consist of between five and seven services a day.

The bulk of the day is spent in devotional reading, prayer, and journaling. But it is punctuated with sessions with the spiritual director and/or worshipping with the monastic community.

Many people try to refresh themselves by getting away for the weekend—skiing, golfing, fishing, or whatever. But you might want to add a prayer retreat to your get-away-weekend options, one that can refresh your spirit at the deepest levels. See Appendix D for more information on possible places to visit.

The Least You Need to Know

◆ In praying with your children, you'll get a theological education.

◆ There are many opportunities within the family for joint prayer, including meals, bedtime, and special church observances.

◆ Prayer chains can help you stay in touch with, and help, a larger group of people.

◆ Prayer partners can encourage and hold each other accountable, and can create spiritual bonds and deep friendships.

◆ Prayer retreats can help us rethink our priorities and get our spiritual lives back on track.

Small Prayer Groups

In This Chapter

- ◆ What constitutes a small group?
- ◆ Why praying in small groups has become so popular
- ◆ How small groups foster a sense of community
- ◆ Three different methods of small-group prayer
- ◆ How to find a small prayer group

"During that time, I grew spiritually more than I ever have before—or since."

"I really bonded with the group, and I have a sense of closeness with them, even years later, that I have with few others."

These are comments of friends of mine, and they are talking about a prayer experience that falls somewhere between the intimacy of one-on-one and the formality of public worship: small groups. Group prayer has been for many people the most meaningful prayer experience of their lives. This chapter explores why that might be true and covers how to participate in such a group.

How Small Is Small?

A "small group" has become almost a technical term in Christian circles: A small group is composed of usually six to twelve people who gather regularly (often weekly), usually in a home, to discuss the Bible or a spiritual book and then pray together. Sometimes they do less and sometimes more (sing, do a service project together, have a potluck dinner).

This is a simple idea with profound consequences. It has become such a meaningful spiritual experience for people that "small group ministry" has become a specialization of ministers. Seminaries offer classes in it; national conferences promote it; dozens of books are published on it annually—some teach how to organize and lead groups; others are discussion guides for groups. Some churches promote small groups heavily and don't feel that they've done their job until everyone in the church is involved in a small group.

So what's all the excitement about?

> **Prayer Pearls**
>
> Two went to pray? O rather say One went to brag, the other to pray.
> —Richard Crashaw, English poet

Best of Two Worlds

Like so much of life, small groups aren't for everyone. But they are for more people than many imagine. That's because, when done well, they offer the best of two worlds.

As important as public worship is, it doesn't allow for intimacy. Praying by oneself, on the other hand, can lead to intimacy with God, but it can also lead to loneliness. Small groups offer a compromise: intimate prayer in the fellowship of others.

"You've got to be kidding," I can hear someone say. "What would make me want to get together with a bunch of strangers, let alone pray with them?"

Well, first, rarely do people get together with a bunch of strangers. You're usually invited by a friend who is either starting a group or who is already part of a group, or perhaps you've become a part of a church that is starting up a small group. Second, you don't just join a group and plunge right into prayer. It takes a few weeks to develop trust. Third, each group develops levels of trust appropriate for that group. Some groups eventually feel free to talk about the intimate details of their private lives; others are happy to leave certain matters well enough alone.

But a key to a successful small group is that people grow together spiritually, sharing more and more of themselves, as is appropriate.

From the Good Book _____

During the days of Jesus' life on earth, he offered up prayers and petitions with loud cries and tears to the one who could save him from death, and he was heard because of his reverent submission. Although he was a son, he learned obedience from what he suffered, and, once made perfect, he became the source of eternal salvation for all who obey him.

—Hebrews 5:7–9

A psychologist, no doubt, could give dozens of reasons why small groups are so attractive to so many, and why people find them one of the most meaningful of spiritual experiences. But let's just look at three:

1. **We're not alone.** It's easy to begin imagining that no one else out there is much interested in prayer. At work and in the community, the subject is rarely raised in casual conversation, and everyone seems so busy and satisfied with their lives. Even in church, it can seem as if everyone is just going through the motions, not really interested in more intimate spiritual growth.

   This is simply not true, as the popularity of small groups attests. Lots of people are anxious to grow in prayer, and they want to talk with other people about it. This is true of people when it comes to most any interest.

   I just took up a new hobby: woodworking. I've been reading books and checking out Internet sites, but there's nothing like bumping into someone and discovering that he does woodworking, too. Conversation immediately moves into high gear, especially when it comes to talking about what power tools each has and which tool is highest on the wish list.

   From the Good Book

   Again, I tell you that if two of you on earth agree about anything you ask for, it will be done for you by my father in heaven. For where two or three come together in my name, there am I with them.

   —Jesus, Matthew 18:19, 20

2. **We like support.** Let me continue the woodworking comparison. Let's say that now you're the one tackling a big project, such as making a bookcase or cabinet. You're bound to run into problems, and you're not quite sure the best way to tackle them. Books and TV shows can take you only so far: Often your woodworking problem is unique to you and your project. You'll find it beneficial to take a class or to have someone to turn to for advice.

Small groups are simply a formal and regular means for people to get together and talk about the spiritual challenges they face and to share with one another solutions that have worked for them.

3. **God is there.** Jesus taught that "where two or three or gathered in my name, I am in the midst of them." (Matthew 18:20) This didn't make much sense to me for the longest time, except to say that in some historical sense (because we were meeting "in Jesus' name"—that is, in his memory) he was with us, just as Shakespeare is with us when we read one of his plays. Certainly, Christ is with us spiritually, I thought, but not any more specially than when we're alone.

> **Prayer Pearls**
>
> Prayer doesn't consist of thinking a great deal, but of loving a great deal.
>
> —St. Teresa of Avila

And then I became friends with Doug, a recovering alcoholic who was in a small group with me. We had long talks about the spiritual life. I'd often talk to him about theology and the importance of reading the Bible and of prayer. He never disagreed with me, but neither did he seem enthusiastic about my suggestions. One day he told me why: "Mark, I'll tell you when I feel God's presence the most: when I'm with other people. That's when I grow spiritually the most."

That's when I realized that was often true of me as well. I just hadn't put my finger on it, and it helped me see that Jesus was not merely speaking metaphorically about being present with those who gather in his name.

Community with a Capital C

A few years ago, a friend of mine, writer and businessman David Goetz, wrote an article in *Leadership* journal about the benefits of small groups in his own life. I quote him at length because he does a good job of showing the many-textured nature of small groups:

> I've always wondered what makes community biblical—as opposed to community that is merely social. Often churches provide social community, called fellowship, which meets a genuine need for friendships and a place where, like the *Cheers* theme, "everyone knows your name."

> That's all well and good. I certainly want my children, for example, to build healthy friendships with other kids from our church.

> But recently I experienced, for the first time, a more profound sense of biblical community. For the past 7 years, my wife and I have participated in a small

group, which at present comprises five couples. This past year, our group celebrated the birth of a child to one of the couples. We also cheered raucously this
year when two other women in the group announced their pregnancies, and
then we prayed fervently for safe deliveries and healthy babies. Both women
were due within weeks of each other.

In October, the woman who was due first became concerned when her due date
came and went. She said the baby seemed to be moving less. That was Saturday.
But the ultrasound detected a strong heartbeat on Monday. On Tuesday, there
was no heartbeat. On Wednesday morning, she gave birth to Ian Patrick Lincoln, whom we would never get to know. The umbilical cord was wrapped twice
around his neck.

My wife and I—and several others from our small group—were at the hospital
Wednesday morning when Ian was born. First his grandpa came out to the waiting room, then his dad, then the doctor. We huddled together, sobbing, staring
down at our shoes. We attempted to pray. Then we all went to the delivery
room to see Ian's mom and his body.

The week dragged by. After the funeral, we collapsed from exhaustion. It was
the saddest week in my life since my grandfather died 12 years ago. In grieving
with the parents and the other members of my small group, I learned an old
truth: Much of our spiritual development happens only through suffering. But
in this life, suffering is not evenly meted out. Especially in the suburbs, which
tend to secret away suffering and death, one can go for long stretches without
smelling the stench of death. But isolation from suffering stunts spiritual forma-
tion. I had gone 12 years without deep mourning.

Community forced me into relationship with a small circle of people who are
becoming closer than family. I was forced to suffer loss—vicariously but real
nonetheless.

Community is not just a place for the suffering to find comfort but for the comfortable to find suffering. Together we
join Christ in his suffering, and as a result,
as 2 Corinthians 1:4 says, "we can comfort
those in any trouble with the comfort we
ourselves have received from God."

Snapshots of Answered Prayers

King Saul sent soldiers to watch
David's house in order to kill him.
David prayed in Psalm 59 to be
rescued from these criminals and
murderers, appealing to God's
unfailing love, and God protected him.

Conversational Prayer

Small groups can pray together in many ways, but let me talk about three that have been most meaningful to me. First, there is "conversational prayer." Here the idea is to pray to God as we talk to one another: conversationally. In conversation, we don't begin and end formally, nor is our language stilted. For another thing, people don't take turns talking in this way.

An absurd example will show how divorced much prayer is from conversation. Let's say my wife and I are entertaining a couple of friends. If we were to conduct a conversation as we do prayer, it might go something like this:

"Dear Barbara, good wife and most excellent mother to my children," I say. "I must thank you for the bountiful meal you've set before us tonight. Your grace and mercy to us are marvelous. Amen."

"Barbara, most excellent cook and gracious host," chimes in one friend, "let me add my abundant thanksgiving and petition you, in your mercy, to reveal to me the recipe for the lasagna, which was a most splendid dish indeed. Amen."

To which Barbara replies: "O most blessed friends and husband, cherished companions in the journey of life: Knock it off." (I wonder if God, after hearing our formal prayers, sometimes says, "Knock it off.")

Conversational prayer takes a more informal, intimate approach to prayer. It's not quite as casual as conversation—we are speaking to the Creator of heaven and earth, after all—but neither does it fall into "thees" and "thous."

Usually the leader begins by introducing topics in prayer, and then individuals add comments until the topic runs itself out. At this point, someone else opens a subject, and individuals add a sentence or two on that topic. And on it goes. An example would be this:

> Person 1: Lord, thank you for the time together, and we pray for Mary, who wasn't able to be here with us tonight. Keep her safe on her trip to Atlanta.

> Person 2: Help her, Lord, too, with her son Eric. She's been struggling to understand how to communicate with him. We know that can be tough with teenagers. Give her wisdom.

> Person 3: Lord, I pray for John, who mentioned tonight that he'll be looking for a new job. Give him wisdom in going about this, and guide him to the right position for him.

> Person 2: And help him be patient in the process, and to trust your guidance throughout.

And so on. Sometimes each person will add "Amen" to his prayer to signal he's done, but sometimes silence is the signal that someone else can pray.

It sounds simple, and it is. But conversational prayer is one of the most revolutionary and meaningful ways to pray with others.

One-Word Prayers

Some groups are uncomfortable plunging into conversational prayer. In such instances, I've introduced the idea of conversational prayer by encouraging people to pray one-word prayers.

I introduce a topic, and then people are encouraged to offer one- or two-word prayers—no more—on this topic.

As we go into prayer, after thanking God for the time together and the opportunity to pray, I might say, "Lord, we begin by praising and thanking you for your goodness."

> **Prayer Pearls**
>
> We should spend as much time in thanking God for his benefits as we do in asking him for them.
> —Vincent de Paul, Roman Catholic priest and spiritual writer

At which point, one person might say, "For health," another might say, "For this group," and another still might say, "For my children."

Then I might say, "Lord, we pray for Mary."

At which point, various individuals would chime in. One might say, "Safety;" another, "Healing;" another still, "Wisdom."

This can be a very powerful form of prayer. It gets right to the heart of issues, without people feeling pressured into saying something holy or eloquent.

Silence Can Be Golden

Another method of group prayer is to pray together in silence. Often this type of prayer is preceded with an introductory prayer and/or concluded with a final prayer. In the meantime, people sit in silence for anywhere from 5 minutes to 20 minutes and commune with God or try to listen to God together.

The first time you do this, five minutes will seem like an eternity. When you've done it for a while, and have learned how to use the time, 20 minutes will seem too short.

After praying together, it's important for the group to talk together about their impressions. This is no foolproof way to discern the voice of God, but it is often surprising to see how many thoughts and images people have in common during such times. Often, after talking things through, the group has a much clearer idea of what God wants.

How do you use the time well? You simply observe what goes on in your mind and emotions as you sit there. Sometimes it helps to have a Bible reading in front of you to guide your meditation. Sometimes you want to keep returning your mind to the main topic of the prayer, if there is one. For example, sometimes a church governing body will sit in prayer for many minutes before making a major decision (such as whether to invite a certain minister to become their pastor). One way to keep focused in this instance would be to keep the person in question focused in your mind, and then observe the thoughts, images, and feelings that come to you.

Where to Find a Group

Small groups aren't heaven on earth. Sometimes one person begins to dominate the group. Groups can be plagued by disagreements and pettiness. They often have a life span that must be respected: To carry the group on longer than it was meant to grow only makes everyone uncomfortable.

That said, small groups are a wonderful way to experience prayer. Unfortunately, I can't tell you simply to look up "Small Prayer Groups" in the phone book and find one. You'll either have to know someone who is already in one, or you'll have to start attending a church in which small groups are a regular feature of its life. Don't hesitate to visit a group in which you know no one. You're not marrying the group, and they will not kidnap you into some cult. Go for a week or two, and if you feel comfortable with the group, continue. Otherwise, search elsewhere.

If you have no luck finding a small prayer group, consider starting your own. Talk with friends who you think might be interested. Agree on a time, place, and format, and you're off and running. To ensure that the group has a focus, you'd be wise to choose a book on the spiritual to read and discuss together, or get input from your local pastor or priest. The hosts can offer modest refreshments; meetings usually last an hour and a half to two hours if refreshments, book study, and prayer are all included.

The Least You Need to Know

♦ Small prayer groups of six to twelve people are becoming increasingly popular.

♦ Small groups remind us that there are others who are on the same spiritual journey, ready to share the common experience of God in their midst.

♦ A community of support and accountability can be created by small groups.

♦ Conversational prayers, short prayers, and silence all work in a group setting that is diverse and that needs order.

♦ It's not hard to find (or start your own) small prayer group; but be aware of disagreements or domination by certain personalities.

34

Prayer in the Free Church Tradition

In This Chapter

- ◆ How to worship in the free church tradition
- ◆ What the different parts of the service are designed to do
- ◆ How free church worship can enhance your prayer life
- ◆ The "seeker-sensitive" church
- ◆ What "speaking in tongues" is all about

If we're going to learn prayer from other Christian pray-ers, we're wise to go to church. But which one? There are more denominations than cable stations.

When it comes to prayer, however, it's not the denomination that's critical but the type of worship the church practices. That simplifies things immensely because there are basically two traditions: liturgical and free church. Let's first look at the free church tradition, which is the most popular in Protestant circles.

Free from What?

The "free church tradition" simply refers to those churches that have declared themselves free from having to use a formal liturgy. (Roman Catholic, Orthodox, Episcopal, Lutheran, and some Methodist and Presbyterian churches use mostly liturgical worship.)

It's a funny thing, though: No church is free from liturgy. For all practical purposes, *liturgy*, which comes from the Greek word for "public service," means "order of service." Every church has an order of service it follows week after week, unless a special occasion preempts it. But the free church tradition relies less on prayer books, favors extemporaneous prayers, requires fewer responses from the congregation, and devotes more of the service to the sermon, thus de-emphasizing Communion. Simplicity is its goal.

> ### Prayer Pearls
>
> Is prayer your steering wheel or your spare tire?
>
> —Corrie Ten Boom, devotional writer

As some examples, you'll find free church worship in many Baptist, Nazarene, Evangelical Free, Church of God in Christ, Covenant, and Assembly of God services, though many Presbyterian, Congregational, and Methodist churches participate in the free church tradition as well. So do nearly all the independent, nondenominational churches across the United States.

What Happens When and Why

A typical order of service is … well, that's one thing about the free church worship; it can go in all sorts of directions. But there does seem to be a general pattern. At its core, the service looks like this. (But again, not all free church services have all these parts, nor do they all put them in the same order.)

- Songs and prayers
- Bible reading
- Sermon

The service moves toward the sermon, the climax both in placement and in proportion; it can be as long as 40 minutes in a 1-hour service. (That's not as bad as the old Puritan sermons, which could sometimes go on for 4 or 5 hours; count your blessings when the sermon starts creeping over 30 minutes.) The sermon is an exposition, or commentary, on the Bible, so the free church service is structured primarily to help people hear God's word as it comes through the preacher.

Abraham Lincoln said, "I don't like to hear cut-and-dried sermons. When I hear a man preach, I like to see him act as if he were fighting bees." Well, whether the preacher fights bees or not, the sermon does have an uncanny way of communicating God to us. As the apostle Paul put it: "How can they call on him [Christ] to save them unless they believe in him? And how can they believe in him if they have never heard of him? And how can they hear about him unless someone tells them?" (Romans 10:14)

Prayer Hotline

Rarely does a sermon grab me from start to finish. Instead I listen for a sentence, an illustration, just one idea I can take away and ruminate on. There is always something God wants to tell me through the sermon, even if it's just a phrase.

Aside from the sermon, here are the other parts in a typical free church service:

◆ **Call to worship and invocation.** *A call to worship* is usually taken from Scripture and "calls" the congregation to worship, something like, "Come, let us sing to the Lord, come into his presence with thanksgiving …," which is from the Psalms.

An *invocation* is a prayer that "invokes" God's presence and aid in worship. Sometimes the call to worship/invocation does not happen until after the opening song.

◆ **Hymn of praise or opening song.** This is the opening song or hymn. A *hymn* is technically a song of praise or thanksgiving to God, but it commonly refers to older songs of praise, those written before the 1960s. This song gives God praise or thanks him for his goodness. Because God is so incredibly good, this seems like a good note to start on.

Some churches have expanded this part of the service and string three or four songs together so that they move gracefully one into another. These are often called "praise choruses," songs with only a verse or two, much of which comes straight out of the Bible.

◆ **Prayer of confession.** After noticing once again the glory and goodness of God (as expressed in the opening hymn or songs), we are made aware of how far we fall short of God, which, not to put too fine a point on it, is pretty far. Thus, we need to confess our sins.

This confession sometimes is said by a worship leader, sometimes is read together, and sometimes is done silently—or a combination thereof. Afterward, a passage is read from the Bible announcing that our sins are forgiven, and this is followed by a song of praise. In Presbyterian circles, for example, the "Doxology" is sung:

Praise God from whom all blessings flow,

Praise him all creatures here below,

Praise him above, ye heavenly host.

Praise Father, Son, and Holy Ghost. Amen.

- **Offering.** For the longest time, I thought the offering was the most offensive part of worship. The sight of ushers passing plates down the aisles for people to put in money was just a tad too mercenary for me. My feeling was, "We're here to worship God, so what does money have to do with it?"

  Unfortunately, I found out it has everything to do with it. The old saying that you can tell a person's priorities by scanning the entries in their checkbook is still true—though we'd probably want to look at their Visa statement as well. I've been telling you that prayer is not about some ethereal religious experience, but about real life. If in prayer we're dedicating our entire selves to God ("thy will be done …"), we cannot hope to avoid dedicating our possessions to him.

  The offering is a moment when we do that. Okay, it's also a convenient way for the church to collect money. But it's a time when I'm reminded that all my life, including my finances—*especially* my finances—belong to God.

  Does that mean I give something every week? No—though I do drop a larger check in the plate about once a quarter.

  This part of the service is sometimes called "tithes and offerings." *Tithes* means "one-tenth" and refers to the long-standing practice of giving 10 percent of one's income back to God, through the church or other charities. Not all Christians tithe, but many do. It is simply a concrete way to say thanks to God for all his blessings, to help other people, and to be reminded that God, in fact, is in charge of everything in our lives.

- **Benediction.** After the sermon, and maybe after another prayer or song, comes the benediction. *Benediction* merely means "blessing," in which the pastor either prays or quotes a Bible verse that is intended to sum up the service or send us on our way back into the world.

  Some people pay little attention to the benediction—they're already thinking about who they need to talk with at coffee hour or whether they're going to get home in time to see the opening kickoff. But sometimes it's worth listening to, as I was embarrassed to learn one Sunday.

  I was a guest preacher at a church in British Columbia, and I was anxious to impress my friends, who were members there. I prepared well, but the sermon apparently didn't cut it. After the service, I asked one of my friends how it went. She is known for her frankness, and she didn't disappoint: She said, "I didn't get much out of the sermon, but one phrase from your benediction really got me thinking."

Oh well.

Communion

In the free church tradition, Communion (also called the Eucharist, from the Greek for "thanksgiving," or the Lord's Supper) is celebrated usually once a month, usually the first Sunday of the month. Some churches celebrate it only once a quarter. Depending on the tradition of the church, it is seen either as a memorial meal, in which people are merely reminded about what Christ did, or a moment in which Christ becomes present in some special form.

Communion is patterned after the final supper Jesus had with his disciples. During that meal, he passed around bread and said that it signified his body "which is given for you." Then he passed around wine, saying it signified his blood "shed for the forgiveness of sins." Jesus was foreshadowing his crucifixion, of course, and after his death and resurrection this meal came to represent for Christians his death, the supreme act of love and sacrifice that made our forgiveness possible.

History, however, has bumped into the church and made one change, at least in many churches in this tradition. Wine has been replaced by grape juice. This is the result, among other things, of the temperance movement, when drinking alcohol under any circumstances was viewed as a sin. Today, long after temperance, and even after many members of these churches enjoy wine with their family dinners, the grape juice tradition continues in some churches.

> **Prayer Pearls**
>
> Never make the blunder of trying to forecast the way God is going to answer your prayer.
>
> —Oswald Chambers, English devotional writer

Table Manners

If you haven't been to church in a while—or if you've never been to church—you'll want a few tips so as not to embarrass yourself at your first Communion. The bread will be passed around on little plates, usually broken in small pieces or as discs of unleavened bread. Simply take a piece when the plate comes your way; if it's a loaf of bread, simply pull off a small piece. Now comes the awkward part: What are you supposed to do?

Sometimes the minister is good enough to say ahead of time, "Partake individually," which means eat it when you want, or "We'll partake together," which means to hold on to the bread until the minister tells you to eat it. In either case, as the plates continue to be passed, this is a time of meditation and for making your own prayers of thanksgiving or dedication.

The same goes for the wine or grape juice, which will come around in trays with little cups. After drinking, look for a mini-shelf, with holes the size of the base of the cups, on the back of the pew in front of you. That's where the empty cup goes. If the church doesn't have those, just watch what everyone else does with theirs.

No matter the logistics, Communion is a most intimate moment with Christ. We by no means have to be in a perfect state of holiness when we partake, but before we come to worship (or as the service leads up to Communion) we are wise to prepare heart and mind to receive not just the bread and juice, but even Christ himself. Communion is prayer—with a capital *P*.

Dancing in Church?

There are not as many bodily motions in a free church service as in the more liturgical service, but there are a few you should understand.

During praise choruses especially, you'll notice some people raising their hands. Some raise them only waist high with palms up—this is an act of offering themselves to God. Others will lift their hands high above their heads with palms facing out—this is a bodily way of directing praise and honor to God.

Snapshots of Answered Prayers
The Philistines seized David in Gath but David prays in Psalm 56 that he will not fear mere mortals and God delivers him.

Others might sway left and right, or up and back, as they sing—and so on. You don't have to do any of this if people around you start up. Nor do you have to feel uncomfortable if other people do it. They're not going to go weird on you; they're just "getting into it." Think of it as a form of dance in which people are letting their bodies participate in worship.

During prayers, most people will shut their eyes. This is considered more reverent and can help with concentration. But an old custom of Christian worship is keeping eyes open during prayer—God is present among us, after all; why not look around to see what he's up to? So, it's your call on that, no matter what people do around you.

Can you clap in worship? Some churches encourage it; others frown upon it. I'd play "follow the leader" on this one.

In most African American churches, the tongue becomes a very important part of worship, especially during the sermon. The sermon is a dialogue, with the pastor preaching and the people responding with words of encouragement: "Amen," "Yes, Lord," "Oh, yes," and the like. Again, there is no law that says you have to join in, nor one that says newcomers can't join in.

Should You Attend a Seeker-Sensitive Church?

Seeker-sensitive churches arose because a lot of people find traditional worship services boring, irrelevant, and incomprehensible—and that's on the good Sundays. Some pastors decided to start services that were "user-friendly," especially to people outside the faith who are seeking to know God better but who are unfamiliar with church culture.

Seeker-sensitive services are popping up all over the place. They are usually found in independent churches (those not affiliated with a denomination), and the most famous—the granddaddy of them all, Willow Creek Community Church in Barrington, Illinois, a suburb of Chicago—attracts about 14,000 people each weekend. Not bad. As a result of such success, a lot of denominational churches are starting to create seeker-sensitive services as well.

What's the difference? Instead of an organ and/or piano, they use guitar, bass, drums, and other "contemporary" instruments to lead singing. They reject hymns in favor of songs that have a contemporary feel, everything from folk to jazz and light rock. People dress casually, many arriving in shorts in the summer. Reverent silence is the exception, not the rule, and clapping can erupt at many times in the service. There is no pulpit, and if there is one, it's made of transparent Plexiglas—and often the preacher wanders away from it freely. Christian jargon is cut to a minimum—for example, the sermon is often called the "morning message."

The goal is to help "seekers" break through the clutter of church culture to hear the essential message of Christ in a way that makes sense to them. The upside is that it is really easy to become acquainted with praying again. The downside is that, over the long haul, because such churches downplay so much of the church's rich tradition, they often are unable to take people more deeply into worship or prayer. I write, however, as one who worships in the liturgical tradition, so I may be biased here.

It Sounds Like Gibberish to Me

One more thing you should be aware of: In some churches, people may start "speaking in tongues" during prayer, and the place will sound like a buzz of gibberish. So what is happening here?

To speak in tongues is to speak in a "heavenly language." This language is given to believers as a gift of the Holy Spirit. It is as if the Spirit is praying through the person as the person is praying to God, and this allows the person to express things that are too deep for words. (Remember that stuff about the mystery of prayer and the Trinity?) Though this is something the church has experienced in every age, speaking in tongues has been a special feature of twentieth-century Christianity.

> **Prayer Pearls**
>
> Many a person is praying for rain with his tub the wrong side up.
>
> —Sam Jones, American revivalist

The gift is expressed in a number of ways. Many simply use this prayer language in their private prayers at home. Others use it with other Christians, and afterward, someone who is said to have the "gift of interpretation" interprets what the prayer said. Tongues are also used in public worship, with everyone speaking (or even singing) in tongues at the same time.

You'll find tongues used in Pentecostal churches (*Pentecostal* refers back to the Day of Pentecost, a Jewish holiday when early Christians first experienced the gift of tongues) and in "Charismatic" circles (*Charismatic* comes from the Greek word *charas*, which means "gift" and refers to the gifts given by the Holy Spirit, especially the gift of tongues). Many mainline churches—Presbyterian, Methodist, Episcopalian, and the like—have Charismatic fellowships within them, who meet to pray together in tongues and for healing.

Is speaking in tongues a prayer practice you should experience? Some Pentecostals will tell you that you *must* speak in tongues to be an obedient Christian. Others will invite you to speak in tongues as a way of experiencing God more fully. Others still will say that if you desire the gift, you can pray for it and receive it; otherwise, don't worry about it. This last option happens to be my take on it: If you are interested in a full prayer life, you should be open to it. I have prayed for this gift, but have not received it.

Talk to your local Pentecostal or Charismatic church for more information.

From the Good Book

Therefore confess your sins to each other and pray for each other so that you may be healed. The prayer of a righteous man is powerful and effective. Elijah was a man just like us. He prayed earnestly that it would not rain, and it did not rain on the land for three and a half years. Again he prayed, and the heavens gave rain, and the earth produced its crops.

—James, James 5:16

The Least You Need to Know

◆ Participating in the free church tradition is one way to enhance your prayer life.

◆ Some of the most important parts of a free church service include the hymns, confessions, sermon, offering, and Communion.

◆ Some aspects of free church worship allow us to be more involved by raising our hands, clapping, or even dancing to express our love and gratitude to God.

◆ Seeker-sensitive churches try to offer worship without seeming "churchy."

◆ Speaking in tongues is a mysterious experience that many people find spiritually enriching.

Chapter 35

Prayer in the Liturgical Tradition

In This Chapter

- ◆ What is unique about liturgical worship

- ◆ How a liturgical service flows

- ◆ The various ways liturgical worship enhances the life of prayer

- ◆ Tips for those who are new to (or coming back to) church

As noted in the last chapter, all churches have a liturgy, an order of service they follow week after week. But some churches—Roman Catholic, Episcopal, Lutheran, and Orthodox (and sometimes Presbyterian and Methodist)—*really* have a liturgy. In contrast to the free church tradition, the liturgical tradition relies more on prayer books, favors written over extemporaneous prayers, requires more responses from the congregation, and puts a lesser emphasis on the sermon and a much higher emphasis on Communion.

Now for the details.

Prayer Book Religion

Liturgical churches each have a prayer book; for Roman Catholics it's called the missal (from a Latin word meaning "of the Mass," which is what Catholics call their worship service). For Episcopalians it's called *The Book of Common Prayer,* or BCP for short. And so on. These prayer books not only guide the order of worship, but they also include the prayers and Scripture readings for each Sunday.

> **Prayer Pearls**
>
> Prayer does not change God, but changes him who prays.
>
> —Søren Kierkegaard, Danish philosopher and theologian

That doesn't mean there isn't some flexibility in the service. Some services are decidedly "low church," meaning that the service is stripped to its bare essentials. "High church" worship comes with all the bells and whistles, or, as we say in the liturgical tradition, "bells and smells"—a reference to the ringing of bells during various parts of the service and the use of incense. (More on that later in the chapter.)

The more strict adherence to a set order of worship and the use of formal, written prayers strikes some Christians as odd. They wonder how, if prayer is about an intimate relationship with God, you can foster that in what seems to be such a rigid and formal service. The answer lies in the purpose of the service. If the free church tradition's service is designed to appear as spontaneous (albeit guided) thanksgiving, then in the liturgical tradition, worship is more a well-thought-out offering made to God. It sacrifices informality to present to God something that is beautiful and worthy of God's greatness.

> **Prayer Pearls**
>
> May we bring this eternal life to the poor, deprived as they are of all comfort, of material possessions; may they come to know you, love you, possess you, share in your life, you who are the God and father of men and of my Lord Jesus Christ, source of all truth and goodness and happiness.
>
> —Mother Teresa of Calcutta

The written prayers have been crafted and fine-tuned through the centuries so that many of them express succinctly and movingly the very personal thoughts and feelings of the worshippers. Just as a sonnet of William Shakespeare is often the most profound and intimate way to express one's love to another, so liturgical prayers help people express their deepest thoughts to God.

Let's not get too idealistic about this: Liturgical worship can be dreary, thoughtless, routine, and boring as hell. (Excuse the expression, but I think I mean it.) Then again, free church services can be dreary, thoughtless, routine, and—you get it. It's not the tradition as much as those enacting the tradition that makes the difference.

The Word of God

Let me take you through a typical Episcopal service. This is very similar to services in other liturgical traditions, using many of the same prayers, in fact. It is also one I'm familiar with. If you know Episcopal worship, you can probably fake it most anywhere.

There are two parts to a liturgical service. The first part is called "The Word of God." The focus of this part is the reading of the Bible and the preaching of the sermon.

The Episcopal service begins with reciting various Scripture verses and prayers, with some said in unison, some responsively (the worship leader reads one line, the congregation the next), and some by the worship leader (called "the celebrant" in the BCP) alone. The prayer book is usually clear about who does what, so you simply have to follow the book. (Once in a while, however, the liturgy is unclear; when I was new to this tradition, I'd just hang back and wait for a phrase or two before deciding whether I was supposed to join in or not.)

All this leads up to the "Collect of the Day," which is a short prayer that "collects" or sums up the theme of the service of that Sunday. For example, on Christmas Day, the collect reads:

> O God, you make us glad by the yearly festival of the birth of your only Son, Jesus Christ: Grant that we, who joyfully receive him as our Redeemer, may with sure confidence behold him when he comes to be our Judge; who lives and reigns with you and the Holy Spirit, one God, now and forever. Amen.

Every Sunday has a theme that is summarized by the collect and highlighted in the Scripture readings. There are usually four Bible readings, one each from the Old Testament, the Psalms, the epistles (which can come from any book of the New Testament except the Gospels or Acts of the Apostles), and the Gospels.

Then comes the sermon, which tends to be considerably shorter than in most free church services, usually lasting 10 to 15 minutes (versus 25 to 40 minutes).

Prayer Hotline

When you go to a liturgical church, sit toward the front, but make sure there are a good number of people still sitting in front of you. You want to sit toward the front because you'll hear and see better and can get a lot more out of the service. But you want people in front of you so that you know when to stand or kneel. Just follow their lead.

After the sermon, everyone stands and reads together the Nicene Creed, a brief summary of Christian belief that goes back to the year 381. Though a statement of faith, it is prayerlike in its cadences and sums up the story and message of Christian faith:

> We believe in one God,
>
> the Father, the Almighty,
>
> maker of heaven and earth,
>
> of all that is seen and unseen.
>
> We believe in one Lord, Jesus Christ,
>
> the only Son of God,
>
> eternally begotten of the Father,
>
> God from God, Light from Light,
>
> true God from true God,
>
> begotten, not made,
>
> of one Being with the Father.
>
> Through him all things were made.
>
> For us and for our salvation
>
> he came down from heaven:
>
> By the power of the Holy Spirit
>
> he became incarnate of the Virgin Mary,
>
> and was made man.
>
> For our sake he was crucified under Pontius Pilate:
>
> He suffered death and was buried.
>
> On the third day he rose again
>
> in accordance with the Scriptures;
>
> he ascended into heaven
>
> and is seated at the right hand of the Father.
>
> He will come again to judge the living and the dead,
>
> and his kingdom will have no end.

We believe in the Holy Spirit, the Lord, the giver of life,

who proceeds from the Father and the Son.

With the Father and the Son he is worshipped and glorified.

He has spoken through the prophets.

We believe in one holy catholic and apostolic church.

We acknowledge one baptism for the forgiveness of sins.

We look forward to the resurrection of the dead,

and the life of the world to come. Amen.

This is followed by the "Prayers of the People," which usually includes a prayer of confession. Again, let me quote from the BCP, because you really can't appreciate the power of this tradition without reading some of the prayers (I'd encourage you to read them aloud, in fact). There are two or three prayers of confession in the BCP, but the most common one used is this:

Most merciful God,

we confess that we have sinned against you

in thought, word, and deed,

by what we have done,

and by what we have left undone.

We have not loved you with our whole heart;

we have not loved our neighbors as ourselves.

We are truly sorry and we humbly repent,

For the sake of your Son, Jesus Christ,

have mercy on us and forgive us; that
we may delight in your will,

and walk in your ways,

to the glory of your name. Amen.

This has always struck me as a succinct and yet complete inventory of my life, and it never ceases to amaze me how well it expresses what I'm feeling. That is liturgical prayer at its best.

From the Good Book

This is the confidence we have in approaching God: that if we ask anything according to his will, he hears us. And if we know that he hears us—whatever we ask—we know that we have what we asked of him.

—John, 1 John 5:14

Holy Communion

The second half of the service focuses on Communion, which the BCP calls the Holy Eucharist (from the Greek word for "thanksgiving").

Communion begins with the eucharistic prayer, or "The Great Thanksgiving." It's called "great" because it's important and, well, it's long. If you understand what's going on in the prayer, you'll get a lot out of it.

Communion continues with a responsive greeting between the priest and the people and then moves into the prayer proper. There are three parts: In the first, God is praised for his glory and for his creation of the world. In the second, Christ is thanked for coming to the world, for "offering himself ... a perfect sacrifice for the whole world," and for rising from the grave. In the third part, the Holy Spirit is the center of attention, especially his power to sustain our faith. So you see, the prayer is trinitarian.

Then to sum up this prayer, and all the prayers of the service so far, everyone prays the Lord's Prayer.

Then the elements are received, usually with people going forward row by row, kneeling at the altar and receiving the bread and the wine. Churches have different customs in how exactly the elements are received, so I just follow what others do and then I do the same.

Then comes another prayer, a hymn, and the benediction.

Bells and Smells

One of the things I like about the liturgical tradition is that it tries to engage all the senses in worship:

♦ *Hearing:* Listening to Scriptures, prayers, sermon, song, organ, bells

♦ *Sight:* Stained-glass windows, priestly dress, colorful banners, religious art around the sanctuary

♦ *Touch* (that is, bodily movement): Kneeling, standing, sitting, crossing yourself, walking, bowing

♦ *Taste:* Bread and wine

♦ *Smell:* The aroma of burning incense

> **Snapshots of Answered Prayers**
>
> David pretended to be insane in front of King Abimelech in order to go free. He praises God in Psalm 34 for rescuing him from his suffering.

Jesus commands us to love God with heart, mind, soul, and strength. Well, liturgical churches try to worship God with the same holistic devotion.

The Church Year

In addition to engaging all of our bodies, the liturgical tradition wants us to rethink our concept of time. The church, in fact, keeps its own calendar with its own seasons, and they only loosely correspond to winter, spring, summer, and fall. Each season has a theme that addresses major events in biblical history and our own life in Christ. This aspect of liturgical worship can really enhance the life of prayer.

- *Advent* begins in late November or early December and lasts for four Sundays. The focus of the readings and the prayers is the first coming of Christ and his eventual second coming.

- *Christmas* begins on December 25, of course, and lasts two Sundays. The focus is, of course, the incarnation ("becoming flesh") of Christ.

- *Epiphany* begins on January 6, or "Three Kings Day," and lasts between 8 and 11 weeks. The services highlight Jesus as the light of the whole world and the church's mission to reach out in love to all.

- *Lent* lasts 40 days (not counting Sundays), beginning with Ash Wednesday, continuing through Good Friday, and ending on Holy Saturday (the day before Easter). The theme is Christ's suffering and death and our need for self-examination, confession, and repentance.

- *Easter* begins on, you got it, Easter Sunday and goes for eight weeks. The focus is the resurrection of Christ and the new life we have in him.

- *Pentecost* begins usually in late May or early June and lasts until Advent. It celebrates the coming of the Holy Spirit and our dependence on his power to sustain us in the Christian walk.

In the midst of these seasons, other themes are celebrated: the baptism of Christ, the Trinity, the death of a saint. The nice thing about all this for prayer is that it gives structure and rhythm to prayer life, both in worship and at home.

Worship for Those Who Haven't Worshipped in a While

If you haven't been to church in a while (or ever), it can be pretty intimidating to start going again. Here are a few tips to ease you into your first few Sundays:

1. Go with a friend who already attends church. There's nothing like having someone show you the ropes. Or you can phone the minister during the week before you visit and ask him or her to find a member to sit with you. This sounds like an inconvenience for the church, but, believe me, it's not. I don't know of any church that would not welcome you in this way.

2. On the other hand, if you just want to blend in with the stained-glass windows, pick a large church. It's easy to get lost in a crowd, and people may not bother you for weeks—until you're ready to get to know them.

3. Get there early and read over the bulletin, or program, the usher will hand you. Scope out the service; you may even want to mark the hymns in the hymnbook ahead of time.

4. During the service, be alert to the rhythm of worship. Christian worship, like prayer, is a dialogue. As such, it has a certain rhythm; if you understand that, you can get a whole lot more out of it. It's a two-step: God speaks; we respond. God speaks to us, as I've mentioned, in the Scripture and sermon especially, but also in various other parts of the service. We respond with prayers, songs, and offering. These two aspects go back and forth in different ways, depending on the worship tradition, but every Christian service has them. If you are aware of them, you'll get a lot more out of the service.

5. If you can't find the hymn or prayer that everyone else is saying, just listen. You're not going to get kicked out if you don't join in. Besides, better to listen to the words being sung or said than to be thumbing through the book, cursing yourself because you can't find the right page.

6. Be patient. C. S. Lewis put it this way: "As long as you notice and have to count the steps, you are not yet dancing but only learning to dance. A good shoe is a shoe you don't notice. Good reading becomes possible when you need not consciously think about eyes, or light, or print, or spelling. The perfect church service would be one we were almost unaware of; our attention would have been on God."

Feeling comfortable in church may not happen overnight, but it will happen. Hang in there!

The Least You Need to Know

◆ The liturgical tradition relies more on written prayers and centers on Communion more than the sermon.

◆ The liturgical tradition is one that can be considered a sensual experience with "smells and bells," sacraments, and pageantry.

◆ The seasons of the church can bring a refreshing spiritual rhythm to the year.

◆ It takes time and practice to worship well in the liturgical tradition.

Prayers for Various People and Occasions

The following prayers are meant only as starters for longer prayers for various people, special church days, etc. Once you get the idea, it should be easier to start praying for still other people, occasions, and needs in your life and the lives of others.

Prayers for Loved Ones

A good prayer for our loved ones is: "Almighty God, we entrust all who are dear to us to thy never-failing care and love, for this life and the life to come, knowing that thou art doing for them better things than we can desire or pray for; through Jesus Christ, our Lord. Amen." Here are some other more specific prayers.

For Husbands

I pray for my husband that the desires of his heart will coincide with your desires. Grant him grace, patience, and great faith to wait upon you and trust you to fulfill your wonderful purpose for his life. Thank you for allowing me to be his companion and helpmate as we walk this spiritual journey together. May your love shine through us and restore the divine image in us as we meet one another's needs.

For Wives

Thank you for the privilege of being your son and for giving me someone who truly blesses my life. Thank you for calling us together to share your love for us. May we be a reflection of how Christ loved the church and how the church responds to Christ. Help me to be the kind of husband who is seeking your glory in all things and keeping my wife's interests above my own. May I love her as I love and care for myself.

For Couples

Many times we fail to look to you as the answer to our difficulties. We thank you for the many blessings you have given to us in your gift of marriage. Please continue to bless us and help us to always remember where our strength comes from. Draw each of us closer to you so that we might be close to each other. May our time together bring honor to you. Help us to remain faithful to each other and to you.

For Sons

Thank you for giving us a son. Thank you for the energy, integrity, and unique qualities our son brings into our lives. Let us have balance in the way that we love him and give him advice. May he grow to be a man after your own heart. Direct his heart into all that you desire for the plan you have for him—his future career, potential spouse, and deepening relationship with you. Help us, by word and example, to give him all that he needs to bear fruit for you, Lord, and fulfill your will.

For Daughters

We pray first and foremost that you would fill her with your Spirit and grant that she would be the kind of woman that would seek to love you with her full heart, mind, and strength. May she not be squeezed into the world's way of thinking, but be a woman of deep faith, courage, and love. May she bring you great glory, honor, and praise and lead others to know of your salvation. Help her through all the trials and temptations of this life and keep her in the everlasting way of your grace, mercy, and love, bringing her to yourself on the final and great day.

For Children

Our Father, we thank you for giving us children. They are our joy, and help us to love them sincerely. Through us you gave them life; from eternity you knew them and loved them. Give us the wisdom to guide them, patience to teach them, vigilance to let them see goodness lived out through our example. Help us to receive them back when they have strayed. Sometimes it is difficult to understand them, so help us provide discipline and guidance. Grant that they may always see our home as a haven in their time of need.

For Fathers

Thank you for our earthly father who in so many ways represents who you are to us. Thank you for his faithfulness and strength, loyalty and love. We ask that you would continue to give him health, wisdom, and direction to be a good husband, father, and leader. May we remember to thank him by our continuing service and prayers as well as kind words. May he be a mirror of the attributes of you, heavenly father, who has given him the gifts and talents that have motivated his self-sacrifice and strength in our lives.

For Mothers

Thank you for a mother who expresses so much compassion, acceptance, and nurturing love in our lives throughout the years. She combines strength with gentleness and warmth. Please bless her abundantly for all the labor of love and hospitality she has shown us, taking care of so many needs—from the physical to the mental and spiritual. Please give her back tenfold what she has invested in her husband and children throughout the years that too often has not been appreciated enough. Give her your supernatural grace, mercy, and peace. Help her to truly enjoy and drink in the love that you and her family have for her, to provide sustenance for her soul.

Prayers from *The Book of Common Prayer*

The following prayers are taken from *The Book of Common Prayer*, the official prayer book used in the liturgy of the Episcopal Church, United States of America.

For the Mission of the Church

O God, who hast made of one blood all the peoples of the earth and who didst send thy blessed Son to preach peace to those who are far off and to those who are near: Grant that people everywhere may seek after thee and find thee, bring the nations into thy fold, pour out thy spirit upon all flesh, and hasten the coming of thy kingdom; through the same thy Son, Jesus Christ, our Lord, who liveth and reigneth with thee and the same Spirit, one God now and forever. Amen.

For the Nation

Lord God almighty, who hast made all peoples of the earth for thy glory, to serve thee in freedom and peace: Grant to the people of our country a zeal for justice and the strength of forbearance, that we may use our liberty in accordance with thy gracious will; through Jesus Christ, our Lord, who liveth and reigneth with thee and the Holy Spirit, one God, forever and ever. Amen.

At Baptism

Almighty God, who by our baptism into the death and resurrection of thy Son, Jesus Christ, dost turn us from the old life of sin: Grant that we, being reborn to new life in him, may live in righteousness and holiness all our days; through the same thy Son, Jesus Christ, our Lord, who liveth and reigneth with thee and the Holy Spirit, one God, now and forever. Amen.

At Confirmation

Grant, almighty God, that we who have been redeemed from the old life of sin by our baptism into the death and resurrection of thy Son, Jesus Christ, may be renewed in thy Holy Spirit and live in righteousness and true holiness; through the same Jesus Christ, our Lord, who liveth and reigneth with thee and the same Spirit, one God, now and forever. Amen.

For the Departed

O eternal Lord God, who holdest all souls in life: Give, we beseech thee, to thy whole church in paradise and on earth thy light and thy peace; and grant that we, following the good examples of those who have served thee here and are now at rest, may at the last enter with them into thine unending joy; through Jesus Christ, our Lord, who liveth and reigneth with thee in the unity of the Holy Spirit, one God, now and forever. Amen.

Of the Holy Eucharist

God our Father, whose Son, our Lord Jesus Christ, in a wonderful sacrament hath left unto us a memorial of his passion: Grant us so to venerate the sacred mysteries of his body and blood, that we may ever perceive within ourselves the fruit of his redemption; who liveth and reigneth with thee and the Holy Spirit, one God, forever and ever. Amen.

Thanksgiving Day

Almighty and gracious Father, we give thee thanks for the fruits of the earth in their season and for the labors of those who harvest them. Make us, we beseech thee, faithful stewards of thy great bounty, for the provision of our necessities and the relief of all who are in need, to the glory of thy name; through Jesus Christ, our Lord, who liveth and reigneth with thee and the Holy Spirit, one God, now and forever. Amen.

Independence Day (July 4)

Lord God almighty, in whose name the founders of this country won liberty for themselves and for us, and lit the torch of freedom for nations then unborn: Grant, we beseech thee, that we and all the people of this land may have grace to maintain these liberties in righteousness and peace; through Jesus Christ, our Lord, who liveth and reigneth with thee and the Holy Spirit, one God, forever and ever. Amen.

Easter Sunday

O God, who for our redemption didst give thine only-begotten Son to the death of the cross, and by his glorious resurrection hast delivered us from the power of our enemy: Grant us so to die daily to sin, that we may evermore live with him in the joy of his resurrection; through the same thy Son, Christ, our Lord, who liveth and reigneth with thee and the Holy Spirit, one God, now and forever. Amen.

Holy Thursday

Almighty Father, whose dear Son, on the night before he suffered, did institute the sacrament of his body and blood: Mercifully grant that we may thankfully receive the same in remembrance of him who in these holy mysteries giveth us a pledge of life eternal, the same thy Son, Jesus Christ, our Lord; who now liveth and reigneth with thee and the Holy Spirit ever, one God, world without end. Amen.

Good Friday

Almighty God, we beseech thee graciously to behold this thy family, for which our Lord, Jesus Christ, was contented to be betrayed and given up into the hands of sinners, and to suffer death upon the cross; who now liveth and reigneth with thee and the Holy Ghost ever, one God, world without end. Amen.

The Nativity of Our Lord: Christmas Day (December 25)

O God, who makest us glad with the yearly remembrance of the birth of thy only Son, Jesus Christ: Grant that as we joyfully receive him for our Redeemer, so we may with sure confidence behold him when he shall come to be our judge; who liveth and reigneth with thee and the Holy Ghost, one God, world without end. Amen.

For Social Justice

Almighty God, who hast created us in thine image: Grant us grace fearlessly to contend against evil and to make no peace with oppression; and, that we may reverently use our freedom, help us to employ it in the maintenance of justice in our communities and among the nations, to the glory of thy holy name; through Jesus Christ, our Lord, who liveth and reigneth with thee and the Holy Spirit, one God, now and forever. Amen.

For Education

Almighty God, the fountain of all wisdom: Enlighten by thy Holy Spirit those who teach and those who learn, that, rejoicing in the knowledge of thy truth, they may worship thee and serve thee from generation to generation; through Jesus Christ, our Lord, who liveth and reigneth with thee and the same Spirit, one God, forever and ever. Amen.

For the Sick

Heavenly Father, giver of life and health: Comfort and relieve thy sick servants, and give thy power of healing to those who minister to their needs, that those (or name or names) for whom our prayers are offered may be strengthened in their weakness and have confidence in thy loving care; through Jesus Christ, our Lord, who liveth and reigneth with thee and the Holy Spirit, one God, now and forever. Amen.

For Labor Day

Almighty God, who hast so linked our lives one with another that all we do affecteth, for good or ill, all other lives: So guide us in the work we do, that we may do it not for self alone, but for the common good; and, as we seek a proper return for our own labor, make us mindful of the rightful aspirations of other workers, and arouse our concern for those who are out of work; through Jesus Christ, our Lord, who liveth and reigneth with thee and the Holy Spirit, one God, forever and ever. Amen.

For Our Country

Almighty God, who hast given us this good land for our heritage: We humbly beseech thee that we may always prove ourselves a people mindful of thy favor and glad to do thy will. Bless our land with honorable industry, sound learning, and pure manners. Save us from violence, discord, and confusion; from pride and arrogance, and from every evil way. Defend our liberties, and fashion into one united people the multitudes brought hither out of many kindreds and tongues. Endue with the spirit of wisdom those to whom in thy name we entrust the authority of government, that there may be justice and peace at home, and that, through obedience to thy law, we may show forth thy praise among the nations of the earth. In the time of prosperity, fill our hearts with thankfulness, and in the day of trouble, suffer not our trust in thee to fail; all which we ask through Jesus Christ, our Lord. Amen.

For the President of the United States and All in Civil Authority

O Lord, our governor, whose glory is in all the world: We commend this nation to thy merciful care, that, being guided by thy providence, we may dwell secure in thy peace. Grant to the President of the United States, the governor of this state (or commonwealth), and to all in authority wisdom and strength to know and to do thy will. Fill them with the love of truth and righteousness, and make them ever mindful of their calling to serve this people in thy fear; through Jesus Christ, our Lord, who liveth and reigneth with thee and the Holy Spirit, one God, world without end. Amen.

For Congress or a State Legislature

O God, the fountain of wisdom, whose will is good and gracious, and whose law is truth: We beseech thee so to guide and bless our senators and representatives in Congress assembled (or in the legislature of this state or commonwealth), that they may enact such laws as shall please thee, to the glory of thy name and the welfare of this people; through Jesus Christ, our Lord. Amen.

For Courts of Justice

Almighty God, who sittest in the throne judging right: We humbly beseech thee to bless the courts of justice and the magistrates in all this land; and give unto them the spirit of wisdom and understanding, that they may discern the truth and impartially administer the law in the fear of thee alone; through him who shall come to be our judge, thy Son, our Savior, Jesus Christ. Amen.

For Local Government

Almighty God, our heavenly Father, send down upon those who hold office in this state (commonwealth, city, county, town) the spirit of wisdom, charity, and justice, that with steadfast purpose they may faithfully serve in their offices to promote the well-being of all people; through Jesus Christ, our Lord. Amen.

For an Election

Almighty God, to whom we must account for all our powers and privileges: Guide the people of the United States (or of this community) in the election of officials and representatives; that, by faithful administration and wise laws, the rights of all may be protected and our nation be enabled to fulfill your purposes; through Jesus Christ, our Lord. Amen.

For Those in the Armed Forces of Our Country

Almighty God, we commend to your gracious care and keeping all the men and women of our armed forces at home and abroad. Defend them day by day with your heavenly grace; strengthen them in their trials and temptations; give them courage to face the perils which beset them; and grant them a sense of your abiding presence wherever they may be; through Jesus Christ, our Lord. Amen.

For Those Who Suffer for the Sake of Conscience

God, our Father, whose Son forgave his enemies while he was suffering shame and death: Strengthen those who suffer for the sake of conscience; when they are accused, save them from speaking in hate; when they are rejected, save them from bitterness; when they are imprisoned, save them from despair; and to us your servants, give grace to respect their witness and to discern the truth, that our society may be cleansed and strengthened. This we ask for the sake of Jesus Christ, our merciful and righteous judge. Amen.

For Reconciliation

Grant, O God, that your holy and life-giving spirit may so move every human heart (and especially the hearts of the people of this land), that barriers which divide us may crumble, suspicions disappear, and hatreds cease; that our divisions being healed, we may live in justice and peace; through Jesus Christ, our Lord. Amen.

For the Unemployed

Heavenly Father, we remember before you those who suffer want and anxiety from lack of work. Guide the people of this land so to use our public and private wealth that all may find suitable and fulfilling employment and receive just payment for their labor; through Jesus Christ, our Lord. Amen.

For Schools and Colleges

O eternal God, bless all schools, colleges, and universities that they may be lively centers for sound learning, new discovery, and the pursuit of wisdom; and grant that those who teach and those who learn may find you to be the source of all truth; through Jesus Christ, our Lord. Amen.

For the Good Use of Leisure

O God, in the course of this busy life, give us times of refreshment and peace; and grant that we may so use our leisure to rebuild our bodies and renew our minds, that our spirits may be opened to the goodness of your creation; through Jesus Christ, our Lord. Amen.

For the Poor and the Neglected

Almighty and most merciful God, we remember before you all poor and neglected persons whom it would be easy for us to forget: the homeless and the destitute, the old and the sick, and all who have none to care for them. Help us to heal those who are broken in body or spirit, and to turn their sorrow into joy. Grant this, Father, for the love of your Son, who for our sake became poor, Jesus Christ, our Lord. Amen.

For the Oppressed

Look with pity, O heavenly Father, upon the people in this land who live with injustice, terror, disease, and death as their constant companions. Have mercy upon us. Help us to eliminate our cruelty to these our neighbors. Strengthen those who spend their lives establishing equal protection of the law and equal opportunities for all. And grant that every one of us may enjoy a fair portion of the riches of this land; through Jesus Christ our Lord. Amen.

For Prisons and Correctional Institutions

Lord Jesus, for our sake you were condemned as a criminal: Visit our jails and prisons with your pity and judgment. Remember all prisoners, and bring the guilty to repentance and amendment of life according to your will, and give them hope for their future. When any are held unjustly, bring them release; forgive us, and teach us to improve our justice. Remember those who work in these institutions; keep them humane and compassionate; and save them from becoming brutal or callous. And since what we do for those in prison, O Lord, we do for you, constrain us to improve their lot. All this we ask for your mercy's sake. Amen.

For Families

Almighty God, our heavenly Father, who settlest the solitary in families: We commend to thy continual care the homes in which thy people dwell. Put far from them, we beseech thee, every root of bitterness, the desire of vainglory, and the pride of life. Fill them with faith, virtue, knowledge, temperance, patience, godliness. Knit together in constant affection those who, in holy wedlock, have been made one flesh. Turn the hearts of the parents to the children, and the hearts of the children to the parents; and so enkindle fervent charity among us all, that we may evermore be kindly affectioned one to another; through Jesus Christ, our Lord. Amen.

For the Care of Children

Almighty God, heavenly Father, you have blessed us with the joy and care of children: Give us calm strength and patient wisdom as we bring them up, that we may teach them to love whatever is just and true and good, following the example of our Savior, Jesus Christ. Amen.

For Young Persons

God, our Father, you see your children growing up in an unsteady and confusing world: Show them that your ways give more life than the ways of the world, and that following you is better than chasing after selfish goals. Help them to take failure not as a measure of their worth, but as a chance for a new start. Give them strength to hold their faith in you and to keep alive their joy in your creation; through Jesus Christ, our Lord. Amen.

For the Aged

Look with mercy, O God our Father, on all whose increasing years bring them weakness, distress, or isolation. Provide for them homes of dignity and peace; give them understanding helpers and the willingness to accept help; and, as their strength diminishes, increase their faith and their assurance of your love. This we ask in the name of Jesus Christ, our Lord. Amen.

For a Birthday

O God, our times are in your hands: Look with favor, we pray, on your servant (insert name) as he begins another year. Grant that he may grow in wisdom and grace, and strengthen his trust in your goodness all the days of his life; through Jesus Christ, our Lord. Amen.

For Guidance

O God, by whom the meek are guided in judgment and light riseth up in darkness for the godly: Grant us, in all our doubts and uncertainties, the grace to ask what thou wouldst have us to do, that the spirit of wisdom may save us from all false choices, and that in thy light we may see light, and in thy straight path may not stumble; through Jesus Christ, our Lord. Amen.

For Quiet Confidence

O God of peace, who hast taught us that in returning and rest we shall be saved, in quietness and in confidence shall be our strength: By the might of thy spirit lift us, we pray thee, to thy presence, where we may be still and know that thou art God; through Jesus Christ, our Lord. Amen.

For Protection

Assist us mercifully, O Lord, in these our supplications and prayers, and dispose the way of thy servants toward the attainment of everlasting salvation; that, among all the changes and chances of this mortal life, they may ever be defended by thy gracious and ready help; through Jesus Christ, our Lord. Amen.

A Prayer of Self-Dedication

Almighty and eternal God, so draw our hearts to thee, so guide our minds, so fill our imaginations, so control our wills, that we may be wholly and utterly dedicated unto thee; and then use us, we pray thee, as thou wilt, and always to thy glory and the welfare of thy people; through our Lord and Savior, Jesus Christ. Amen.

A Prayer Attributed to St. Francis

Lord, make us instruments of your peace. Where there is hatred, let us sow love; where there is injury, pardon; where there is discord, union; where there is doubt, faith; where there is despair, hope; where there is darkness, light; where there is sadness, joy. Grant that we may not so much seek to be consoled as to console; to be understood as to understand; to be loved as to love. For it is in giving that we receive; it is in pardoning that we are pardoned; and it is in dying that we are born to eternal life. Amen.

In the Evening

O Lord, support us all the day long, until the shadows lengthen and the evening comes, and the busy world is hushed, and the fever of life is over, and our work is done. Then in thy mercy, grant us a safe lodging, and a holy rest, and peace at the last. Amen.

Before Worship

O almighty God, who pourest out on all who desire it the spirit of grace and of supplication: Deliver us, when we draw near to thee, from coldness of heart and wanderings of mind, that with steadfast thoughts and kindled affections we may worship thee in spirit and in truth; through Jesus Christ, our Lord. Amen.

For the Answering of Prayer

Almighty God, who hast promised to hear the petitions of those who ask in thy Son's name: We beseech thee mercifully to incline thine ear to us who have now made our prayers and supplications unto thee; and grant that those things which we have faithfully asked according to thy will may effectually be obtained to the relief of our necessity and to the setting forth of thy glory; through Jesus Christ, our Lord. Amen.

On Sunday

O God, our King, by the resurrection of your Son, Jesus Christ, on the first day of the week, you conquered sin, put death to flight, and gave us the hope of everlasting life: Redeem all our days by this victory; forgive our sins, banish our fears, make us bold to praise you and to do your will; and steel us to wait for the consummation of your kingdom on the last great day; through the same Jesus Christ, our Lord. Amen.

Grace at Meals

Blessed are you, O Lord God, King of the universe, for you give us food to sustain our lives and make our hearts glad; through Jesus Christ, our Lord. Amen.

The Greatest Prayer Books of All Time (Besides This One!)

The following bibliography is a resource tool to help you delve further into the spiritual discipline of prayer, both alone and with others.

Arthur, Kay. *Lord, Teach Me to Pray in 28 Days*. Eugene, OR: Harvest House Publishers, 1995.

Barrier, Roger. *Listening to the Voice of God*. Minneapolis: Bethany House, 1998.

Bodishbaugh, Signa. *The Journey to Wholeness in Christ*. Grand Rapids: Chosen Books, 1997.

Bounds, E. M. *Prayer and Revival*. Grand Rapids: Baker Book House, 1993.

Chambers, Oswald. *If You Will Ask*. Grand Rapids: Discovery House, 1989.

DeBlassie, Paul. *Deep Prayer*. New York: Crossroad, 1990.

Duewel, Wesley L. *Touch the World Through Prayer*. Grand Rapids: Francis Asbury Press, 1986.

Eastman, Dick. *Love on its Knees*. Old Tappan, NJ: Chosen Books, 1989.

Garlock, Ruthanne, and Sherrer, Quin. *Prayer Partnerships*. Ann Arbor: Vine Books, 2001.

Graf, Jonathan. *The Power of Personal Prayer*. Colorado Springs: NavPress, 2002.

Hassel, David J. *Radical Prayer*. New York: Paulist Press, 1983.

Hawthorne, Steve C., and Kendrick, Graham. *Prayer-walking*. Orlando: Creation House, 1993.

Hayford, Jack W. *Prayer Is Invading the Impossible*. Plainfield, NJ: Logos International, 1977.

Holloway, Jane. *Prayer for Amateurs*. London: Hodder & Stoughton, 2000.

Hulstrand, Donald M. *The Praying Church*. New York: Seabury Press, 1977.

Hybels, Bill, and Nystrom, Carolyn. *Too Busy not to Pray Journal*. Downers Grove, IL: InterVarsity Press, 1998.

Kroll, Woodrow. *When God Doesn't Answer*. Grand Rapids: Baker Book House, 1997.

Merton, Thomas. *Contemplative Prayer*. New York: Herder & Herder, 1969.

Murray, Andrew. *The Inner Life*. Springdale, PA: Whitaker House, 1984.

Omartian, Stormie. *The Power of a Praying Wife*. Eugene, OR: Harvest House Publishers, 1997.

Peterson, Eugene. *Answering God*. San Francisco: Harper & Row, 1989.

Sanders, J. Oswald. *Prayer Power Unlimited*. Chicago: Moody Press, 1988.

Sumrall, Lester. *Secrets of Unanswered Prayer*. Nashville: Thomas Nelson Publishers, 1985.

Torrey, R. A. *Power of Prayer*. Grand Rapids: Zondervan Publishers, 1971.

Internet Sites

The following Internet sites will allow you to interact with others in terms of prayer as well as give you resources to aid your prayer life.

Bible.com—What does the Bible say about prayer?
www.bible.com

Book of Common Prayer—Resources for the 1979 Prayer Book.
www.justus.anglican.org

Centering Prayer—Based on Thomas Keating. Christian contemplative prayer.
www.centeringprayer.com

Christian Prayer—The Lord's Prayer is Christ's model for us all to deepen our communication with Him.
www.christian-prayer.net

Crosswalk.com—Prayer requests answered, private or public.
www.crosswalk.com/community/prayer

Daily Guideposts—Prayer requests taken. (*Guideposts* magazine).
www.guideposts.org/prayer/

Evening Prayer—Daily evening prayer from *The Book of Common Prayer*.
www.episcopalnet.org

Healing Prayer—Prayer is witness to the presence of God in our lives.
www.healingprayer.org

Healing Scripture Prayers—Learn how to pray for healing and miracles from Bible teacher Warren Wiersbe.
www.healingscripture.com

Jesus Teaches on Prayer—Ray Stedman's sermons on prayer.
www.pbc.org/dp/stedman/jprayer

Mission America Coalition—To bring prayer into every family in America.
www.lighthouse.org

NDP Home Page—National Day of Prayer Task Force.
www.ndptf.org

Persecution prayer requests—Pray for the persecuted church around the world.
www.persecution.org/prayer/

Portals of Prayer—A daily devotional for Bible reading, meditation, and prayer.
www.cph.org/forms/portals.asp

Prayer 101—Collection of articles and lessons on prayer.
www.harvestprayer.com/pray101/

Prayer Changes Things Chat Room—Live chat and prayer board.
Chat.prayercanada.com

Prayer of Jabez—Enlarge your territory and increase your impact.
www.prayer-of-jabez.net

Prayer of the Day—Give thanks for God's care.
www.methodism.org/uk

Prayer Quotes, Stories, and Sayings—Experience a personal transformation.
www.inspirationalprayer.com

Prayer Thoughts—Daily reflections that focus on daily Bible readings.
www.prayingchurch.org/thoughts.html

Promise Keepers prayer page—World prayer team at the Promise Keepers men's group.
www.promisekeepers.org

Seven basic steps to successful fasting and prayer—Destroy the strongholds of evil.
www.ccci.org

Sinner's Prayer—Become a sinner saved by grace.
www.sinner-prayer.com

The Serenity Prayer—For inspiration, addiction, and recovery.
Open-mind.org/Serenity.htm

Walk Thru the Bible—Prayer to get you through your day.
www.walkthru.org

What is prayer?—The Billy Graham Organization answers your questions.
www.billygraham.org/qna.asp

Prayer Retreat Centers in the United States and Canada

Our friend Timothy Jones has given us permission to list a selection of the more than 250 retreat centers throughout the United States and Canada that he recommends. We recommend strongly that you purchase his book, *A Place for God*, and use it as a directory to choose a retreat center for a period of concentrated prayer—whether that be a day or even a week. If possible, once a year is the best time period in which to make a commitment. Go with your Bible, a good devotional book, and a journal for notes. Just spend time in quiet solitude, talking to God. Bring to him all your fears, desires, and decisions that you face. It will change your perspective when you return and if God speaks to your heart, it might just change your life.

Most of these retreat centers are Roman Catholic because of the strong tradition of prayer combined with solitude. But in these ecumenical days they have many visitors who are not of their denomination and yet they allow you to "be yourself" in whatever Christian context you prefer.

In the United States

A Quiet Place
Contemplative Prayer Center
PO Box 158
Milford, IN 46542
219-658-4831

Abbey of Gethsemani Retreat Center
Trappist, KY 40051
502-549-4129

Bon Secours Spiritual Center
525 Marriottsville Road
Marriottsville, MD 21104
410-442-8219
www.erols.com/bssc

Christ the King Retreat Center
621 South First Avenue
Buffalo, MN 55313
612-682-1394

Community of the Holy Spirit
Saint Hilda's House
621 West 113th Street
New York, NY 10025

Desert House of Prayer
7350 W. Picture Rocks Road
Tucson, AZ 85743
520-744-0774

Franciscan Center
3010 Perry Avenue
Tampa, FL 33603
813-229-2695

Franciscan Spirituality Center
920 Market Street
LaCrosse, WI 54601
608-791-5295

Glorieta Baptist Conference Center
PO Box 8
Glorieta, NM 87535
800-797-4222

Good Counsel Friary
493 Tyrone Road
Morgantown, WV 26505
304-594-9247

Iona House
4577 Billy Maher Road
Memphis, TN 38135
901-377-9284

Knowles Mercy Center
2304 Campanile Road
Waterloo, NE 68069
402-359-4288

Laurelville Mennonite Church Center
Route 5, Box 145
Mount Pleasant, PA 15666
800-839-1021
www.laurelville.org

Manna House of Prayer
323 East Fifth Street
PO Box 675
Concordia, KS 66901
785-243-4428

Milford Spiritual Center
5361 S. Milford Road
Milford, OH 45150
513-248-3500

My Father's House Spiritual Retreat Center
39 N. Moodus Road, Box 22
Moodus, CT 06469
203-873-2357

New Camoldoli Retreat House
Big Sur, CA 93920
408-667-0209

New Melleray Abbey
6500 Melleray Circle
Peosta, IA 52068
319-588-2319

Oblate Renewal Center
5700 Blanco Road
San Antonio, TX 78216
210-349-4281

Priory Spirituality Center
500 College Street NE
Lacey, WA 98516
360-438-2595

Sacred Renewal Center
26 Wyoming Avenue
PO Box 153
Billings, MT 59103
406-252-0322

Saint Anselm Abbey
100 Saint Anselm Drive
Manchester, NH 03102
603-641-7115
www.anselm.edu/abbey.html

Saint Augustine's House
3316 East Drahner Road
PO Box 125
Oxford, MI 48371
248-628-5155

**Saint Bernard Conference and
Hospitality Center**
1600 Street Bernard Drive SE
Cullman, AL 35055-3057
205-734-2925

Saint Gregory's Abbey
1900 West MacArthur Drive
Shawnee, OK 74801
405-878-5490

Saint Ignatius House
Jesuit Retreat Center
6700 Riverside Drive NW
Atlanta, GA 30328
404-255-0503

Saint Scholastica Center
1205 S. Albert Pike
PO Box 3489
Fort Smith, AR 72913
501-783-1135

Sea of Peace House of Prayer
802 Jungle Road
Edisto Island, SC 29438
843-869-0513

Shalom Prayer Center
840 South Main Street
Mount Angel, OR 97362
503-845-6585

Stillpoint Ministries, Inc.
51 Laurel Lane
Black Mountain, NC 28711
828-669-0606

Tabor Retreat Center
2125 Langhorne Road
Lynchburg, VA 24501
804-846-6475

Techny Conference Center
2001 Waukegan Road
PO Box 176
Techny, IL 60082
847-272-9363

The Community of Jesus
PO Box 1094
Orleans, MA 02653
508-255-9490
www.cofj.net

The Glen Eyrie Conference Center
PO Box 6000
Colorado Springs, CO 80934
719-594-2285

The Spiritual Life Center
1020 S. Beretania Street
Honolulu, HI 96814
808-523-1170

The Vincentian Renewal Center
PO Box 757
Plainsboro, NJ 08536
609-452-2851

Thomas the Apostle Center
45 Road 3CX-S
Cody, WY 82414
307-587-4400

Washington Retreat House
400 Harewood Road, NE
Washington, DC 20017-1595
202-529-2102

Wellspring Retreat House
PO Box 60818
701 Park Place
Boulder City, NV 89006
702-293-7208

In Canada

Abbaye Saint-Benoit
Saint-Benoit-Du-Lac
Quebec, Canada QC J0B 2M0
819-843-0480

King's Fold
Box 758
Cochrane, Alberta, Canada AL T0L 0W0
403-932-9531

Marguerite Centre
700 Mackay Street
Pembroke, Ontario, Canada ON K8A 1G6
613-732-2408

Queenswood House
2494 Arbutus Road
Victoria, British Columbia, Canada BC V8N 1V8
250-477-3891

Saint Benedict's Retreat and Conference Centre
225 Masters Avenue
Winnepeg, Manitoba, Canada MB R4A 2A1
204-334-8840

Index

U–V

W–X–Y–Z

Special offer for readers of
The Complete Idiot's Guide® to Prayer, Second Edition

Receive your **FREE** copy of *Devotional Prayers: Enriching Your Daily Walk with God.*

Compiled and edited by the authors of *The Complete Idiot's Guide® to Prayer, Second Edition*, this little book offers 30 days of morning prayers to help you experience daily life with deeper meaning. Fill in the information requested below, and mail the form to:

Alpha Books
The Complete Idiot's Guide® to Prayer, Second Edition, offer
800 East 96th Street
3rd Floor
Indianapolis, IN 46240

Or e-mail your name and address and your responses to the questions below to: **alphapublicity@pearsoned.com.**
You'll receive your copy of *Devotional Prayers* within 6-8 weeks.

Name _____

Address _____

City/State/Zip _____

Have you ever purchased any other *Complete Idiot's Guides®*? _____

If yes, what other titles? _____

Please check the primary influencing factors for purchasing this book:

☐ Front or back cover information   ☐ Table of contents
☐ Authors' reputations   ☐ Completeness/approach of content
☐ *The Complete Idiot's Guide®* brand reputation   ☐ Cover design
☐ Price   Other _____

How did you first learn about this book?

☐ Saw the book on the shelf at store   ☐ Read book review
☐ Recommended by a friend   ☐ Familiar with *The Complete Idiot's Guide®* series
☐ Recommended by store personnel   ☐ Familiar with authors' work
☐ Internet site   Other _____

What other topics would you like to see as *Complete Idiot's Guides®*? _____

_____

_____

Please tell us about yourself:

Age: ☐ Under 21   ☐ 21-34   ☐ 35-50   ☐ 50+

Sex: ☐ Male   ☐ Female

Education: ☐ High school   ☐ College   ☐ Graduate school

Occupation: _____

Alpha Books

The Complete Idiot's Guide® to Prayer, Second Edition, offer

800 East 96th Street

3rd Floor

Indianapolis, IN 46240